John Willmuth Hill

The Purification of Public Water Supplies

John Willmuth Hill

The Purification of Public Water Supplies

ISBN/EAN: 9783744649957

Printed in Europe, USA, Canada, Australia, Japan

Cover: Foto ©ninafisch / pixelio.de

More available books at **www.hansebooks.com**

THE PURIFICATION

OF

PUBLIC WATER

SUPPLIES

BY

JOHN W. HILL

CONSULTING ENGINEER

MEMBER AMERICAN SOCIETY OF CIVIL ENGINEERS, MEMBER AMERICAN WATER WORKS ASSOCIATION,
MEMBER AMERICAN PUBLIC HEALTH ASSOCIATION

NEW YORK

D. VAN NOSTRAND COMPANY

LONDON

E. & F. N. SPON, 125 STRAND

1898

PREFACE.

THIS work is in continuation of a series of lectures and papers on the *Quality of Public Water Supplies*, which the author has had the honor to read before several scientific societies and universities during the past five years, and is intended to present in a brief way, (1), the fact and causes of pollution of sources of public water supply; (2), the effect of this pollution on the typhoid fever rates of our larger cities; and (3), to illustrate by a few examples how the typhoid rates have been reduced by the introduction of water from purer natural sources and by filtration of polluted waters. In connection with the subject of water quality, brief reference is made to the water bacteria, and some data are given on the methods of construction and operation of sand filters, together with the cost of filter construction in different water-works, and the cost per million gallons of water treated.

The principal object in bringing out this work at the present time is to impress upon city officials, health officers, and others connected with or interested in works of public water supply, the necessity of a more vigorous attack of the problems of "Water Pollution," and "Purification of Water" intended for drinking and other dietetic uses.

The statistics of population and typhoid fever death rates (Appendix A) have been obtained from health officers, water-works managers, and official published reports.

The author has endeavored to acknowledge all sources of information in the body of the book; but especial thanks are due Dr. Dunbar of the Hamburg Hygienic Institute for several valuable original papers on water supply in Germany; Mr. Rud Schroder, inspector of the Hamburg water-works, for much valuable information on the operation of these filters; and Mr. Thomas W. Boughen of Cincinnati, who by the author's request kindly undertook to collect exact information upon the details of filter construction and operation during a recent tour of Europe.

In the translation of German, French, and Spanish papers and reports on European water-works and the hygiene of water, he has had kind and valuable assistance from Dr. Philip Hillkowitz, Charles E. Rasinsky, and Adolph G. Wulff, graduates of the University of Cincinnati. Valuable assistance has also been rendered by Mr. Paul Hamilton, a graduate of the University of Michigan, in the preparation of tabular matter on recent filter practice, etc.

All the illustrations, excepting Figs. 10, 11, and 12, were prepared especially for this work by his son, Mr. Henry C. Hill, to whom the author is also largely indebted for patient assistance, and many valuable suggestions in connection with the experimental work and collation of authorities for matter which appears in the book.

Chapter I. was originally read as a lecture before the Cincinnati Section of the American Chemical Society at the Cincinnati University, Jan. 15, 1897; and Chapter II. was originally read as a lecture before the Academy of Medicine, Cincinnati, May 3, 1897. Chapter IX. was originally read as a paper on the "Sterilization of Drinking-Water as a Means of Reducing the Typhoid Fever Rates" at Buda-Pest, September, 1894.

J. W. H.

CINCINNATI, *June*, 1897.

CONTENTS.

CHAPTER III.

CHAPTER IV.

CHAPTER XVII.

APPENDIX A.

APPENDIX B.

APPENDIX C.

LIST OF ILLUSTRATIONS.

THE PURIFICATION OF WATER.

CHAPTER I.

INTRODUCTION.

WATER is an essential of human existence. According to Landois,* 58.5 per cent of the body weight is water, and nearly 70 per cent of the blood corpuscles is water; of the serum of the blood, 90 per cent is water.† No other article of diet enters so completely into the construction and support of the animal system. A very early writer held that the blood of an animal was life, ‡ and the use of it as an article of food was interdicted by holy law. Water being the main constituent of the blood, it may also be regarded as the principal element of animal life; and all diligence should be exercised in procuring for dietetic purposes a water which, while readily assimilable by the system, shall not be the cause of disease.

It is a curious fact, borne out by the many costly and pains-taking investigations into the resources of cities for public water supply, that, after all, we are not thoroughly informed upon the question of water quality. This is not in disparagement of the labors of the many able investigators along this line of scientific research; but while in nearly every other branch of physics satis-factory proof of certain qualities of matter can be had, the absolute proof of the hygienic quality of water supplies is still beyond the reach of our most modern methods of research. If one is disposed to question this statement, his careful attention is invited to the

---

* Landois' *Human Physiology.*
† *Transactions American Society of Civil Engineers,* vol. xxxii., p. 151.
‡ Genesis, chap. ix., v. 4.

1

views of some of the ablest water analysts of England, as shown by the exhaustive investigation of the Royal Commission on Metropolitan Water Supply.*

If one is in doubt as to the strength of a bar of steel, he can easily resolve his doubts by putting a specimen into a testing-machine and breaking it. The results will satisfy him upon all the physical properties of the metal. If he desires to pursue the inquiry further, he can obtain very satisfactory evidence of the composition of' this steel, and reasoning *a priori*, can make as many bars substantially like his specimen as may be desired.

Examinations of water samples, however, are not so satisfactorily conducted. The results obtained at one time are not often verified by subsequent tests. Changes in the chemical and biological condition of the water are constantly going on ; and it is not unlikely that a public water supply might comply with all the recognized standards of potability at one time, and be subject to just condemnation at another. And right here lies the danger to communities which depend upon water from a common source.

The experience at Plymouth, Penn. (1885), shows how a hitherto satisfactory source of water supply may become an agent of destruction, with no preliminary indications of the time or nature of the changes which were taking place in the previously pure water of this little mountain reservoir.

The terms "pure" and "impure" with reference to water are used advisedly. If the water is safe for drinking and dietetic purposes, it is "pure" although such water, if from natural sources, would not be found chemically and bacterially "pure ;" while an "impure" water is one that is the cause of disease, even though the chemist and bacteriologist might not be able to decide upon the evidence or nature of the impurity. Impurities may come into water from the atmosphere, from surface drainage, and from sewage. But the impurities which are feared in water are the pathogenic and putrefactive bacteria, and the ptomains.

The pathogenic bacteria are those specifically concerned in disease, and held to be a part of its etiology. The putrefactive bacteria found in all water rich in organic matter, especially from

* London, Eyre & Spottiswoode, 1893.

sewage sources, may produce disorders of the ªdigestive tract, although not held to be the specific agents of disease. The ptomains have never within the author's knowledge been found in water, although it is reasonable to suppose that such may come into water from putrefying organic matter lying upon the fore-shores of rivers and lakes; but the dilution of these will be very great in all ordinary instances of rivers and lakes constituting sources of water supply.

The biologist and bacteriologist deal in matter found only in suspension in water; and dangerous substances may exist in solution, and their methods of search would not disclose the fact. If ptomains ever occur in a water supply they will be in solution, and the ordinary chemical water analysis will not reveal them. Indeed, the proof by chemical means of a ptomain or toxic substance in water will be found upon investigation to be very difficult, if not altogether impossible, by any known process.* It is a disputed question whether Brieger and his co-laborers have really precipitated the toxic substances of bouillon cultures of the pathogenic bacteria,† and altogether it may be held that the absolute proof of water quality is still an unattainable result.

This fact, however, should not diminish the perseverance of the workers in the field of water analysis and purification, but rather serve as a stimulus to stronger and higher efforts in behalf of the thousands who annually perish from water-borne diseases.

That certain waters, when judged by our present standards, are held to be safe for drinking and other dietetic purposes, while other waters, judged by the same standards, are held to be unfitted for such uses, we all know; but general confidence in these same standards is still to be established.

Absolutely pure water is not found in nature. All water, from whatever source, even freshly fallen rain-water, contains some evidences of contamination; but according to our standards, water fit to drink is often found in natural sources. It is not essential that water for drinking and dietetic purposes be chemically and

---

* Royal Commission on Metropolitan Water Supply, London, 1893. Professor E. Ray Lankester, *Appendices to Evidence*, p. 452.

† *Annales de l'Institut Pasteur*, Sanarelli, April, 1894.

bacterially pure ; but it is essential that it contains no pathogenic organisms, and shall be free from ptomains due to the action of bacteria upon decaying organic matter.   Whether the latter have really occurred in drinking-water is not certainly known, but some investigators at the present time seem to suspect the possibility of it.

The pumping of water for domestic uses from a source known to be polluted by sewage or otherwise should be severely condemned.   The delivery of water containing the elements of fatal disease to a confiding and helpless community should be ranked with the sale of intoxicating liquors to minors and confirmed inebriates.   An attempt to kill people by the systematic distribution of a poison would be met by the apprehension and punishment of the offender ; while the delivery of water for drinking and other dietetic uses, as fatal to some as a dose of strychnine, is going on in nearly every large city of the land.   Shall we shut our eyes to the fact that polluted water is dangerous to health, or shall we recognize the evil, and address ourselves to its remedy?

Every city which continues to supply a tainted water without earnest and intelligent efforts at abatement, is guilty of a barbarism not tolerable in this age of enlightenment and progress.   The interest taken in the quality of public water supplies during the past ten years is well shown by the work of the Royal Commission on Metropolitan Water Supply, London (1893) ; by the magnificent and far-reaching work of the Massachusetts State Board of Health, 1890, *et seq.*, and of several important commissions upon city water supply in this country and abroad ; and, finally, by the independent labors of many able and patient investigators, like Professor Frankland, Dr. Miquel, Dr. Prudden, and others.

The Royal Commission on Water Supply to London covered more ground, and was more searching in its investigations, than any similar body that has hitherto acted on behalf of a municipal corporation ; and without regard to its conclusions, which may be open to discussion, there can be no doubt of the great ability of the commission and of the men called to give evidence before it.

The whole field of inquiry, from the available capacity of the London watershed to the quality of the water which may be had from the most perfect works for filtration, was fully covered. The ablest men of England, in geology, medicine, chemistry, biology, bacteriology, and sanitary and hydraulic engineering, were called before the commission, and evidence was taken upon every point which by any means could affect the quantity or quality of the water required by the metropolis; and minute inquiry was made into the possibility of transmitting certain zymotic infectious diseases by drinking-water.

The Hygienic Laboratory of Hamburg, so far as it relates to a supervision of the quality of water supplied to the citizens, is perhaps more complete than that of any other city in the world. Dr. Dunbar, a former resident of St. Paul, Minn., and now a citizen of Germany, is in charge of the laboratory; and every facility is afforded him for complete surveillance and control of the quality of the city water supply.

The management of the filters, and maintenance of the quality of the water supplied to the chief cities of Holland, are as carefully conducted in the interest of the public health as are the boilers and pumping-engines operated in the interest of the public purse. By the combined efforts of the engineers, chemists, and bacteriologists connected with the water-works of Holland, the water is pumped with the greatest ecomony of fuel, and is consumed by the people with the least loss of life from water-carried diseases.

The city of Manchester, Eng., realizing the value to its prosperity of an unimpeachable public water supply, has recently bought a lake (Thirlmere) in County Cumberland, and much of the proximate drainage ground, and conducts this water to the city through conduits aggregating in length one hundred and two miles. Vienna, from a city having at times typhoid fever rates as high as any in Europe, by abandoning its former sources (the Danube and wells), and seeking its water in the Austrian Alps, has become one of the least typhoid fever infected centers in the world.

· The extensive labors of the Massachusetts State Board of Health at its Lawrence experiment station have been guided by two chief objects, — one the treatment of urban sewage by practical methods, which will render the effluents innocuous to health, and the other the development of information upon practical methods of sand filtration of polluted waters.

Independent investigators have been seeking information upon the exact chemical and biological character of various waters all over the world. Research has been conducted along the line of water transmission of disease ; and the organisms concerned in the etiology of infectious disease have been patiently and carefully studied.

The practical work of cities, and the scientific work of the analysts, clearly point to great changes along the line of public water supply. Thirty years ago the sand filters, which we now find in the London water-works, were filtering water from the rivers Thames and Lea, as they are now ; but no one at that time suspected what these filters really were doing. The water companies and consumers believed that the filters were making a great improvement in the quality of the polluted river waters, but the physics of sand filtration were at that time not written and not known.

Naturally enough, processes conducted in ignorance of the rationale of every step and each reaction seldom attain the high efficiency which follows manipulation along lines based upon a clear knowledge of all the causes operating to produce a common result. And if the filters of the London water-works, as operated thirty years ago, failed to furnish water of a quality equal to that now obtained, the fault was not in the principle of the filter, but in the lack of experimental information upon the part of the eminent engineers, who, like Mr. James Simpson, designed and operated them. This knowledge has since been supplied by the Pasteurs, the Kochs, the Franklands, and the Mills, who have each in his way furnished some of the material by means of which the practice of water purification has reached a firm foundation.

When Mr. James P. Kirkwood went abroad in the spring of 1866, to examine the works of water purification at that time in use in several European cities, notably London, the subject of water quality rested entirely upon the chemical tests for organic matter. The filter was regarded as a fine strainer, or as Mr. Kirkwood says,* "They (the sand filters) become indeed screens of the greatest delicacy, intercepting all material impurities, not the least of which are the very small fish with which all waters are crowded at certain seasons."

Something smaller than fish were then held back by the London filters; this much was known, but no mention had then been made of the action of bacteria in water on organic matter, of the "Schmutzdecke," which in Germany is regarded at once as the evidence and cause of successful sand filtration, or of the action of the nitrifying organisms in converting compounds of ammonia into nitrous and nitric acids.

These things were being done by the London sand filters in 1866, not so perfectly, perhaps, but in a measure as they are now; yet the bacteria were in the London water then as at present, but no one was conducting gelatin plate cultivations, and searching in drops of water for little organisms, so small in any dimension as to be beneath notice.†

Organic matter in suspension in the water was being split up into carbon dioxide and other gases and into nitrogenous compounds by bacterial action; but no one, not even Dr. Letheby, mentioned it to Mr. Kirkwood upon the occasion of his visit to London. The gelatinous Schmutzdecke, which Herr Piefke ‡ writes upon so ably, and argues as the very essence of· successful sand filtration, was being formed on the sand-beds; but the British workman, who shoveled off the upper one-half or three-quarters of an inch of sand from a clogged filter bed, never noticed it. The partial or complete aëration of a filter when it was temporarily out of service was never suspected as a means of maintaining the nitrifying organisms in the sand-bed. In short, the real action of a sand filter was then unsuspected, the bed of sand being considered somewhat superior to a molder's sieve for the interception of suspended matter in the water.

The celebrated Dr. Letheby § freely admitted "that we have

---

* *Filtration of River Waters*, by James P. Kirkwood, New York, 1869, p. 7.
† This term is not here used in the same sense as under observation.
‡ *Die Principien der Reinwassergewinnung vermittelst Filtration*, Berlin, 1887.
§ *Filtration of River Waters*, by James P. Kirkwood, New York, 1869, p. 26. .

not at the present time any absolute test for discovering organic matters in water, much less the nature of these organic matters;" but great as has been the progress in the chemistry, biology, and bacteriology of water since Dr. Letheby penned these lines, much remains to be done in applying the knowledge gained in a practical way.

If it be true that by proper prophylaxis certain zymotic diseases may be made to disappear, why are we so slow in adopting the remedies which science and history have pointed out ? Are we in doubt of the correctness of our conclusions, or are we indifferent to the sacrifice of human life ?

It is not the author's purpose at this time to discuss any special methods of purification for polluted waters. This will be done under their respective headings; but the fact has been demonstrated so often, especially abroad, that methods upon a large scale can be so conducted as to command the quality of a water supply, and one who opposes the purification of water supplies upon the ground of impracticability must be set down as not being well informed on water purification or as an enemy of the public health.

Professor Percy Frankland,[*] after comparing the operation of the London filters for a series of years with certain deductions which he had drawn from an earlier investigation of these filters, stated : —

"The importance of these results lies in their proving that in the matter of sand filtration we are no longer working in the dark, but that we now know the factors upon which the success of the process depends, and by attention to which its efficiency may be maintained or even increased."

The tracing of disease through a sewage-polluted water may be obscure to some; but if a certain source of water supply is known to be polluted at some point with the organisms concerned in disease, and it is further known that such organisms, or some of them, can live in water for a length of time sufficient to pass from the place where they enter this source of water supply to another place where water is taken up for domestic uses, is it difficult to conceive that some of the people who drink this water at the sec-

---

[*] *Micro-organisms in Water*, by Percy and Grace Frankland, London, 1894, p. 131.

ond place may take these organisms into their system and lay the foundation of disease?

The typhoid bacillus is seldom found in water, and the failure to find it is too often taken as an evidence of its non-existence there.* Dr. T. M. Prudden, however, in a conversation with the author, very aptly disposes of this objection by stating, "If I were to go down to the Battery and throw a coin into New York Harbor, do you think I could ever find it again?" The coin is there; this we know because he threw it into the water, and the failure to recover it cannot be taken as proof of its non-existence in the bay, but as an indication of the inefficiency of our methods of search. The same argument will hold good in case of failure to find, among a lot of vigorous water bacteria, the typhoid or any other disease germ which can sustain at best only a limited, migratory existence in any kind of water.

It is also held by opponents of the water transmission of infectious disease that the evidence is lacking of the actual infection by this means. Of course no one sees the germ in water, and therefore is never distinctly aware of taking it into the system in this way; but circumstantial evidence of the transmission of disease is sometimes as potent as circumstantial evidence of crime, and must be accepted accordingly.

Upon another occasion the author attempted to illustrate the passage of disease germs from one point to another in water in the following manner : —

If we were to take an iron pipe two or three feet long, put a marble in one end, tilt the pipe slightly, and make the marble appear at the other end, you would say that the marble had passed through the pipe. You saw it put in at one end, and in due time it appeared at the other, but you have not really seen the marble passing through the pipe. The inference, however, that the marble did pass through the pipe is correct; there is no other way in which, after it was put in at one end, it could reach the other.

Let the marble be replaced by the typhoid bacillus, and let the pipe be a river, or a lake, or a reservoir (as at Plymouth, Penn., in 1885). We can prove by examination of the fæces of typhoid patients in the early stages of the disease that the Eberth germ is passing into our sewers,† and, of course, into our

---

* *Twenty-fourth Annual Report Massachusetts State Board of Health,* p. 531.

† "Report of Royal Commission on Metropolitan Water Supply," *Minutes of Evidence,* p. 404.

larger sources of water supply. Eventually we will find, upon post-mortem examination of persons dying in the early stages of typhoid, this same bacillus in cultures made from the spleen and sometimes from the intestine.

How has it come there? We saw it go into the sewer, and we find it in the body of the typhoid victim. We know it went from the sewer to the river, and we infer that the river was the carrier of the germ. We did not see it passing through the water, neither did we see our marble passing through the pipe. We know that the marble did go through the pipe, and I think the evidence now before us sufficiently demonstrates that water is the carrier of the typhoid bacillus from the sick to the well.

It is strange that, in spite of our exact information upon the matters which convert water into sewage, we are so willing to drink this dilute mixture of filth. We know sewage consists of the wastes from the household and factory, and from the wash of the streets and roads, and still we drink the mixture, often with no misgiving, and rarely indeed with complaint.

At the same time, if I were to take a glass of distilled water which is wholly destitute of dangerous organic matter and bacteria, and in your presence put into it even the slightest amount of any of the objectionable wastes which constitutes sewage, there is not one person who would care to drink it. Sentiment revolts at the bare suggestion of drinking a water with which we have seen filth mixed, and at the same time we swallow just such stuff when we drink the water of many of our large cities.

The whole theory of water purification is based upon the conviction that pure water cannot create a disturbance of the animal system or be the cause of ill health, and that certain organic matter, or the products of organic matter, or organisms in water, is the cause of certain disorders, or are concerned in the etiology of specific disease. It is not necessary for one to believe in the germ theory of disease before he can become an advocate of pure water supplies. Long before the ptomains and bacteria were known, certain able men had pointed out that water from sources apparently beyond the reach of pollution was more healthful to drink than water which was known to be polluted. But to those who do believe in the transmission of some infectious diseases by living organisms, it is not difficult to perceive how sewage-polluted waters may become very dangerous distributers of infection.

Pure water is held by some to be better than purified water. This undoubtedly is true; but the sources from which pure water is available are so few, that it can safely be assumed if cities are to have pure water, they must adopt artificial means to make it so.

Thus filtration and sedimentation are not adopted at the present time by any city simply to improve the appearance of water, and make it more welcome to the bodily senses, but as distinct safe-guards against water-borne diseases.

No one should be deceived upon the influence of sedimentation or filtration of polluted waters. These means never have rendered, and probably never will render, such waters pure ; but they can be devised and operated in such a manner that nearly every natural water can be rendered less likely to injure the human system, and at a cost which will not be prohibitory to their use. A claim such as is sometimes put forth, that the water from the filters of Lon-don has not or cannot be the cause of typhoid fever,* cannot be universally admitted.

Organisms larger than the typhoid bacillus have repeatedly been detected in the filtered London water ; † and while the typhoid bacillus has not been found among them, neither has it been found upon careful investigation in the raw water before it has gone to the filters.‡ (According to Dr. G. Sims Woodhead,§ it has never been found in any rapidly flowing river.) At the same time, with greater care in operation of the filters, and with improved methods of water analysis and higher standards of purity, the typhoid rates of London have shown a marked decline.

Thus for the decade 1861–1870 ‖ the annual typhoid fever death rate for London was 90 per 100,000 of population. For the following decade the annual typhoid fever death rate was 24 per 100,000 of population, and for the decade ending with 1890 the annual typhoid fever death rate was 19 per 100,000 of population.

During the seven years ending Dec. 31, 1896, the average annual typhoid fever death rate for London was 14.4 per 100,000 of population, or was then one-sixth of the rate which prevailed thirty years before. This remarkable reduction in the typhoid rates cannot be credited to improvements in the filters, so much as

---

* "Report of Royal Commission on Metropolitan Water Supply," 1893, *Minutes of Evidence,* p. 404 ; also *Potable Water,* by Floyd Davis, New York, 1891, p. 40.

† *Analytical Investigation of London Water Supply,* 1896, p. 10.

‡ "Report Royal Commission," *Minutes of Evidence,* p. 405.

§ *Ibid.,* p. 505.

‖ *Engineering Record,* Oct. 27, 1894.

to a better knowledge of how they should be operated, and to the methods of water analysis developed during the past fifteen years.

Thirty years ago the London filters were operated to secure a clarified water, clear water seeming at that time to mean pure water, or water safe for drinking and other dietetic uses. We know better now, and limpidity is no longer taken as an evidence of purity in water.

When we consider that the death rate from typhoid fever has been as low as three persons per 100,000 of population in Munich (1892), while it has been as high as 154 persons per 100,000 of population in Chicago (1891), the most obtuse must admit that there is something wrong in our sanitary works or regulations which will permit of a death rate from typhoid fever in any city of this country *fifty* times as great as that of a certain city in Europe. While the Munich rate is very low, still it is not exceptional, as is shown by the following rates for that city, Berlin, and Vienna : —

DEATHS PER 100,000 OF POPULATION FROM TYPHOID FEVER.

Year,	1890.	1891.	1892.	1893.	1894.	1895.	1896.
Munich,	8	7	3	15	2–3	3	3
Berlin,	9	10	8	9	4	5	5
Vienna,	9	6	8	7	5	6	5

Now compare these rates for the same years with those of three cities of the United States.

DEATHS PER 100,000 OF POPULATION FROM TYPHOID FEVER.

Year,	1890.	1891.	1892.	1893.	1894.	1895.	1896.
Chicago,	92	154	106	45	31	32	46
Pittsburg,	. .	100	100	111	56	77	61
Louisville,	88	81	72	84	72	77	45

Vienna and Munich are supplied with the purest of natural waters from mountain springs, and the city of Berlin takes its supply from the River Spree and Lake Tegel, the waters of both being passed through artificial sand filters before they are served to the consumers.

In comparing the typhoid fever rates of American and German cities, perhaps some allowance should be made for the difference in habits of the populations of the respective localities. Thus Munich is said to be one of the greatest beer-drinking centers of the world, the consumption of this beverage having at one time reached as high as one hundred and twenty-five gallons per capita per annum ; and it is possible that the low typhoid fever rates from the German cities may be due in part to the general abstinence of the populations from the public water for drinking purposes.

If it be true that the low typhoid fever rates of certain cities in Europe are due to the general use of beer and wine as beverages instead of water, then this emphasizes the fact that a typhoid polluted drinking-water is the principal cause of the high typhoid fever rates in cities in this country, and makes it seem remarkable that cities like Munich, Vienna, and The Hague, for examples, where the typhoid rates are very low, and, as some people claim, water is not regarded as a proper thing to drink, should pay so much attention to the quality of their public water supplies.

Why should Vienna, for instance, be at such great expense to bring water from the Alps, distant sixty-five miles, if it is not to be used for dietetic purposes, when the water of the Danube will meet every other requirement quite as well as this " Schneeberg water," and can be obtained at a fraction of the cost involved in the scheme of works by which that city is now supplied ?

The usual manner of introducing the typhoid germ into the human system is by infected drinking-water ; therefore every city should regard it as a duty to itself to see that the water distributed for drinking and other dietetic purposes is not the carrier of the typhoid bacillus or of the organism productive of typhoid fever.

Much has been written upon the subject of water supply and the dangers of polluted waters to health, much also has been written upon methods of purifying polluted waters, and doubtless much remains to be written upon all these subjects ; but from the present view, it can be safely stated that whenever a steady, vigorous effort is made by all municipalities to supply their citizens with water up to the highest standard attainable by practical means, that the case and death rate from water-borne diseases will sink so low as to be no longer the cause of alarm.

CHAPTER II.

SOURCES OF PUBLIC WATER SUPPLY.

THE sources of public water supply for cities are rivers, natural lakes, large impounding reservoirs, usually at elevations sufficient to furnish a supply to cities by gravity ; springs, shallow dug wells, often carried into the drift a depth not much in excess of the maximum suction lift of pumping machinery ; and deep driven wells. Some of the latter may be artesian, and supply into large wells or reservoirs from which the suction of the pumps is taken, or may be connected directly with the pumps.

Of course all water supply must be derived from the rainfall, whether it be taken from streams, lakes, impounding reservoirs, or from springs and wells ; but the water supply of any particular locality may not be wholly dependent upon the local rainfall. This is true where the source of supply is a river draining a large territory, or where it is obtained from springs or deep wells. In localities where the outcrop or denuded rock formation is destitute of soluble materials, such as lime and magnesia, the water gathered in impounding reservoirs will be quite as soft as that of domestic cistern water collected from the roof of a residence or other building.

In the limestone regions surface water, while running off to impounding reservoirs, comes in contact with the outcrop of rock, and takes up some of the lime and magnesia ; and the impounded water will be harder than domestic cistern water. River water in hardness and quality will depend entirely upon the character of the watersheds from which it is derived, and the materials with which it may come in contact after it has reached the channel of discharge.

Aside from the direct sewage pollution of the large rivers of the world by the refuse from the civilization which is collected upon their banks, there is another pollution, due to the contact of the water while running off, with organic matter from various sources collected upon the watershed. Some of this may be carried in solution by the runoff of rainfall into the channel, while other portions may be carried along in mechanical suspension.

The objection to a polluted river or lake water is not limited to the amount of sewage which it may contain. It may be positively objectionable from a sanitary point of view by reason of organic matter, and possibly pathogenic bacteria, which may come into such water from the surface drainage of the tributary watershed. If the opinion entertained by Professor E. Ray Lankester, that the bacillus of typhoid fever may be an exacerbated form of *b. coli communis* (a pathogenic germ which is known to be given off in the dejecta of sheep and other domestic animals, as well as of man), be confirmed by later investigation, then it is very clear that the special sewage pollution of a drinking-water supply is not essential for the propagation of typhoid fever, and that there will be found in the organic matter now coming into streams and other sources of public water supply, from the runoff of rainfall or surface drainage, all the elements essential for the development of this particular disease.

(It does not appear that there are many who share the opinion with Professor Lankester that *b. typhosus* is an exalted form of the colon bacillus, but time may demonstrate that his view is correct ; and if it does, light will be shed upon some of the apparently inexplicable phenomena connected with certain epidemics of typhoid fever.)

Rivers which receive the drainage of cities or towns on their banks and the banks of their tributaries, even in the absence of known sewage pollution, cannot be regarded as uncontaminated sources of public water supply ; and although it may be difficult to show the presence of organic matter or of bacteria inimical to health, still there will always be an amount of organic matter in such rivers in process of decomposition, which may give rise to disorders of the human system, even though they may not be the cause of specific disease.

It is probable that surface water can be impounded in reservoirs from watersheds at elevations so high as to avoid pollution from all sources but the atmosphere ; and such water, although still open to the influence of decomposing organic matter found everywhere in nature, will always be purer than water collected in rivers, lakes, and ponds on the low lands.

Sources of water supply at high elevations with a yield so large as to satisfy the requirements of cities are of rare occurrence; and even in the few cases where such exist, the distance from the municipality to be supplied is so great as to make the development and utilization prohibitory for any but the larger cities. The city of Vienna derives its supply of public water at the present time altogether from large springs found in the Schneeberg, a portion of the Austrian Alps, and brings this water through a conduit sixty-five miles long to the city. The city of Munich obtains its water supply from similiar springs in the Mangfall valley of the Bavarian Alps. A few of the smaller municipalities in this country derive their public water supply from springs or streams at high elevations in sparsely settled or wild districts. But sources of this character are not available by the majority of the cities of this or any country; and recourse must be had to such sources as are available, and these, as stated at the outset in this chapter, are rivers, lakes, ponds, creeks, and dug and driven wells.

Considering rivers as constituting by far the largest source of water supply for municipal corporations, it may be accepted as an axiom "that no river is carrying during times of flood a water which is fit for drinking purposes except it first be artificially purified;" and if such rivers, in addition to the pollution which cannot be avoided by the runoff of rainfall on the drainage areas, receive the sewage of towns and cities, the water is undoubtedly not fit for drinking and culinary uses until it has been dealt with in such a manner as to render it innocuous to health. It is frequently asserted or implied in text-books and reports on sewage and sewage disposal, that the noxious properties of sewage are destroyed by proper dilution; but when sewage is the carrier of disease germs, dilution cannot remove them. It will reduce the number of such germs per unit of volume of the mixed sewage and water; but the germs are still there, and if taken into the system through drinking-water may produce just as serious results to as many people as if no dilution had occurred.

Dilution of sewage undoubtedly reduces the chances of any single individual imbibing a fatal germ in drinking the water ; but the germ itself will be just as dangerous, and in one aspect of the case may be more dangerous, when imbibed.

It is well known to bacteriologists engaged in the analysis of drinking-waters that the typhoid bacillus, for instance, will live for the greatest length of time in a water devoid of other kinds of bacteria, and will live for the least length of time in a concentrated sewage rich in the bacteria of putrefaction. The dilution of sewage therefore reduces the number of bacteria per unit of volume of the water, and favors the vitality of the typhoid bacillus. Considering that some of the bacteria can survive for many days in water of single distillation containing naturally but a very minute amount of organic matter, it will not be difficult to apprehend the possibility of a high dilution of sewage distinctly favoring the longevity of the typhoid germ ; and the theory that a sewage-polluted water may be rendered safe for drinking purposes by dilution must necessarily neglect this fact. Rivers and their tributaries have for generations been the receptacles of sewage, garbage, and all the wastes of civilization ; and even if the water came into these channels free from any objectionable matter, the practice of communities in making them the receptacles of sewage would condemn the water from such sources as altogether unfitted for drinking and some other uses. This, however, is well recognized, not only in England and other countries of Europe, but in certain portions of this country ; and steps are being taken to prevent the pollution of streams by the refuse of organized communities.

Considering that even in its best condition the water of a river is of questionable hygienic quality, one can appreciate the importance of a disposal of sewage, garbage, and other wastes, in a manner that can by no means injure sources which are drawn upon for public water supply.

Dr. G. Sims Woodhead * says : —

"If river water *must* be used, every possible precaution should be taken against its being made a receptacle for unpurified sewage. It is almost im-

* *Report Royal Commission on Metropolitan Water Supply,* Appendix C, p. 491.

possible during periods of flood to obtain it free from large quantities of surface drainage, but it should be insisted that in ordinary weather there should
be no surface drainage directly into the Thames or into its tributaries."

According to Professor Baumeister,[*] we can safely drink a
sewage-polluted water when the sewage and water are mixed in
certain proportions, depending upon the amount of organic matter
in the sewage and of that previously in the water. But he depends
altogether on chemistry for the test of potability of the water,
when it is well known that chemistry is powerless to reveal infectious properties or bacteria in the water. He states upon German
authority that water may carry $2\frac{1}{3}$ grains of organic matter to the
gallon and still be potable. Looking at the question from a chemical standpoint this may be true, but from a sanitary standpoint
any organic matter in drinking water known to be from a sewage
source will render such water unsafe for drinking.

The statement by Professor Baumeister that sewage containing
29.2 grains of organic matter to the gallon may be mixed with
river water containing 1.2 grains of organic matter to the gallon,
in the ratio of 23 gallons of water to 1 gallon of sewage, and the
mixture be safe for drinking purposes, seems to me to be very
dangerous, because the sewage may contain the germs of typhoid
fever which no amount of dilution can eliminate. Moreover,
advice like this, instead of promoting the purity of water supplies
and the public health, is calculated to injure both.

It is but fair to state that Professor Baumeister is looking at
the matter solely from the standpoint of sewage disposal into
running streams ; and it is doubtful if the selfish motive of ridding a
community of sewage by generally the easiest and cheapest method
should be allowed to prevail, when certain disaster to those who
may draw their drinking-water from the stream below is bound
to follow.

In another paragraph Professor Baumeister says : —

" The objection may be raised to these computations [relating to sewage
dilution] that the limiting amounts of organic matter in potable water was not
fixed under a supposition that a part of it was human excrement."

---

[*] " The Quality of Water Supplies," by the author, *Transactions American Society of Civil
Engineers*, vol. xxxii., p. 149 *et seq.*

But all sewers receive some human dejecta; and this at times may contain disease germs, and these germs, mixing with a so-called potable water, are dangerous. Adapting to our purpose the memorable words of Mr. Lincoln, any water likely to be adopted for drinking purposes may be safe to all people at some times, it may be safe to some people at all times, but it may not be safe to all people at all times; and the protection of those who may at some time be susceptible to its deleterious influences should warn us against the use of any drinking-water known to contain organic matter from a sewage source.

What has been said by way of objection to rivers and their tributaries as sources of water supply will apply to lakes which receive the drainage of rivers and the runoff of large watersheds, with the reservation, — that in large bodies of water the reduction of organic matter by subsidence and bacterial action will proceed with a more regular rate than in rivers. In support of this proposition, the experiments of Dr. Miquel upon water taken from the River Seine at a point below the outfall of some of the larger sewers of Paris indicate that polluted water at rest through a long period of time is sufficient to reduce the organic matter to harmless nitrates and nitrites, and remove the bacteria altogether; these (as organic matter) probably disappearing as gases, or forming a part of the residual compounds of nitric or nitrous acid with the inorganic bases.

The time required, however, according to Dr. Miquel, is very great; and excepting in cases of very large, deep bodies of water no such reduction can be expected.

The experiments of Dr. Miquel have not taken into consideration the seasonal disturbances of large bodies of water, which occur in the spring and autumn, and are due to the difference of temperatures of the layers of water at the top and bottom of large lakes and reservoirs, which is calculated to bring organic matter from the bottom of such bodies of water, and distribute it with more or less uniformity throughout all the layers, from the top to the bottom. Aside from these seasonal disturbances, the fact is very well established, that there is a species of purification going on steadily in all large bodies of water, which if uninterrupted by the accession of fresh organic matter from the runoff of rainfall and the discharge from sewage-polluted rivers and streams, such water would eventually become absolutely pure. This of course assumes a regimen for lakes and impounding reservoirs as well as the lesser quiescent bodies of water which is not found in practice, and in the author's opinion, the time has arrived to treat such sources of public water supply in the same manner as we are preparing to treat the water of polluted rivers ; for the same agencies which are operating to increase the natural contamination of river waters are also operating to produce a contamination of our lake and impounded waters, the difference being more in degree than in kind of pollution.

In his testimony before the Royal Commission on Metropolitan Water Supply, Dr. William Odling,* one of the official analysts of the water supplied by the London companies, expressed the opinion that no river or lake water was potable until after filtration, and laid particular stress upon the necessity of filtering lake water before it was used for dietetic purposes.

This fact is well illustrated in the experience of the city of Zurich, which takes its water from Lake Zurich, a large body of water at high elevation in the Swiss Alps, and supposed for many years to be an ideal source of public water supply ; yet it is well known that alarming typhoid fever rates have been traced to the polluted water of the lake, and for a number of years no water has been taken by that city until it has first been passed through a system of sand filters.   It is possible that no natural water supply in the United States is superior to that of Lake Zurich, lying as it does far above the usual sources of contamination ; but despite this fact, we find that even this body of water is not located high enough, or far enough away from the habitation of man, to insure its purity through all time ; and if it be essential to filter the water of Lake Zurich before it is delivered for drinking and other domestic purposes, why should it not be so with any natural body of water now used as a source of public supply in this country?

The commonly accepted opinion that sewage-polluted streams are capable of self-purification by flow through a reasonable dis-

* *Minutes of Evidence*, p. 388.

tance can no longer be seriously entertained. The Sixth Report of the Rivers Pollution Commission of England contains the conclusion "that there is no river in the United Kingdom which is long enough to purify itself of sewage received at its source;" and it might have added, nor in any other country where fresh accessions of sewage are being constantly received by rivers from cities on their banks.

It is often held that aëration of polluted waters has a beneficial effect on their quality. This theory, however, is successfully disputed by the experiments of Dr. T. M. Drown for the Massachusetts State Board of Health. These experiments show no oxydizing effect of aëration on the suspended organic matter in polluted waters, and a water must be very heavily charged with sewage before the dissolved oxygen per unit of volume of the water becomes so low as to have an injurious effect on the bacteria concerned in the destruction of organic matter. Aëration may impart "life," as it were, to water; but it cannot be said to have any marked influence on its quality.

It is probable that the self-purification of rivers occurs in the same way as in lakes, — by subsidence of the heavier organic matter, and by the destructive action of the bacteria; and these effects, as shown by the experiments of Dr. Miquel on the water of the River Seine, require considerable time, and are probably assisted by a quiescent state of the water, — two conditions not consistent with rivers of steep or moderate slope, and exposed from point to point in their course to renewals of organic matter from sewage and drainage sources.

Certain eminent investigators still hold to the opinion that self-purification of polluted streams really occurs, and that this, combined with dilution of the sewage by accession of fresh water, will be sufficient to purify a contaminated water until it is fit for drinking. But no reliance can be placed on self-purification; and if cities are to have a satisfactory drinking-water from a source of known pollution, it must be made satisfactory by some artificial means.

Impounding reservoirs, such as constitute the sources of supply for New York and Liverpool, are not open to the same degree of pollution as lakes and rivers; but excepting the drainage-ground of such sources is laid waste, and rendered free from all animal influences, even such water cannot be regarded as complying with the highest standard of hygiene.

Dug wells sunk a short distance in the drift are open to pollution from surface drainage; and such should never be adopted for a public supply except they be far removed from human habitation, and then only when the materials through which they are dug contains a thick stratum of impervious clay overlying the water-bearing sand or gravel. Wells of this character usually are limited in depth to the suction lift of pumps, and intercept water only in the upper layers of the soil.

Sometimes shallow wells intercept veins of water gathered on distant and higher watersheds, and the water may have been subjected to efficient natural purification before it reaches the well. In such cases, if the materials of the drift and the manner of constructing the well are such as to effectually exclude all local surface drainage, the water may be of high quality and altogether safe. It is not an easy matter, however, to determine from what source intercepted ground water has come; and shallow well water should not be used for public supply until repeated bacterial and chemical tests, through a reasonable length of time, have shown no possible pollution by sewage or local surface drainage.

If it be true that the typhoid fever death rates in any large community is a reliable index of the quality of the public water supply, then we are bound to admit that our great lakes (sewage polluted as they are, especially in the neighborhood of such cities) cannot be accepted as satisfactory sources of public water supply, excepting the water be subjected to careful filtration before it is supplied to the consumers.

TYPHOID FEVER DEATH RATES PER 100,000 OF POPULATION LIVING.

CITIES USING LAKE WATER.

Chicago,	(average for seven years ending December 1896),						71
Milwaukee,	"	"	"	"	"	"	"	29
Detroit,	"	"	"	"	"	"	"	30
Cleveland,	"	"	"	"	"	"	"	46
Buffalo,	"	"	six	"	"	"	"	34
Average,							42

CITIES USING RIVER WATER.

Pittsburg,	(average for seven years ending December, 1896),	84
Philadelphia,	" " " " " " "	45
Cincinnati,	" " " " " " "	49
Louisville,	" " " " " " "	74
St. Louis,	" " " " " " "	39
Average,		58

CITIES USING FILTERED RIVER WATER.

London,	(average for seven years ending December, 1896),	14.4
Berlin,	" " " " " " "	7.1
Rotterdam,	" " " " " " "	5.7
Hamburg,	" " four " " " "	9.7 *
Hamburg,	" " three " " " "	7.0
Altona,	" " six " " " 1895	26.8
Average,		12.2

In addition to the causes of pollution of river and lake waters previously mentioned, certain objectionable properties are sometimes imparted to the water by the subsoil drainage from irrigated and fertilized land. Thus the salts in phosphates and other fertilizers, and the ammonias from land laid with stable compost, are taken up by the water percolating through the arable ground, and eventually find their way by lateral movement through the soil into sources of water supply. While the simple addition of organic matter to water by this cause may never be very objectionable in itself, there is an objection to imparting properties to water which may encourage the growth and development of some of the pathogenic bacteria, and the increase of the alkalinity of water has already been pointed out, at least in one instance, as the cause of the rapid development of the cholera bacillus.† A professor of chemistry in one of our Western universities has stated to the author, that from his investigations typhoid fever seems to be most persistent in those districts where the water is abnormally high in nitrates and nitrites, and it is altogether probable that the subsoil drainage of farm lands is concerned in maintaining this condition of nitrates and nitrites in certain water sources which are drawn upon for domestic supply.

* Filters put in service, May, 1893.
† *Micro Organisms in Water*, by P. F. & G. C. Frankland, London, 1894, p. 306 (Hamburg Epidemic, 1892).

The author does not propose at this time to discuss the influence of nitrates or nitrites on the vitality of the typhoid bacillus, and will simply suggest that what has hitherto been regarded as a matter of no consequence in connection with a public water supply may become, in the light of future developments on the biology of this germ, a question of grave concern. Thousands of acres of farm land are to-day being annually treated with natural and artificial fertilizers, and the subsoil water from such land is going into some of our sources of water supply with possibly no advantage to the water. If the opinion now held by some investigators be confirmed by later experience, — that the addition to water of certain salts from these fertilizers is favorable to the growth of the typhoid bacillus, — then a new and difficult problem will be presented in connection with the other and well-recognized sources of pollution by surface drainage and urban sewage.

It is altogether feasible to provide against the direct contamination of water supplies from sewage by requiring all communities to treat this in such manner that the effluent shall conform to a given standard of hygiene before it is permitted to go into our water courses, lakes, and ponds ; but the objection to surface and subsoil drainage cannot be so easily disposed of. In the light of the present information upon the subject, we are safe in assuming that any dangers to our sources of water supply from these causes must be met by treatment of the water after such pollution has occurred, rather than by efforts to prevent pollution ; and if the theory and operation of sand filtration be accepted as established conditions, and not as propositions still to be proven, we can assume that the filtrate may be brought to any practical standard of hygiene without regard to the quality of the water from which it is obtained.

Filtration to be successful must be able to meet all the varying conditions of any water, and render a filtrate which will be substantially unvarying in quality. While the quality of the water applied to the filter may, and in many cases will vary between wide limits, the quality of the filtered water must be practically uniform. The London standard of bacterial quality of the filtered water is one hundred bacteria per cubic centimeter of the filtrate ;

and while the counts are usually much lower than this, under no condition can the filtered water show more than this number without passing the limits there assigned for potable water.

The London standard is thus not based upon the relation of the numbers of bacteria in the filtrate to the numbers of bacteria in the unfiltered water, but is an absolute standard, to which the filtered water must conform without regard to the bacterial condition of the water as it comes from its natural source. The standard of filtered water, like all standards, is an arbitrary one, and is fixed upon the judgment of men best informed upon the subject ; and as standards of quality for any substance are rarely placed beyond the reach of practical methods, it is reasonable to infer that with increased experience and knowledge of filtration, and with improved results from the application of research and experiment, that the standard of water quality will be placed higher and higher, until the limit of practical methods is attained.

That one hundred bacteria or colonies per cubic centimeter of filtered water is not a rare or difficult achievement is well attested by the operation of the Chelsea filters, which according to Dr. E. Frankland, the official analyst of the water supplied by the London companies, furnished a filtrate that contained for the year 1896, omitting the month of June, an average of 21 colonies of bacteria per cubic centimeter of water, the numbers being as high as 55 in December and as low as 2 in September, while the river water at Hampton Court, the point of intake for the Chelsea water company, contained so few as 1,740 bacteria per cubic centimeter in August, and as many as 160,000 bacteria per cubic centimeter in December of that year.

No operation suffers by care in its performance ; and to the caution as well as skill displayed in the operation of the London filters is due the low numbers of bacteria in the filtered water, and the low typhoid fever rates of that metropolis.

When failures have been recorded in the filtration of public water supplies, it can be set down as being due to ignorance or carelessness in proportioning the filters, or to gross mismanagement in their operation. Many attempts have been made to pass water through sand filters at rates which were not only beyond all precedent, but beyond reason. Thus a certain water company, which is now supplying a city of over 150,000 population east of the Rocky Mountains, has attempted to filter a polluted water at the rate of nearly 200,000,000 gallons per acre per day; a rate one hundred times greater than that for the London filters, and has assumed that this water was fit to go to its consumers, and be used for drinking and other dietetic purposes. The vertical rate of filtration in the London and most of the European works seldom exceeds 8 to 10 feet per day of twenty-four hours, while the estimated rate for this *improved* system of filtration in the Western city was 600 feet per day, or 5 inches per minute.* Natural filtration through the pervious materials of the drift is variously stated to occur at rates of 7 to 40 feet per day of twenty four hours.

Under circumstances like these it is not surprising that the water was really not filtered at all, and went through the mains to the consumers with no actual improvement in its hygienic quality.

The typhoid fever rates for that city were abnormally high for the last six months of the past year (1896), and the health officials very justly charged the unusual rates to this sham filtration.

In another Western city an improved natural filter was recently started to operate at rates of 22,000,000 to 44,000,000 gallons per acre per day, with very satisfactory results, according to report of the designer. No analysis of the water before and after it passed this filter, nor records of the influence of such water filtration on the health of the consumers, are available by the author; but it cannot be doubted that filtration under these conditions is really no filtration at all, and is calculated to hinder rather than encourage proper efforts in the direction of water purification by practical methods.

If the bacterial contents of a water is a fair test of quality, then driven wells sunk to moderate depths in the drift do not always intercept thoroughly filtered water. Professor Sedgwick, of the Massachusetts State Board of Health, has tested the water of a number of driven wells in the vicinity of Boston, with bacterial counts as high as 1,376 per cubic centimeter, while the water from other driven wells was shown to contain so few as 30 bacteria per cubic centimeter.

* *Transactions American Society of Civil Engineers,* vol. xxxi., p. 159.

The author's tests have shown certain driven wells to supply water containing from 2 to 4 bacteria per cubic centimeter, while other wells have shown as many as 1,060 bacteria per cubic centimeter. When chemical analyses have been made by the author contemporaneous with the bacterial tests, the higher counts of bacteria in driven well waters are usually accompanied by evidences of organic matter in the water.

High numbers of bacteria in driven well water is sometimes said to be due to the condition of the casing-pipe rather than to the water. But this scarcely can be correct ; the manner of driving tube wells and the condition of the casing are quite alike in all situations, and counts of bacteria per cubic centimeter of the water as widely separated as 2 to 1,400 cannot be satisfactorily accounted for by growths on the walls of the pipe.

Within the author's practice he has seen no reason to suspect any variation in the condition of the interior surfaces of the iron casings, while great variations in the bacterial counts of driven well water have been recorded. It is quite probable, even with foul casing-pipes, that the continuous passage of water of low bacterial contents over the iron would reduce the bacteria to the kinds and numbers of those naturally in the water ; [*] and since tests of the water for bacteria are usually made after long pumping of such wells, it seems unreasonable to charge high numbers of bacteria in water from tube wells to the growth of species in the organic matter supposed to be on the interior surface of the pipes.

Natural filtration through the materials of the drift must depend (like artificial filtration through prepared beds of sand) upon several factors, chief of which are the thickness of the layers, and size of the grains of sand and gravel, through which the water passes to the lower levels, where it is collected in reservoirs and pockets, or intercepted by strata through which vadose currents are passing.

It cannot be assumed without analysis that natural filtration always produces pure water. In some examples it doubtless does ; in others it may not. If the pervious materials of the drift are quite porous, allowing high rates of vertical percolation, it is possible, indeed probable, that such water, if originally polluted, will still be

---

[*] *Practical Bacteriology*, Dr. W. Migula, London, 1893, pp. 151, 166.

polluted at considerable depths. Beds of coarse gravel below the lower levels of the ground water probably have no influence on the quality of the water passing through them, no straining effect can be expected, nor is the author aware of any biologic action taking place in deep-seated strata of pervious materials.

Dr. Rosenau * of the U. S. M. H. S., during November of 1895, made a very exhaustive examination of the water supplied to the city of San Francisco, and found unmistakable evidence of the presence of the colon bacillus and *b. proteus vulgaris* in the San Andreas and Pilarcitos waters, and evidence of the *proteus* variety in the water from the Crystal Springs Reservoir.

The Visitacion water, from a series of wells 130 to 180 feet deep in the sand and gravel, contained the colon bacillus. Concerning these bacteria Dr. Rosenau says : —

"The presence of the *proteus* indicates fermenting processes, doubtless the decomposition of organic matter in the water. This organism is one of the most common and widely distributed putrefactive bacteria.

"The colon bacillus is an intestinal organism, and its presence in the water means contamination with alvine discharges, either of man or the lower animals."

In the light of what has been said on the inefficiency of natural filtration in certain localities, the discovery of *b. coli communis* in water from the wells of the Visitacion water-works possesses especial significance. The presence of this bacillus in water is an index of sewage pollution, either from man or animals ; and the evidence of sewage pollution at this depth (130 to 180 feet) clearly demonstrates that natural filtration cannot be relied upon in all localities or at all times.

The water from a well sunk in a sand-bar in the Ohio River near the city of Cincinnati, at a depth of 77 feet, contained a putrefactive bacterium resembling *b. proteus vulgaris*, which liquefied 10 per cent gelatin in a cool cupboard within two days.† The water from the Ohio River had a hardness at this time of 2.18 to 2.40 parts per 100,000 parts of water ; while the water from

---

* *Public Health Reports.* Washington, D.C., April 10, 1896.

† *Report of Engineer Commission on Extension and Betterment of Cincinnati Water Works,* 1896, p. 23.

the bottom of the sand-bar had a hardness of 12 to 13 parts per 100,000 parts of water, indicating ground water not well purified by percolation through the pervious materials of the drift.

It is fortunate, however, that the ground water generally adopted for public water supply is gathered originally on suburban or unimproved land, the runoff of which at its worst is never polluted with city sewage, as are our rivers and some other bodies of water; and such water is infinitely less liable to contain the bacteria of disease communicable by drinking-water.

Such waters, while of higher purity than lake and river waters, are not always to be accepted as indices of the efficiency of natural filtration, but as waters which never were seriously polluted.

The distrust of all natural sources of water supply, excepting deep wells, and springs at high elevations, by many of the European authorities, has given a strong impetus to filtration·of water in foreign cities. "With the exception of mountain springs * such as supply Vienna and Munich, or carefully planned works for ground water such as supply Dresden, or deep well water from the chalk strata such as supplies the Kent district of London, the foreign engineers seem to regard nearly all other of the natural sources of water supply as open to suspicion."

Certain standards of quality in articles of diet are recognized the world over, and even the poorer grades of food materials are required by law to be of a quality that will cause no injury to health. All civilized nations insist upon absolute immunity from disease through articles of diet ; and why should people be less concerned about the quality of their domestic water supplies than they are about the quality of articles of food ? No other substance enters so largely into the support of the animal system ; and the same care and safeguards which are applied to the ordinary articles of food should be applied to drinking-water, and water for most of the domestic uses.

The objection to polluted water is not so much to the organic matter which it may contain, as it is to the possibility of the presence of some of the bacteria concerned in the production of disease.

---

* *The Water Supplies of Eight Cities in Relation to Typhoid Fever Rates*, by the author, Chicago, 1896.

At the present time some 23 of the pathogenic organisms have been found in water or sewage, among which are the germs of typhoid fever and cholera.

The latter being a disease not indigenous to this country, and rarely coming even by importation, it is sufficient to consider the typhoid bacillus as the special object to be avoided in selecting sources of water supply, or to be restrained by methods of purification of polluted waters.

While other pathogenic organisms may be imbibed through drinking-water, or be taken into the system through some other form of contact with water, and set up processes which lead to disease, the proof of this is still lacking ; and the distinguishing purpose of pure or purified water is the reduction of the typhoid fever rates. Moreover, the use of a naturally pure water, and the processes resorted to for the purification of polluted waters, will probably have the same influence on all other water-borne pathogenic organisms as on the typhoid bacillus ; and remedies which will be successful in excluding this one germ from our domestic waters will (so far as we now know) operate with equal force against all other water-carried disease germs.

Before discussing the probability of typhoid fever infection by public water supplies, it may be well to remark that other disorders of the animal system may be traced to certain inorganic matters in water. Thus waters high in lime or other bases are not the best for continuous use as a drinking-water. Certain of these minerals may, in very limited quantities and at times, be of advantage to the animal system ; but the continuous use of a water high in mineral contents is recommended by physicians only in special cases, and to correct certain disorders or symptoms to which such waters, or rather their mineral contents, are fitted.

In early life that part of the human system which is intended to eliminate the excess of salts in water and food is very powerful, and capable of a large amount of daily work without injury. As we grow older, and especially in advanced life, this part of the system can be easily overworked ; and when it is, the blood will contain an abnormal amount of these salts or their acid products which lead to very serious results. The excess of salts often is deposited in the capillaries and other blood vessels where the circulation is sluggish, rendering them brittle and easy of rupture by shocks or vascular pressure.

Embolisms, apoplexy, and paralysis may be traced to this deposit of lime or some other base (in excess in the blood), which impedes the movement of the fluid through the vascular system. and produces stresses in some of the more delicate vessels or capillaries, which they are unable to resist. This objection to what are usually termed hard waters for drinking-purposes may be very refined, and too remote for practical consideration in the light of the more pronounced objection to the sewage pollution of waters ; but it is worthy of thought, and continued study of this aspect of drinking-waters may verify the author's opinion, that a soft, pure drinking-water is better for the human system than a hard, pure drinking-water.

While there is a popular sentiment against the use of a water known to be sewage polluted, this is neither as strong nor as well grounded as it must be to secure reforms in the water supplies of many of our cities. When people come to understand that disease and death lurk in sewage-polluted waters, and that to drink such waters, or permit others to drink them, is an invitation to suffering and loss of life, then communities will demand remedies for the evils which in many instances are now but vaguely supposed to exist.

There are several well recognized tests of the quality of a water supply : —

First, the test by chemical methods, which measures the amounts of nitrogenous organic matter in water as ammonias, the chlorides of sodium and potassium as chlorine, the reduction of nitrogenous matters to nitric and nitrous acids, as nitrates and nitrites, and finally determines the presence of minerals, as arsenic, copper, etc., which may be in quantity sufficient to make a given water supply dangerous to health. Chemistry divides up the dissolved and suspended matters, and indicates the nature and amount of each.

Second, the test by biological methods, which deals exclusively with the number and kinds of organisms present, and their probable origin in the water, and more directly and certainly than chemistry determines the fitness of water for domestic uses.

Finally, the quality of a given water supply may be roughly but effectually determined by allowing the people to use it, and noting its influence on their health. This method prevails in nearly all the cities of this country; and a comparison of the typhoid fever rates from these with the rates of other cities where the quality of water supply is the subject of careful and constant supervision, clearly demonstrates the importance to every community of the best water which skill and money can provide.

For many years the cities of Jersey City and Newark, N.J., drew their water supplies from the Passaic River at Belleville. Above this point, as early as 1894, the river was receiving the sewage from two hundred thousand people; and, being subject to tidal influence, some of this sewage was carried up and down past the two water-works intakes, until it went with ebb-tides into Newark Bay, or was deposited by subsidence on the bottom of the river. At the time of the author's examination of the Jersey City water (August, 1894), some destruction of the sewage by the action of the bacteria, infusoria, and other living organisms, in the water evidently was going on, but at a rate too slow to have any marked effect on its quality. In April of 1892 Newark abandoned the Passaic River, and commenced to draw its water supply from impounding reservoirs in the valley of the Pequannock River, while Jersey City continued to take all or part of its water from the Passaic River until November, 1896.

" These two cities are separated principally by a large meadow or swamp.* They are embraced in the same system of electric street railroads, subject to the same climatic conditions, and, excepting their sources of public water supply, there is no known reason why any marked difference in the typhoid fever rates should exist between them."

" A comparison of the typhoid rates for the past seven years from these two cities, however, furnishes important evidence that water is the carrier of the typhoid bacillus, and that the typhoid death rate bears a just relation to the sewage pollution of our sources of public water supply."

---

* *Engineering Record*, March 23, 1895. (Including rates for 1895–1896.)

In the following table are given the death rates from typhoid fever per 100,000 of population living : —

JERSEY CITY, N. J.

Year,	1890.	1891.	1892.	1893.	1894.	1895.	1896.
Death Rate,	91	95	53	60	76	71	61–62

NEWARK, N. J.

Year,	1890.	1891.	1892.	1893.	1894.	1895.	1896.
Death Rate,	60	81	45	28	15	17	21

Until 1892, and for nearly four months of that year, both cities drew their water supplies from the Passaic River, at Belleville. During April of 1892, the supply of Newark was changed to the Pequannock source; while Jersey City continued the use of Passaic water until November of 1896, when the whole supply of that city also was obtained from the Pequannock River. While the influence of the Pequannock water is not so well shown in the annual records of Jersey City, a study of the monthly typhoid mortality for 1896 reveals the remarkable vileness of the water from the old source.

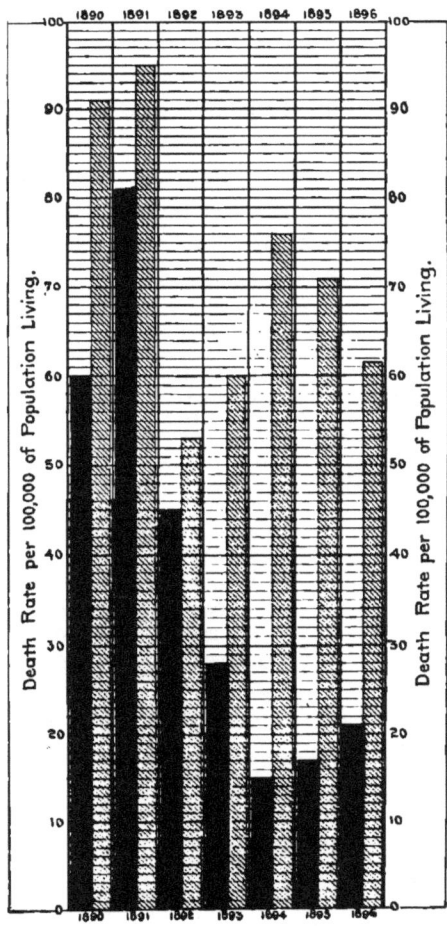

Fig. 1. Comparison of Typhoid Fever Death Rates for Newark and Jersey City, N. J. (Black, Newark; Shaded, Jersey City.)

Considering that the average death rate from typhoid fever in Newark since the introduction of the Pequannock water is still from two and a half to five times what it would be if supplied with water like that of some of the larger cities of Europe, one can understand how objectionable must be the Passaic River as a source of dietetic water supply.

The average rate for Newark for 1890 and 1891 was 70.5; while the average rate for 1892 to 1896 inclusive was 25.2, or a reduction of 64.3 per cent. The average rate for Jersey City for 1890 and 1891 was 93; and the average rate for 1892 to 1896 inclusive was 64.3, a reduction of 30 per cent.

This reduction in the case of Jersey City is due to other causes than the use of Pequannock water; and allowing for the same general influences in the city of Newark, the net reduction in the typhoid fever rates by Pequannock water was 34.3 per cent.

The distinct influence of the Pequannock water when used in Jersey City in comparison with Passaic water, is shown by the following table : —

JERSEY CITY, N. J. (1896). POPULATION, 187,008.

Month.	Pumped from Passaic River. Av. Daily Gals.	By Gravity from Pequannock River. Av. Daily Gals.	Percentage of Pequannock Water.	Deaths from Typhoid Fever.
January,	18,100,000	6,600,000	27	28
February,	15,700,000	10,400,000	40	30
March,	14,700,000	11,500,000	44	16
April,	9,800,000	13,900,000	59	9
May,	13,200,000	13,000,000	50	6
June,	6,300,000	21,000,000	76	7
July,	5,700,000	22,400,000	80	3
August,	6,900,000	22,100,000	76	3
September,	7,900,000	19,900,000	72	3
October,	3,500,000	22,500,000	86	4
November,	. . .	25,500,000	100	1
December,	. . .	28,400,000	100	5

Of the 115 deaths from typhoid for the year (1896), 74 occurred during the first three months, for which time the average proportion of Pequannock water was 39 per cent.

On comparing January and February, when 67 per cent of the

water supply was drawn from the Passaic River, with the months of November and December, when all the water was from the Pequannock River, the reduction in the typhoid rates was nearly 90 per cent.

From the following table it appears that the typhoid death rate is generally higher in Jersey City for the months of October, November, and December, than for the months of January, February, and March, as it usually is for other cities ; and assuming this to be true for the year 1896, then with an increased or complete substitution of Pequannock water for the sewage polluted Passaic water, there was a reduction of over 86 per cent in the typhoid death rates.

DEATHS FROM TYPHOID FEVER, JERSEY CITY, N. J.

YEAR,	1893.	1894.	1895.	1896.	1897.
POPULATION,	175,000.	179,939.	184,173.	187,098.	190,000?
January,	12	16	12	28	1
February,	3	5	9	30	6
March,	15	1	20	16	2
April,	7	6	19	9	2
May,	2	3	9	6	2
June,	11	4	7	7	3
July,	6	10	7	3	1
August,	13	14	11	3	2
September,	8	16	6	3	2
October,	9	23	13	4	3
November,	11	7	9	1	· ·
December,	8	14	14	5	· ·

The average deaths from typhoid for the months of November and December for the years 1893 to 1895 inclusive, during which time Passaic water alone was used (corrected for population of 1896), were 22, compared with which months the deaths for 1896, using Pequannock water alone, were 6, or the reduction was 73 per cent. Comparing the deaths for January and February, 1893 to 1896 inclusive, with the deaths for the same months of 1897, the reduction of the death rate was over 76 per cent, by reason of the complete substitution of Pequannock for Passaic water. The water from the Pequannock was first turned into the Jersey City mains Jan. 10, 1896.

The city of Lawrence, Mass., with a population (1896) of 55,000, draws its water supply from the Merrimac River, after it has received the sewage from Lowell, nine miles above. The city of Lowell, with a population (1896) of 85,700, draws its water supply partly from the Merrimac River, and partly from a system of driven wells. Lawrence, however, has filtered its water since September of 1893, while Lowell uses such water as is drawn from the river in its natural state.

The typhoid fever death rates per 100,000 of population living, for these two cities, since 1890, are shown in the following table : —

Year,	1890.	1891.	1892.	1893.	1894.	1895.	1896.
Lowell,	158	98	90	61	55	39	42
Lawrence,	123	115	102	93	48	31	15

The average death rates for the years 1890 to 1892 inclusive, before filtered water was used in Lawrence, were for Lowell 115, and for Lawrence 113, or quite the same ; while for the three years, 1894 to 1896 inclusive, during which time filtered water was used in Lawrence, the average rates were for Lowell 45, and for Lawrence 31. The percentage of reduction in the rates for Lowell was 40, and for Lawrence over 72, leaving a net reduction of 32 per cent to be credited to the filtered water of the latter city.

This is not all that the filtered water is entitled to, according to reports from Lawrence, which show that many of the mill operatives continue to use canal water, which is unfiltered Merrimac water, in defiance of the notices posted conspicuously in the mills that canal water is dangerous to health, and should not be drunk ; and a fairer comparison will be of the years 1890 to 1892 inclusive, before the filtered water was introduced, with 1896, when the use of filtered water was doubtless more general than for 1893, 1894, and 1895. Upon this comparison, Lowell shows a reduction of 63.5 per cent on the former rates, while Lawrence shows a reduction of nearly 87 per cent on the former rates, or a net reduction in favor of the filtered water of Lawrence of over 23 per cent.

An examination of the table indicates that some influences were at work in Lowell since the filtered water was introduced in Lawrence, which very materially reduced the typhoid fever rates of the former city;* but whatever these influences, they were not so efficient in reducing the death rates as were those of the filtered water supplied to Lawrence.

Standing alone, the filtration of the polluted Merrimac River water has reduced the typhoid rates for Lawrence nearly *ninety* per cent; and by the correction of certain errors in the design of this filter, with total abstinence of the people from unfiltered water, a greater reduction than this is to be expected.

The great difficulty in the way of advancing practical works of water purification is the lack of proof that water is really the cause of disease. A moment's reflection will convince one that apart from transmission by personal contact, as in smallpox, or by food, as milk, etc., all infectious diseases must be transmitted to human beings from the air, the soil, or from water. The evidence now that certain diseases like tuberculosis and diphtheria are due to air-borne germs is very satisfactory. Similarly from the soil we obtain the germs of tetanus and anthrax, and the evidence is very convincing to the majority of investigators that typhoid fever and cholera are almost exclusively water-carried diseases.

Dr. Edmund Rogers, an eminent physician of Denver, Col., classes mountain fever with typhoid fever. Both are continuous fevers, and arise from similar causes. If the fever is light, it is called mountain fever; if it becomes intense, it is called typhoid. Typhoid seems to be endemic in parts of certain States where mountain water constitutes the supply for potable purposes. It is a mistake to assume that mountain water must be pure water, where exposed, as it is in many localities, to the sewage from mining-camps or other permanent or migratory settlements upon the watershed above the points at which such water is taken for domestic supply. Small centers of typhoid are found upon the mountain slopes at all times, and these may furnish material for the infection of cities dependent upon mountain water.

---

* After above paragraph was written, a communication to the author from Mr. R. J. Thomas, superintendent of the Lowell water-works, contained the information that since February, 1896, "No water has been taken from the river, direct nor through the filter [described in Chapter XI.], a sufficient supply of very good water having been obtained from a system of driven wells."

A foot-note in Mr. Preller's paper on the water-works of Zurich, Switzerland, contains the following statement : —

> " Spring water rising in the upper Alpine reaches is, in spite of its crystalline clearness, peculiarly liable to pollution by the scattered droppings of grazing cattle, unless the whole drainage area is inclosed. Although the water purifies itself to a great extent in the course of its flow, it can produce epidemics by the droppings of diseased cattle, of which cases are recorded in the upper Rhine Valley, at Neuchâtel, and at Appenzell."

Here is a danger to which too little attention has been given. In considering the population of a given watershed no mention (within the author's knowledge) has ever been made of the number of domestic animals, while careful enumeration is given of the people per square mile. Domestic animals are not always in a state of health ; and evidently any disease germs which may be in the excreta of these scattered over a given watershed will be washed into the streams, lakes, or reservoirs with each succeeding storm.

It is not likely that any farmer would fancy having the sewage from his stock discharged into his domestic well, yet the same thing really occurs when the runoff of rainfall on perhaps every watershed carries this same sewage from domestic animals into our sources of potable water supply.

Some of the diseases of cattle and sheep, for instance, are recognized as diseases of man ; and while no evidence exists that these are infectious by water carriage, still it is certainly very imprudent to assume that no danger can exist in this direction simply because it has not been proven.

It is sometimes held that all typhoid fever cannot be charged to impure water supplies : this may or may not be true ; but in any family the only things that are common to all its members are the water, the soil, and the air surrounding the premises — all other possible causes of disease infection are affected by the personal habits of the members. Nearly all articles of diet, excepting water and milk (as a beverage), are sterilized by cooking and baking before they are ingested ; and such articles as are not sterilized are usually washed with water before they are brought to the table.

Other causes than domestic water supplies have been shown to be responsible for typhoid epidemics, but water only has been shown to be the cause of our high continuous typhoid fever rates.

The investigation of epidemics of typhoid fever in isolated localities has suggested that in many of these the cause must have been local; and it has been held that when no known pollution of the water supply by domestic sewage has occurred, the water supply was blameless.

A little thought upon the subject suggests that, in settlements far removed from the ordinary channels of typhoid infection, the same causes may be at work that we find in more populous centers.

The colon bacillus may be found in any water open to pollution from the excremental refuse of domestic animals; and may it not be possible that the colon bacillus from a sheep or hog, when taken into the human system, becomes the active cause of typhoid fever? and if it does, is it not easy to understand how epidemics can arise, even when no apparent cause may exist? It is not known to the author that any one excepting Professor Lankester believes that the colon bacillus may become the typhoid bacillus; and no one but Harvey, two hundred and fifty years ago, believed in the circulation of the blood. Harvey, however, was right, while the others were wrong; and Lankester may be right to-day. Many steps must be taken to prove his views; and if proven by time, the cause of these isolated typhoid cases will be made very clear, and water again will be shown to be the carrier of the infection.

The fact has been repeatedly shown, that certain so-called pathogenic organisms have their virulence exalted by contact with certain other so-called non-pathogenic organisms; and the combined effect of the action of the colon bacillus normal to the human intestine and the colon bacillus from domestic animals may be the symptoms and lesions characteristic of typhoid fever.

Proof of this is lacking, but certain epidemics seem to be accountable for in no other way.

CHAPTER III.

BACTERIAL CONTENTS OF VARIOUS WATERS.

THE great variation in the numbers of bacteria counted from the same source on different dates of the same month, or upon a series of plates all inoculated in the same manner at the same time, has frequently been noted, and is probably due primarily to the lack of uniformity in the distribution of the bacteria throughout the water sample, and somewhat to the nutrient properties of the media employed, and temperature of growth.

When the nutrient media are from the same solution for a series of three or more plates, and the conditions in other respects the same, the author has frequently found a great difference in the number of bacteria from successive drops of water from the same sample, which can be reconciled only upon the theory of a lack of uniform distribution of the organisms in the water sample. It is well known, in the case of a water sample allowed to stand for a few minutes, that the number of organisms varies considerably with the depth at which they are taken by the dropping tube, the smaller number being found near the surface of the water, and the larger number at the bottom.   To avoid an error due to depth of water when the sample is taken up for inoculation of the nutrient media, it is customary to shake the bottle thoroughly before it is opened and the sample taken, to distribute as well as possible the organisms throughout the whole volume of water.

The number of bacteria per cubic centimeter of a water sample also depends upon how the inoculation is made ; whether the water is taken from the collecting bottle and quickly dropped into the gelatin, or is given time to permit of the bacteria settling to the point of the pipette before inoculating the tube.   A test for the effect of gravitation of the bacteria after the sample of water has been taken up in the dropping tube is given below : —

PLATE I. — Water taken from the beaker into the tube, and a few minutes allowed for the bacteria to settle to the point of the tube before the inoculation was made.

PLATE II. — Inoculation quickly made after the sample of water was taken into the dropping tube.

PLATE III. — Same as PLATE II.

WATER FROM DOMESTIC CISTERN.

PLATE	I. — Bacteria per cubic centimeter,					1,330
PLATE	II. —	"	"	"	"	460
PLATE	III. —	"	"	"	"	480

Tests of Ohio River water as it comes through the taps of Cincinnati have been made by the author with the following results :

BACTERIAL CONTENTS OF OHIO RIVER WATER AS SUPPLIED TO THE CITY OF CINCINNATI.

DATE.	DAYS OF GROWTH.	COLONIES PER C. C. OF WATER.
July 18, 1894,	4 on gelatin,	7,665– 9,570
" 24, "	5 " "	94,050–103,000
Aug. 1, "	7 " "	1,680
Oct. 4, "	4 " agar,	9,856
" 15, "	5 " . "	1,872
" 15, "	5 " gelatin,	5,820
" 29, "	5 " "	1,760
Nov. 7, "	5 " "	2,674
Mar. 13, 1895,	6 " "	20,724
July 23, "	4 " "	2,835– 2,910
Aug. 30, "	4 " "	561
Nov. 29, "	4 " "	8,448– 9,120
Dec. 12, "	5 " "	2,455– 3,295
Jan. 15, 1896,	7½ " "	3,146– 4,825
" 22, "	5 " "	1,248– 1,704
" 27, "	4 " "	1,498– 1,701
Feb. 1, "	4 " "	5,025– 5,100
" 9, "	4¾ " "	1,596– 1,717
" 10, "	6 " "	2,030– 2,155
" 16, "	7½ " "	1,442– 1,680
" 16, "	4½ " "	1,458– 1,593
Mar. 1, "	3¾ " "	842– 1,446
" 2, "	5 " "	1,051– 1,821
Apr. 12, "	5½ " "	1,657– 1,883
June 29, "	4 " "	2,304– 2,832
July 4, "	4 " "	495– 644
Dec. 11, "	4 " "	10,742– 11,300
" 13, "	4 " "	6,333– 9,637

There is nothing unusual about the bacterial contents of the Ohio River water. All rivers receiving sewage, or the wash of soil, contain relatively large numbers of bacteria, most of which are the common water species, and concerned in the breaking up of organic matter. The water supply of Cincinnati is subjected to no kind of purification before it is delivered to the consumers, and any objection which may exist to it before it is pumped from the river still exists when it reaches the consumer. Cincinnati is one of the cities of this country which has a high typhoid fever rate.

According to Mr. M. N. Baker,* who has given very serious consideration to the subject of sewage disposal and water purification, "When sewage-polluted water must be used, means should be adopted for its purification."

With large dilution of sewage containing pathogenic organisms, the chance of taking any of these into the stomach through the medium of drinking-water is diminished, but the longevity of the organisms is increased. In an undiluted sewage the typhoid bacillus would probably perish within a short time. In pure water, that is, water free from the energetic putrefactive organisms, the typhoid bacillus would live for weeks. If other organisms be absent from the water, i.e., if the water is sterile, the typhoid bacillus has been known to survive for three months.†

Dr. Abbott states that no bacteria are found in deep well water,‡ but the author's experience has been quite to the contrary ; no well water, however deep the well, has failed to contain some bacteria, and some moderately deep driven wells have shown considerable numbers upon bacterial test.

The examinations by Professor Sedgwick, and the table of results by the author which are given on pp. 44 and 45, throw some light on the bacterial contents of well water.

Certain experiments have been made to determine the effect of domestic filters on Ohio River water. These filters are all sold as germ-proof apparatus, and the purchaser in most instances really

* *New Jersey Sanitary Association, Proceedings,* 1895, p. 75.
† *Water Supply for Cities,* by author, University of Illinois, 1896, p. 12.
‡ *Principles of Bacteriology,* by A. C. Abbott, M.D., Philadelphia, 1894, pp. 419–436.

believes in their efficiency in the prevention of the passage of bacteria. The best domestic filter is the Pasteur, with which at this time nearly every person is familiar; but even this will not restrain the passage of bacteria for any length of time. Variations in the porosity of the porcelain tubes will increase or diminish the rate of delivery of water through the unglazed material, and correspondingly affect the rapidity with which certain of the bacteria will grow through the pores of the tubes.

BACTERIAL CONTENTS OF WATER.

PASTEUR–CHAMBERLAND FILTERS, —

DATE.	DAYS OF GROWTH ON GELATIN.	COLONIES PER C. C. OF WATER.
1. June 16, 1894,	7	62
Tube sterilized just before use.		
2. Oct. 10, 1894,	5	580–974–1,536
This filter in restaurant, and probably not well attended to.		
3. Oct. 10, 1894,	5	2
This is a new filter with freshly sterilized tubes.		
4. Oct. 15, 1894,	10	4
Sample from new filter.		–
5. Oct. 24, 1894,	5	180–209–436
This filter is in a popular hotel, and carefully attended to.		
6. Nov. 25, 1894,	19	4–8
This filter in drug-store, water used for prescription purposes.		
7. May 23, 1895,	7	201–236–287
Same as No. 6, water still used for prescription purposes.		
8. May 23, 1895,	7	167–182–293
Same as No. 2, tubes renewed.		

Freudenrich [*] has made some experiments with the Pasteur filter to determine the sterility of the filtrate at different dates after sterilization of the tubes, and for different temperatures of the room in which the filters were kept, and finds that at a temperature of 35° C. the filter delivered sterile water at the end of six days, while at a temperature of 22° C. the filtrate in some cases was, and in others was not, sterile at the end of ten days. The cause of one filter furnishing sterile water, and another operating under the same conditions giving a filtrate containing bacteria, is

---

[*] *Centralblatt für Bacteriologie*, vol. xii., 1892, p. 240.

explained by the investigator as being due to the difference in the density or porosity of the tubes, and to differences in the micro-organisms in the water at different times.

It has been the author's experience with water from filters of this type that they never furnish *absolutely* sterile water ; for upon a series of plates inoculated with such water, while some may re-

BACTERIAL CONTENTS OF WELL WATER, EASTERN MASSACHUSETTS.

(From Examinations by PROFESSOR W. T. SEDGWICK. *)

LOCATION OF WELL.	DEPTH IN FEET.	COLONIES PER C. C. OF WATER.
Cambridge,	193	254– 269
"	100	30
"	454	206– 214
"	254	135– 150
Lowell,	. .	228
"	. .	178 (Gly. Agar.)
Cambridgeport,	198	116
"	198	192– 193
"	198	258– 262
Boston,	213	138– 139
"	213	130– 140
"	213	101– 106
"	377	48– 54
"	377	149– 158
Cambridgeport,	277	1,240–1,376
"	277	486
Boston,	130	440– 480
"	200	525
Roxbury,	180	57– 60
Somerville,	67	165
Roxbury,	750	38

main sterile for several days, in due time they will develop one or more colonies.   An entirely sterile plate he has never met with. Professor Percy Frankland, in discussing this filter, says : —

"It must be regarded, therefore, still as an open question whether patho-
· genic organisms, such as typhoid bacilli, can or cannot grow through the pores of the Chamberland (Pasteur) filter ; and until this question has been answered in the negative, it is obvious that in using these cylinders they should be frequently cleaned and sterilized."

* *Twenty-sixth Annual Report Massachusetts State Board of Health*, p. 435.

Not having the details of the Freudenrich tests, it is impossible to compare the results from abroad with those obtained here. Tests of Pasteur filters, in such condition as they are found in hotels and restaurants, have given from 180 to 1,500 bacteria per

BACTERIAL CONTENTS OF WATER FROM DRIVEN WELLS.

(From Examinations by Author.)

Date.	Location.	Growth on Gelatin, Days.	Depth of Well in Feet.	Colonies per C. C. of Water.		Remarks.
1895	Lebanon, O.	5	62	260–1060		Boring No. 7.
1895	Wyoming, O.	3½	146	109		. . .
1895	Lebanon, O.	5	115	7		Boring No. 12.
"	"	8	115	4		"
"	"	11	115	8		"
1895	St. Mary's, O.	5	265	3–	14	In lime rock.
"	"	7½	265	3–	14	"
"	"	9½	265	6–	14	"
"	"	5	280	53–	67	"
1896	Dayton, Ky.	5½	82	34		Dayton sandbar.
"	"	5½	82	38		"
"	"	5½	82	39		"
1896	Dayton, O.	4½	70	1		Pumping.
"	"	4½	70	52		. . .
"	"	4½	70	60		Natural flow.
"	"	4½	70	66		"
"	"	4	70	146–	149	"
"	"	5	70	31–	39	After 72 hours of pumping.
1896	Wyoming, O.	4	146	7		From discharge pipe of pump while pumping.
"	"	4	146	73–	75	From tap, residence.
1897	Wyoming, O.	4	146	285–	305	" " "
"	"	9	146	2.6–	7.8	From discharge pipe of pump.

cubic centimeter; and the low counts of 2 to 4 bacteria per cubic centimeter have been obtained from tubes not previously used.

In regard to Freudenrich's * experiments with water from the Pasteur filter, unfortunately we have the results of his investigations without the details as to nutrient media employed, or tem-

---

* *Fire and Water*, Nov. 3, 1894.

perature and time allowed for the colonies to develop in the inoculated gelatin (or other media). If Freudenrich's inoculations were made in the standard gelatin-peptone solution, and the plates or dishes were examined, as is customary, at the end of three or four days, one can understand how such plates might show no growth at all; but if the examinations be delayed for a week or ten days, we should expect to find colonies of water bacteria appearing on such plates.

From his own experiments with water from new Pasteur filter-tubes, the author has never failed to find colonies of water bacteria, if sufficient time is given for these to develop; and this may be partly accounted for by the nutrient properties of the gelatin, and the great difference in time of growth between different bacteria found in water, some appearing in twenty-four hours, while others require from one to three weeks to grow. If a plate is planted with slow-growing bacteria, an examination of such plate at the end of four days may reveal no colonies at all, and such water would incorrectly be declared sterile. For, evidently, if any water bacteria are found growing on the plate after being kept for two or three weeks in the moist chamber at room temperature, such bacteria must have been in the water when the plate was inoculated. Of course it is assumed in such cases that the plate has been carefully guarded against the introduction of adventitious germs.

Stone disk and tube filters, of which quite a number of forms are now being made and sold, are not to be regarded as germ proof, although so labeled; and from the treatment which they receive after being introduced into a residence, they usually become a positive menace to the health of the family dependent upon them for their drinking-water. It is not denied that these filters are successful in clarifying turbid waters; but a collection of sponges will do the same thing, and no one supposes that a sponge filter will restrain the passage of bacteria. Water may be rendered perfectly limpid by filtration; but colorless or clear water, and pure or purified water, are not the same.

Clarified water may be the carrier of pathogenic bacteria quite as well as turbid water; while turbid water, apart from the inorganic substances (in solution or suspension) which gives it color, may be very pure. Clarification and filtration are not one and the same thing ; although, as a rule, properly filtered water usually is colorless, unless the color is derived from peaty substances, in which event the hygienic quality may be greatly improved by filtration without removing the color.

BACTERIA IN WATER FROM DOMESTIC FILTERS.

STONE DISK FILTERS, —

DATE.	DAYS OF GROWTH ON GELATIN.	COLONIES PER C. C. OF WATER.
1. Sept.　2, 1894,	5¾	19,035–48,600

This filter in a very popular restaurant, with the legend on the menu : "The water of this establishment is filtered through —— stone filter, and is absolutely pure."

2. Dec.　18, 1894,	5	3,859–5,733

This filter in private residence filtering cistern water.

3. July　12, 1895,	4	11,704–14,605

Same as No. 2.

4. July　20, 1895,	4	29,765

Same as Nos. 2 and 3.

5. April 12, 1896,	5½	2,873–3,628

New filter in service few hours before sample was taken; this also is in a restaurant which offers its patrons pure *filtered* water.

6. Dec.　9, 1896,	5	1,299–1,308

Filter in residence.

STONE TUBE FILTER, —

7. July　17, 1895,	4	125–175	Showing effect of
8. July　19, 1895,	6	335–440	time on development
9. July　21, 1895,	8	410–535	of colonies.

SAND FILTERS, —

10. May　21, 1895,	4	153–176–180	Without coagulant.
In restaurant.			
11. Dec.　17, 1895,	7	30–34–36	With coagulant.
Experimental filter.			
12. Jan.　1, 1896,	7	20–85	"　　"
Experimental filter.			
13. Sept.　20, 1896,	2½	77–105	"　　"

This sample of water reported by chemist as being free from alb. ammonia.

SAND AND CHARCOAL FILTER, —

14. March 30, 1896,	3	2,445–2,512
Filter in residence.		

It will be noted that the number of colonies from a given water sample depends upon the days which the plate is permitted to grow before the count is made. Referring to the stone tube filter, the water from which was tested July, 1895, by prolonging the growth from four to eight days, the count was increased more than three times ; and all the colonies finally found on these plates were due to bacteria in the water at the time of inoculation. The same increased growth due to time of inoculation is strikingly shown in the following table of bacteria from spring waters, where in one instance the count rose from 424 at the end of two days to 1,440 at the end of six days. Other illustrations of the influence of time on the counts will be noted in the several tables of bacterial contents of various waters.

Spring waters sold in Cincinnati for table use have given the following results when tested for bacterial contents : —

SPRING WATER.

(Samples collected at the source, and planted within two hours.)

DATE.	SPRINGS.	DAYS OF GROWTH ON GELATIN.	BACTERIA PER C. C. OF WATER.
Sept. 2, 1895,	Tallewanda, Ohio,	4	128–148
Nov. 3, "	" "	4	85–402

(From Bottled Spring Water.)

Geneva bottled spring water, planted Aug. 1, 1895, gave the following results : —

Counted at end of 2 days,   424 colonies per c. c. of water.
"   "   4 "   1,024   "   "   "   "
"   "   5 "   1,160   "   "   "   "
"   "   6 "   1,440   "   "   "   "

Dr. T. M. Drown, from analyses of forty-one spring waters in Massachusetts,[*] found : —

2 springs contained   1 bacteria per c. c. of water each.
5   "   "   2   "   "   "
7   "   "   an average of   7   "   "   "
6   "   "   "   "   16   "   "   "
7   "   "   "   "   29   "   "   "
6   "   "   "   "   70   "   "   "

---

[*] *Twenty-third Annual Report Massachusetts State Board of Health*, p. 356.

3 springs contained an average of 159 bacteria per C. C. of water each.
1   "   "   "   250   "   "   "
1   "   "   "   416   "   "   "
1   "   "   "   973   "   "   "
2   "   "   "   1,844   "   "   "

Professor W. T. Sedgwick * has examined the water in a number of springs in the country district of southern New Hampshire with the following results : —

No.	Date of Analysis.	Bacteria per C. C. of Water	
		On Gelatin.	On Agar.
1	Nov. 29, 1894,	252–258	145–167
2	"	134–163	133
3	"	92–105	72– 79
4	"	95–106	89– 96
5	"	193–218	203–217
6	"	43–100	36– 72

The author, in searching for *b. typhosus* and allied organisms in the Ohio River water, has made several tests with the solution proposed by Parietti for destruction of the non-pathogenic bacteria in water, with the results as given in the table on page 50. The influence of varying quantities of the acid solution is distinctly shown by the test of Jan. 5, 1896.

The test of Aug. 7, 1895, indicates the influence of time on plates inoculated with Ohio River water, after treatment of the gelatin with a strong dose ($\frac{5}{13}$ c.c.) of the Parietti solution. At the end of four days (the usual time of incubation of water bacteria at room temperature) no growth at all had occurred, while three days later twelve colonies had appeared, and three days later than this the growth had increased six times. In endeavoring to reduce the number of bacteria in a water sample by dosing the gelatin with the Parietti solution, considerable care must be exercised to avoid the destruction of the typhoid bacillus if it be present. It is well known that several other organisms will resist larger doses of the acid solution ; and upon any plate, when search is being made for *b. typhosus*, one must expect to find several other

* *Twenty-sixth Annual Report Massachusetts State Board of Health*, p. 436 *et seq.*

bacteria, if the latter happen, as is usual, to be present in the water.

It is commonly supposed that freshly fallen rain-water contains few bacteria. According to Miquel (Paris), rain-water at Mont-souris, in the suburbs of the city, contained 4.3 bacteria per cubic centimeter, while rain-water caught in the middle of the city contained 19 bacteria per cubic centimeter.

INFLUENCE OF PARIETTI SOLUTION ON GROWTH OF BACTERIA.

CINCINNATI, OHIO, TAP WATER.

DATE.	DAYS OF GROWTH ON GELATIN.	KIND OF WATER.	COLONIES PER C. C. OF WATER.
Aug. 7, 1895,	4	Plain water,	804
Aug. 7, "	4	City water in 10 c. c. of 15% gelatin treated with $\frac{5}{12}$ c. c. of Parietti solution,	No growth.
Aug. 10, 1895,	7	"	12
Aug. 13, "	10	"	72
Dec. 12, "	5	Plain water,	2,455–3,205
Dec. 12, "	5	City water treated with 6 drops = $\frac{1}{4}$ c. c. of Parietti solution in 10 c. c. of 10% gelatin,	25– 29
Dec. 15, 1895,	$7\frac{1}{2}$	Plain water,	3,146–4,825
Dec. 15, "	$7\frac{1}{2}$	City water treated with 6 drops = $\frac{1}{4}$ c. c. of Parietti solution in 10 c. c. of 10% gelatin,	59– 119
Jan. 5, 1896,	18	City water treated with 4 drops = $\frac{1}{6}$ c. c. of Parietti solution in 10 c. c. of 10% gelatin,	853
Jan. 5, 1896,	18	City water treated with 5 drops = $\frac{1}{5}$ c. c. of Parietti solution in 10 c. c. of 10% gelatin,	658
Jan. 5, 1896,	18	City water treated with 6 drops = $\frac{1}{4}$ c. c. of Parietti solution in 10 c. c. of 10% gelatin,	227

The author, however, finds that the numbers of bacteria in rain-water depend upon the time at which the collection of the sample is made. If at the beginning of a shower, the numbers may be high, while after a few hours of rainfall the atmosphere appears to have been washed of its bacterial contents, when the

numbers become very low. The notes below illustrate the influence of time of rainfall upon the bacterial contents of the water.
The author's samples were collected in the suburbs of Cincinnati,
where the conditions were quite like those of the country.

Fresh rain-water from short shower caught in sterilized bottle placed
on the ground clear of trees and houses.

DATE OF TEST.	DAYS OF GROWTH.	COLONIES PER C. C.
July 22, 1895.	4	5,495–5,759.

A sample of rain-water collected July 28, 1895, on 4 days'
growth, gave 414 molds and 624 colonies per cubic centimeter.

Rain-water collected at end of twelve hours of rainfall.

DATE.	DAYS OF GROWTH.	COLONIES PER C. C.
July 12, 1896,	3¼	15–18
July 13, 1896,	4½	54–57

As further interesting information upon the chemical quality of
freshly fallen rain-water, the following analyses by Dr. Thomas M.
Drown are quoted : —

CHEMICAL ANALYSIS OF RAIN-WATER.[*]

(Parts per 100,000.)

DATE.	STATION.	AMMONIA.		NITROGEN AS		CHLO-RINE.
		Free.	Albuminoid.	Nitrates.	Nitrites.	
1888.						
July 7,	North Andover,	.0047	.0038	.0070	.0000	. . .
Sept. 18,	" "	.0016	.0026	.0040	.0000	. . .
Sept. 12,	Lawrence,	.0298	.0024	.0000	.0000	.007
Oct. 2,	"	.0414	.0030	.0100	.0000	. . .
Nov. 27,	"	.0164	.0014	.0050	.0002	.360
1889.						
May 21,	Lawrence,	.0086	.0026	.0030	.0001	.070
June 17,	Jamaica Plain, Boston,	.0564	.0152	.0180	.0004	.130
1890.						
Mar. 28,	Newton Highlands,	.0154	.0034	.0050	.0001	.060
1887.						
Dec. 26,	Boston (snow),	.0258	.0038	.0030	. . .	. . .

[*] *Massachusetts State Board of Health*, 1890, Part I., "Report on Water Supply and
Sewerage," p. 562.

Quite a profitable business has been established in several of the larger cities in the manufacture and sale for table use of distilled water. A test of such water as supplied in Cincinnati gives a very favorable result : —

DISTILLED WATER. (Single Distillation.)

DATE.	DAYS OF GROWTH ON GELATIN.	BACTERIA PER C. C. OF WATER.
Oct. 29, 1895,	4	30–52
Oct. 31, 1895,	6	38–80

The following water was suspected of having caused typhoid fever in one of the State institutions of Ohio : —

(Sample taken from tap in Superintendent's Office.)

DATE.	DAYS OF GROWTH ON GELATIN.	BACTERIA PER C. C. OF WATER.
Sept. 11, 1896,	3	845–862–897

Many of the above colonies were rapid liquefiers, compelling the count of the dishes at end of three days to avoid complete loss of test.

Same water tested Sept. 29, four days growth on gelatin.

One dish gave 239 bacteria per cubic centimeter of water.

Second dish, gelatin wholly liquefied and count impossible.

Some tests of the influence of a small Anderson Revolving Iron Purifier on water from the Ohio River gave results as follows : —

ANDERSON REVOLVING IRON PURIFIER.

(Laboratory Test of Ohio River Water.)

DATE.	KIND OF WATER.	DAYS OF GROWTH ON GELATIN.	COLONIES PER C. C. OF WATER.
June 29, 1896,	Plain city water,	4	2,304–2,832
" "	Anderson Purifier,	4	50– 90
July 4, 1896,	Plain city water,	4	495– 644
" "	Anderson Purifier,	4	39– 119

Reference will be made to this performance again in discussion of this mode of water purification ; but at this point it should be remarked, that the conditions under which the experiments were conducted did not favor the best performance of the device, but were deemed sufficient to indicate, in a rough way, how the contact of the fragments of iron in the purifier aided in the removal, by subsequent sand filtration, of the larger percentage of the bacteria contained in the raw water.

Artificial ice made from distilled water is now largely sold in many cities, particularly where the climate is prohibitory of the collection of ice from lakes and ponds. A test of such ice, as supplied in the city of Cincinnati and vicinity, is given below : —

TESTS OF ARTIFICIAL ICE SUPPLIED IN CINCINNATI.

DATE.	DAYS OF GROWTH ON 15% GELATIN.	COLONIES PER C. C. OF WATER.
July 12, 1896,	3¼	17– 37
July 13, 1896,	4¼	99–105

In testing water samples for bacterial contents, in addition to the usual precautions to avoid contamination from the atmosphere, it is advisable to make an occasional test of the air of the workroom, as a guide to the probable amount and kinds of organisms which might accidentally come into a sample under observation. Such tests by the author indicate a considerable variation in the numbers of air germs which will fall on an open sterile gelatin plate in the same room at different times.

BACTERIAL CONDITION OF AIR OF WORKROOM.

DATE.	TIME OF EXPOSURE.	GROWTH.	MOLDS.	COLONIES.
July 14, 1894,	10 minutes,	4 days,	26	69
Nov. 15, 1895,	15 "	9 "	2	43
Mar. 29, 1896,	15 "	7 "	2	4

Certain experiments have shown sunlight to be a powerful agent in the destruction of nearly all forms of bacterial life. With respect to the influence of sunlight on the bacterial life in river water, Dr. E. Frankland, in his " Report on the Quality of London Waters for 1895," says : * —

"With regard to the effect of sunshine upon bacterial life, the interesting observations of Dr. Marshall Ward leave no doubt that sunlight is a powerful germicide; but it is obvious that its potency in this respect must be greatly

* *Annual Summary of Vital Statistics*, London, 1895, p. 67.

diminished, if not entirely annulled, when the solar rays have passed through a stratum of water even of comparatively small thickness before they reach the living organisms. By a series of ingeniously contrived experiments Mr. Burgess has demonstrated the correctness of this view. A sterile bottle was half filled with Thames water, and violently agitated for five minutes to insure equal distribution of the organisms. Immediately afterwards a number of sterile glass tubes were partially filled with this water, and sealed hermetically. Three of these tubes were immediately packed in ice, and the remainder were attached in duplicate, at different distances apart, to a light wire frame, which was then suspended vertically in the river. The experiments were made near the Grand Junction Water Company's intake, at a place favorable for the sun's rays to fall on the river without any obstruction. The river was at that time in a very clear condition, and contained but little suspended matter, while the day was fine, although clouds obscured the sun occasionally. The tubes were exposed to light in the river for four and a half hours (from 10.30 A.M. to 3 P.M., on May 15, 1895). At the end of this time the tubes were packed in ice for transport to the laboratory, where the cultivation was started immediately. The colonies were counted on the fourth day, and yielded the following numbers : —

	COLONIES PER C. C. OF WATER.
Thames water packed in ice immediately after collection,	2,127
" " after exposure to sunlight for 4½ hours at surface of river,	1,140
" " after exposure to sunlight for 4½ hours at 6 inches below surface of river,	1,940
" " after exposure to sunlight for 4½ hours at 1 foot below surface of river,	2,150
" " after exposure to sunlight for 4½ hours at 2 feet below surface of river,	2,430
" " after exposure to sunlight for 4½ hours at 3 feet below surface of river,	2,440

These experiments show that on the 15th of May the germicidal effect of sunlight on Thames microbes was *nil* at depths of one foot and upwards from the surface of the water. It cannot therefore excite surprise that the effect of sunshine upon bacterial life in the great mass of Thames water should be nearly, if not quite, imperceptible.

Upon the contrary, the influence of sunlight on the contents of shallow reservoirs has been held to exert a very perceptible effect on bacterial life in the water. Bacteriological cultivation is usually conducted in cupboards or incubators, from which the light is rigorously excluded to avoid the inhibiting influence of light upon the cultures, and this effect is known to be due to light independent of heat from the sun's rays ; and one would have supposed that in clear water, through which the light would penetrate for some distance, a stronger influence would have been manifested than is shown by the experiment quoted.

That the effect of sunlight is held by some experienced investigators to be of value in the reduction of bacterial life in polluted waters, is apparent by the following quotation from a letter to the author by Mr. Rud Schroder, inspector of the Hamburg Water-Works : —

"In such places, where the winter temperatures do not vary from ours [Hamburg], I believe open filters are to be preferred on account of their facility in being worked and cleaned ; and last, but not least, in regard to their bacteriological efficiency due to the rays of the sun."

CHAPTER IV.

THE TYPHOID BACILLUS AND TYPHOID FEVER.

THE connection of *b. typhosus* with the etiology of typhoid fever is now so well established, and the relation of polluted water supplies to typhoid fever so generally recognized, that a brief review of the chief characteristics of this bacillus and allied organisms found in water will not be inappropriate.

B. typhosus, obtained from a human spleen, will give the following characteristics : —

(1) The bacillus will not liquefy gelatin.

(2) It will not coagulate sterilized milk.

(3) It will not produce gas when cultivated in glucose bouillon in the fermentation tube.

(4) It will not give the indol reaction.

(5) When grown in a peptone solution containing potassium nitrate, it is said to reduce nitrate to nitrite.[*]

(6) Under the microscope drop cultures show great activity of the bacillus. (This the author finds depends upon the age of the culture ; cultures near the original source (spleen) exhibit greater motility than old cultures, and in degenerate cultures motility seems to be no longer a property of the bacillus.)

(7) The vacuoles, or unstained spaces in the plasma, are rarely absent.

(8) Filaments are often found in stained young cultures.

The invisible growth on sterilized potato is no longer regarded as a test in differentiation of the typhoid bacillus. Other germs will give the same effect, and the invisible growth is not constant even with the typhoid organism.

In chemical composition the typhoid bacillus is not known to differ from the harmless bacteria. Under the microscope it resem-

[*] *Annual Report Massachusetts State Board of Health,* 1891, p. 641.

bles a diminutive rod with round ends, of length about three times the width. The length, however, is not uniformly three times the width; for longer and shorter individuals will be seen on cover glass preparations, and not infrequently long threads or undivided filaments will be noticed in preparations from young cultures. Numerous flagella, or whiplike appendages, spring from the cellulose envelope, and endow the bacillus with motility. When stained with carbol-fuchsin the bacillus appears as a brilliant red rod.

In looking for the typhoid bacillus in a sewage-polluted water, in addition to certain non-pathogenic organisms resembling *b. typhosus* in some respects, one is very liable to encounter two other germs nearly identical with the typhoid bacillus. These are *b. coli communis* and *b. lactis aerogenes.*

These three bacilli resemble (or differ from) each other in the following respects : —

(1) All are non-liquefiers. That is to say, all bacteria will either (*a*), grow in gelatin and liquefy the material, or (*b*), will grow in the material without liquefying it.

(2) While there is a distinct difference between the three bacilli in microscopic appearance, and *b. coli communis* and *b. lactis aerogenes* seem to have definite proportions not easily mistaken, the typhoid bacillus possesses such vagaries of proportion that at times it seems to resemble closely the other germs. Although *b. coli communis* is always thinner than the typhoid bacillus, and *b. lactis aerogenes* always shorter, the length of *b. coli communis* often agrees with the length (from a parallel culture) of the typhoid bacillus, and the width of *b. lactis aerogenes* is about the same as the typical typhoid rod, while all have rounded ends.

(3) All grow in gelatin stick cultures quite alike; *b. lactis aerogenes* the quickest and most luxuriantly, and *b. typhosus* the slowest and with least energy. Between *b. typhosus* and *b. lactis aerogenes*, *b. coli communis* occupies a middle ground. All produce a dirty white expansion on sloped agar.

(4) When cultivated in glucose bouillon in the fermentation tube, these organisms grow equally well in the presence or absence of air; the bouillon in the open leg (exposed through the cotton plug to the air), and in the closed leg (from which all air has been

removed during the sterilization of the contents of the tube), exhibiting similar turbidity. When the allied germs, *b. coli communis* and *b. lactis aerogenes*, are cultivated in the fermentation tube, an abundance of gas is produced in the closed leg, while the typhoid bacillus, when so grown, produces no gas ; and this test has been proposed by Dr. Theobald Smith * for the identification of *b. typhosus*.

When the test is one to determine whether a certain germ is the typhoid bacillus or *b. coli communis*, the fermentation tube will settle the question ; but alone it will not determine whether a suspected germ found in water is the typhoid bacillus or some other organism. In Ohio River water the author has found bacilli which grow in the fermentation tube quite like the typhoid bacillus, but which are known by further tests not to be this germ.

(5) When the typhoid bacillus is grown in sterilized milk having a slightly acid reaction, it will increase the acidity perceptibly, but neither in the presence nor absence of heat will the milk be coagulated ; while *b. coli communis*, when grown in milk, produces a large increase of acidity, and sometimes coagulates the milk in the tube at room temperature, and always coagulates the milk upon the application of heat for a few minutes.

(6) When cultivated in gelatin or agar to which one or two per cent of glucose is added, the typhoid bacillus will grow more luxuriantly than in plain gelatin, but produces no gas, while *b. coli communis* and *b. lactis aerogenes*, when so cultivated, produce an abundance of gas.

(7) *B. typhosus* in drop cultures is possessed of great activity, executing within the field of the microscope motions of translation and rotation, and sinuous movements to and fro ; *b. coli communis* has a sluggish motion, wholly unlike that of the typhoid organism ; while *b. lactis aerogenes* is not possessed of motility at all.

(8) All of these organisms are said to be found in the dejecta of man, and *b. coli communis* and *b. lactis aerogenes* also in the dejecta of animals.

* *The Fermentation Tube*, by Theobald Smith, Washington, D.C., 1893.

The following experiments by the author with *b. typhosus* and *b. coli communis* in sterilized milk throw some light upon the respective acid-resisting properties of these organisms : —

TESTS OF B. TYPHOSUS AND B. COLI COMMUNIS IN STERILIZED MILK.

(Acidity of 5 c. c. of milk tested before sterilization with a $\frac{1}{10}$ normal solution of caustic soda.   All cultures grown at room temperature.)

Five cultures were used : —

(A) *B. typhosus* obtained from Dr. T. M. Prudden, New York.
(B) *B. typhosus* obtained from Dr. O. L. Cameron, Cincinnati.
(C) *B. typhosus* obtained from Dr. O. L. Cameron, Cincinnati.
(D) *B. coli communis* obtained from Dr. O. L. Cameron, Cincinnati.
(E) *B. typhosus* obtained from spleen, Cincinnati Hospital.

DATE.	CULTURE.	ORIGINAL ACIDITY OF MILK.	DAYS OF GROWTH.	FINAL ACIDITY OF MILK.*	INCREASE OF ACIDITY.*
1894					
Dec. 24,	A (2)	0.75	4½	0.775	0.025
"	B	0.75	4½	0.825	0.075
"	C	0.75	4½	0.925	0.175
"	C	0.75	4½	0.950	0.200
1895					
Jan. 1,	A	0.80	4	0.910	0.110
"	A	0.80	4	0.930	0.130
"	B	0.80	4	1.100	0.300
Jan. 21,	B (2)	0.70	5	0.800	0.100
"	D	0.70	5	2.400	1.700
"	D	0.70	5	2.500	1.800
Jan. 26,	A	0.70	5	0.950	0.250
"	A	0.70	5	0.850	0.150
Mar. 2,	E	0.70	6	0.900	0.200
"	E	0.70	6	0.880	0.180
Mar. 8,	A	0.70	4	0.975	0.275
"	E	0.70	4	0.925	0.225
June 6,	A	0.70	5	0.900	0.200
"	E (3)	0.70	5	1.000	0.300

While *b. typhosus* will grow side by side with *b. coli communis* in sterilized milk with a slight increase of the acidity of the milk, the latter, on the contrary, will increase the acidity of milk to the point of coagulation.

Culture " A " indicated an increase of 22 per cent in the acid-

* Acidity of milk stated in cubic centimeters of caustic soda solution.

ity of milk; culture " B " an increase of 21 per cent; culture " C " an increase of 25 per cent; culture " E " an increase of 30 per cent; and culture " D " (*b. coli communis*) indicated an increase of 233 per cent in the acidity of milk. The increase of acidity of sterilized milk by *b. coli communis* as compared with *b. typhosus* is nearly ten to one.

Aside from the able demonstration of its untenability by Dr. Dunbar,* the theory which prevailed a few years since that an acid solution might be made in which *b. typhosus* would develop, while *b. coli communis* would perish, is clearly shown to be an impossibility by the experiments detailed above. The difference in the increase of acidity of sterilized milk by *b. typhosus* and *b. coli communis*, however, is an important factor in the differentiation of these organisms.†

A curious circumstance calculated to support Professor Lankester's view of the origin of *b. typhosus* is, that while the colon bacillus has been often found in polluted waters, the typhoid bacillus has been found upon very rare occasions, and considerable uncertainty surrounds quite a number of the alleged discoveries of the latter bacillus in water supplies. Doubtless in all cases of sewage pollution of water, the colon bacillus is much more numerous than the typhoid bacillus, because the former may come into the sewage from many sources, while the latter can come only from those suffering with typhoid fever, and even in such cases the bacillus is said to be given off only during the earlier stages of illness.

B. lactis aerogenes, likewise a bacillus of the intestine, by its resemblance in several respects to *b. typhosus* and *b. coli communis*, is very liable in the earlier stages of differentiation to be mistaken for either. It, however, may be determined much easier that a given organism is *b. coli communis* or *b. lactis aerogenes*, than that it is *b. typhosus ;* and this difficulty in differentiating a germ supposed to be *b. typhosus*, obtained outside the animal body, is a

---

* *Zeitschrift für Hygiene*, 1892, p. 485.
† *Twenty-third Annual Report Massachusetts State Board of Health*, p. 640.

stumbling-block in the way of direct proof that a given water supply contains the typhoid germ.

The rapidity with which the bacillus usually acts when inoculated into the lower animals renders these experiments an uncertain test in differentiation, although the researches of Dr. Alessi * with typhoid cultures on guinea pigs show that considerable time may elapse between inoculation and death of these animals. These experiments indicate that rats which die survived the infection from 12 to 36 hours, rabbits from 24 hours to 4 days, while guinea pigs survived the inoculation from 8 hours to 13 days.

The investigations of Dr. Alessi show that while putrid gases, i.e., sewer gas, may increase the susceptibility of the lower animals to typhoid fever infection, they cannot be considered as a cause. Many animals were experimented upon ; and with the exception of rats first exposed to the influence of putrid gases and then used as controls, all the animals not inoculated with the typhoid culture recovered. The following table contains a *résumé* of the mortality of the animals from these experiments : —

EXPERIMENTS WITH CULTURES OF B. TYPHOSUS AND B. COLI COMMUNIS.

CULTURE USED.	ANIMALS.	PERCENTAGE OF MORTALITY.	
		Inoculated Animals.	Control Animals.
B. typhosus (A),	Rats,	75	7
"	Guinea Pigs,	70	0
"	Rabbits,	100	0
B. typhosus (B),	Guinea Pigs,	80	0
"	Rabbits,	70	0
B. coli communis,	Guinea Pigs,	83.3	0

It is held at the present time by the best-informed students along this line, that if a given source of water supply is exposed to constant or even occasional sewage contamination, and that such sewage contains the dejecta from typhoid patients in hospitals and residences, it is not necessary to have direct proof of the presence of the typhoid bacillus in such water to justify its condemnation.

* "On Putrid Gases as Predisposing Causes of Typhoid Infection," by Dr. Giuseppe Alessi, *Journal of the Sanitary Institute*, London, January, 1896, p. 505.

The circumstantial evidence that the organism ·is in such water is sufficient, and the failure to find the bacillus upon test should not be taken as evidence of its non-existence.

The typhoid bacillus, originally isolated and described by Eberth, has been made the subject of careful study by Koch, Gaffky, Frankell, and Simmonds, and latterly by Joseph Sanarelli, of the Pasteur Institute, Paris.   Several papers by Sanarelli have appeared in discussion of the organism, — its connection with the etiology of typhoid fever, the symptoms and lesions produced, and results of inoculation in the lower animals, — of which the more important deductions and opinions are worthy of mention.

The so-called typhotoxin, described by Brieger as a product of the vital activity of the Eberth bacillus, is considered by Sanarelli only as an ordinary product of decomposition, arising from the changes which occur in the albuminoid substances of the culture media, or to bacterial poisons previously existing in the culture.

Of the Stas-Otto method by which typhotoxin is obtained it has been said : * —

"However, the method is not free from criticism.   The great number of chemical manipulations to which the organic matter is subjected is liable to lead to the formation of some basic substances, and to the destruction of others.   One is justified in considering the isolated base as preëxisting in the original material, only when it produces symptoms identical with those caused by the substance from which it is extracted."

Vaughan and Novy, however, assume that Brieger has actually isolated the poisonous product of the typhoid bacillus ; while Sanarelli rejects typhotoxin, so-called, as a product of the Eberth germ. Sanarelli calls attention to the fact that "recent investigators have shown that evaporation of the albuminous liquids in the presence of hydrochloric acid and their subsequent extraction with alcohol is alone sufficient to produce bodies considered by Brieger as ptomaines, and the typhotoxin does not produce a morbid state comparable with that of typhoid fever," and concludes that all attempts to ascertain the chemical nature of the poison produced by the ·typhoid bacillus are failures.

* *Ptomaines and Leucomaines*, by Vaughan and Novy, Philadelphia, 1891, p. 170.

Sanarelli argues that no matter by what channel the typhoid bacillus enters the system, its seat of operation is not the small intestine (Peyers glands), as heretofore supposed, but the spleen. Here it grows and elaborates the toxin which is taken into the circulation, and produces certain local effects which are characteristic of typhoid fever. He holds that the toxic product of the growth of *b. typhosus* in the spleen, when taken into the circulation, paralyzes the walls of the intestine, and destroys its powers of resistance to the action of *b. coli communis*, and that all local effect in the ileum is to be charged to the latter organism, and not, as has been generally supposed, to the action of *b. typhosus* on the mucosa and vessels of the intestine.

He maintains that all local symptoms of typhoid fever are like the symptoms in the ileum, altogether due to the toxic properties imparted to the circulation by the growth and development of *b. typhosus* in the spleen. He claims that the typhoid bacillus has never been isolated from the dejecta, nor from the anatomical changes in the intestine, and argues that if typhoid fever has its beginning and end in the digestive tract, why do we not find the *b. typhosus* there from the very beginning, before the symptoms characteristic of the disease are noticed. The diarrhea, he insists, is maintained and aggravated by *b. coli communis.* This remarkable series of papers contains the following conclusions : —

" The extraordinary multiplication of the colon bacillus, and its tendency to destroy all other bacteria and become the sole representative of the intestinal species, are the results of an active biologic work, incessant and complex. . . . When the poison (elaborated by *b. typhosus*) has attained the extreme limit of its tolerance by the subject, the fever ceases, and collapse ends the scene. It is this period of collapse which we reproduce experimentally on animals. In them the typhoid virus permeates the system, and manifests its effects too rapidly to give it time to react by means of fever during the early stages of intoxication. If the bacillus of Eberth could produce its toxin in the human system as rapidly as the cholera spirilla do theirs, typhoid fever would be like cholera, — a disease short of duration and without fever."

According to Sanarelli, by reason of their lower powers of resistance, the action of *b. typhosus* on the lower animals is too rapid to produce the train of effects which are recorded of this disease in man.

To the medical practitioner these conclusions of Sanarelli, if confirmed by further investigation, should possess great value, and be an aid to him in revising his methods of treatment of typhoid fever.　To the sanitarian they also possess interest, as showing the manner in which a certain bacterium (*b. coli communis*), always in the human intestine, and frequently found in sewage-polluted waters, may indirectly be endowed with extra pathogenic powers, and sustain a relationship to typhoid fever not heretofore suspected.

The typical typhoid bacillus, the bacillus of Eberth, is found in the spleen, and occasionally in some other organs of one who has died during the early stages of typhoid fever.　This organism, as is well known, has morphological and biological characteristics unlike the colon bacillus ; and considering the well-founded doubts of the several alleged discoveries of the true typhoid germ in water supplies, while many investigators have isolated the colon bacillus from this source, some strength is imparted to Professor Lankester's assumption that *b. typhosus* may be an exacerbated form of *b. coli communis.*

It has been stated that Malvoz of Liège, by successive cultivations of *b. coli communis* in a slightly acid bouillon, produced a species showing the characteristics of Eberth's bacillus.

The influence of environment on species is well known ; and may it be possible that *b. coli communis,* when taken into the human system through the medium of drinking-water, in certain persons finds there the conditions favorable to its development into what we know as *b. typhosus?*　Certain schools * refuse to recognize a difference between these two organisms, although they do not go so far as Professor Lankester, and assume that one may become the other.　They regard the two bacilli as different forms of the same species, and treat *b. coli communis* as a cause of typhoid fever.

Dr. Jordan,† of the University of Chicago, in a very able paper on the characteristics of the typhoid bacillus, says : —

---

* Sanarelli : *Annales de l'Institute Pasteur,* Nov. 25, 1892.

† *The Identification of the Typhoid Fever Bacillus,* by Edwin O. Jordan, Ph.D., Chicago, 1894.

" While the close similarity of the colon bacillus and the typhoid bacillus is necessarily recognized by every one, and while it is admitted that there is no single criterion that absolutely distinguishes the latter from all the perplexing 'varieties' and 'related forms,' it is nevertheless maintained by many that the sum total of the morphological and physiological characters presents a true and unmistakable picture of the specific organism of typhoid fever. These investigators hold that, although the varieties may approach more or less closely to the typical typhoid germ, they may always be distinguished from it by at least some one character which is not shared by the genuine typhoid organism."

In his summary on the existing information upon the differentiation of the typhoid organism from the colon bacillus and allied germs, among other conclusions he states : —

(1) "There is usually found in the spleen and other organs of an individual dying with typhoid fever, a bacillus which possesses certain definite morphological and physiological characters. . . .

(5) " The cases of alleged conversion of one 'species' or 'variety' (*b. coli communis*) into another (*b. typhosus*) do not carry conviction, and are susceptible of other interpretations than those advanced regarding them."

So far as protection to our public water supplies is concerned, this diversity of opinion on the typhoid bacillus as an independent organism can have little weight. The means adopted for the exclusion of *b. typhosus* from our drinking-waters will also exclude the colon bacillus. At least, it is not now known that a filter properly constructed and operated will not be equally effective in restraining the passage of either germ ; and methods of sterilization such as are in use on sea-going vessels are bound to eliminate both organisms from our drinking-waters. There is, however, this difference to be considered between the generally accepted theory of the transmission of the typhoid bacillus from the sick to the well through the direct sewage pollution of drinking-waters, and the theory of Professor Lankester of the colon bacillus under proper conditions becoming the typhoid bacillus, that if the latter should be substantiated, the exposure to typhoid fever from water sources is much greater than has generally been supposed ; and no surface water supply, the drainage area of which is inhabited by domestic animals, can be regarded as proof against a possible contamination by *b. coli communis*.

The percentage of mortality from typhoid fever is variously stated in text-books, and some statistics from the later experience of American cities with this disease are given in the table which follows : —

TYPHOID FEVER MORTALITY.

CITY.	PERIOD TAKEN.	CASES REPORTED.	DEATHS.	PERCENTAGE OF MORTALITY.
Lowell, Mass.,	Sept., 1890, to Jan. 1891,	550	89	16.2
" "	Nov., 1892, to Feb., 1893,	141	30	21.3
Lawrence, Mass.,	Nov., 1892, to Feb., 1893,	141	28	20.0
Springfield, Mass.,	July, 1892, to Sept., 1892,	155	32	20.6
St. Louis, Mo.,	April, 1892, to Mar., 1893,	3,624	514	14.2
" "	Aug., 1892, to Jan., 1893,	3,455	453	13.1
Pittsburg, Pa.,	1891,	1,047	248	23.7
" "	1892,	1,145	256	22.4
" "	1893,	2,398	294	12.3
Schenectady, N.Y.,	July, 1890, to April, 1891,	300	70	23.3
Cincinnati Hospital,	1891,	85	11	13.0
" "	1892,	59	7	12.0
" "	1893,	108	4	3.7
" "	1894,	117	14	12.0
" "	1895,	98	10	10.2

It is a fact well known to physicians and investigators, that typhoid fever is everywhere a disease which sets in late in summer or early in autumn, and continues above the normal rate until midwinter, after which it usually shows a decline, falling to the lowest case and death rates during the months of spring. The theory of Pettenkofer and others of the Munich school,* that the disease rises and falls in intensity as the level of the ground water falls and rises, is partly supported by the usual seasonal distribution of typhoid.

In spring the level of ground water is high, and the typhoid rates low. In the autumn the level of the ground water is low, while the typhoid rates are high ; but so many proofs are at hand showing high typhoid rates with high levels of ground water, and low typhoid rates accompanied by low levels of ground water, that the Pettenkofer theory of a connection between the level of the

* *Cholera,* by Dr. Max Von Pettenkofer, translated by Dr. T. M. Hime, London, 1883 (chart facing title-page).

ground water and typhoid fever is not of general application, and cannot point to a probable general cause for this disease in the lowering of the level of ground water.

Another theory of the cause of the rise in the typhoid fever rates during autumn is based on the assumption that the early rains carry into the streams and lakes which constitute so many sources of water supply, sewage and offal which has accumulated upon the ground and along the banks of streams during the period of drought. Opposed to this theory, however, is the almost uniform condition that the typhoid rates begin to rise before the fall rains occur. Indeed, the maximum rate is often reached in the autumn, before rains have fallen sufficient in volume to swell the streams, and wash organic refuse from the banks.

Dr. Woodhead * has indirectly suggested a theory which, properly expanded, seems to furnish a good reason for the seasonal influence on the typhoid rate ; viz., that the development of the typhoid bacillus in water will depend upon the temperature of the water in which it is migrating, low temperature discouraging the growth of the bacillus, while high temperature favors it. During the early autumn the lakes and rivers are at the highest temperature, which continues with slow diminution (in the temperate zone) well into the winter. During this period of high natural water temperature, typhoid fever usually rises to its greatest intensity for the year ; and when the temperature of the water naturally declines, and approaches its lowest point after midwinter, the typhoid rates also subside and reach their minimum.

This theory of the rise and fall of typhoid rates does not depend upon floods nor upon the level of the ground water, and is entirely consistent with the information upon the growth of the typhoid bacillus in the human body and in the usual culture media.

The influence of proper preventive measures on typhoid fever is shown by the experience of Vienna and Munich.

Professor Von Zeimssen † of the latter city a few years ago stated "that the reduction in the cases in the hospital had almost

---

* Royal Commission on Metropolitan Water Supply, London, 1893, *Minutes of Evidence*, p. 506.

† *On Typhoid Fever in Baltimore*, by Dr. William Osler, 1892.

changed the character of the service, and they had scarcely patients enough to illustrate the disease in the clinical courses." Dr. Osler is disposed to credit this reduction in the typhoid rates in these cities to improved sewerage, when it is really due largely to the remarkable improvements in their public water supplies, Munich having abandoned its old sources in wells and the River Isar for mountain springs in the Mangfall valley, and Vienna having abandoned its wells and the Danube for the Schneeberg springs in the Alps.

Improvements in sewerage should reduce the susceptibility of a people to typhoid infection, but the cause is removed when pure water is substituted for polluted water.

The channels of typhoid fever infection for a large city are clearly indicated in a recent paper by Dr. J. J. Reincke, *On the Epidemiology of Typhoid Fever in Hamburg and Altona ;* * and as applicable especially to Hamburg before filtration of the Elbe water was adopted, he mentions : —

(1) Importation of typhoid by way of the sea and the upper Elbe, and infection of the water of the river in front of the city by travelers.

(2) Infection of the water of the Elbe by patients in the city, whose disinfected dejecta is carried by the sewage into the river.

(3) Infection of the Elbe water from people on the ships, city dock laborers, and bathers.

(4) Infection by means of food which had come in contact with the Elbe water.

(5) Infection through the unfiltered Elbe water distributed to the people prior to May, 1893.

(6) Infection by patients and food brought into Hamburg from neighboring places.

(7) Secondary infection within the city by direct transmission, or infection of food and wells. [Causes which he holds were peculiarly numerous and effective in the second half of the great epidemics.]

Concerning the seasonal distribution of typhoid, he shows how the number of cases increase in autumn and decline towards spring. He points to the fact that in Germany the years 1857, 1865, and the early 70's were years of high typhoid fever rates, and the years of 1860 and 1867 were years of phenomenally low typhoid fever

* Hamburg, 1896.

rates ; and suggests that "there must be certain influences at work (here) that are more far-reaching than the predisposing causes."

He mentions conditions heretofore remarked, that the epidemics of typhoid which originate in the autumn have a gradual decline, while epidemics which originate during the late winter or early spring months show a sharp rise and fall of intensity and a sudden disappearance. Seasons of drought with low levels of ground water he considers as favoring high typhoid rates, while wet seasons and high ground water levels he regards as unfavorable. During dry seasons there is greater body heat with more thirst, and a larger consumpion of water for drinking and bathing purposes, which increases the liability to infection.

Dr. Reincke combats Pettenkofer's theory of the cause of typhoid fever, while agreeing with him that the proper prophylaxis for the disease is to be found in high quality of public water supplies and efficient sewerage and drainage. The very significant statement is made, that if typhoid fever epidemics are prevented in the cities there will be none in the country, and as a consequence there can be no reimportation of cases into the cities.

The author, after careful investigation, reached the conclusion several years ago that the sewage-polluted waters of the cities were largely responsible for typhoid fever in the country districts, and agrees with Dr. Reincke that the typhoid rates of any city is a measure of the efficiency of its works of sanitation.

Speaking of Hamburg, he says "that the present favorable and heretofore unattainable status of typhoid fever is to be largely credited to the filtered water supply, as indicated by the fact that this disease has not diminished among the people on the vessels arriving at the port."

CHAPTER V.

CLASSIFICATION OF CITIES BY TYPHOID FEVER STATISTICS.

It has been held (and correctly in the author's opinion) that the best test of the quality of a city water supply was the typhoid fever rates of that city. Thus a city with water of high quality should show low typhoid rates, and a city with water of known sewage pollution should show high typhoid rates. The final test of all public water supplies is the influence of these on the health of the consumers ; and in order to institute a comparison of cities upon the basis of quality of water supply, the author proposed, in a lecture recently delivered before the faculty and students of the University of Illinois,* to classify the larger cities of the world, embraced within the scope of modern health statistics, upon their typhoid fever death rates.

Thus cities of the first class must show a death rate from typhoid fever of not more than 10 per 100,000 of population living.

Cities of the second class must show a rate not higher than 20 per 100,000 of population living.

Cities of the third class must show a rate not higher than 30 per 100,000 of population living, and in like manner by tens until the sixth class was reached. All cities having a typhoid death rate in excess of 60 per 100,000 of population living are grouped in the seventh class. The classification is made upon the average rates for the years 1890 to 1896, inclusive, for the principal cities of the United States, Canada, and Europe, including two cities in Egypt and two cities in Australia. The statistics from which the classification is made will be found in the table of Typhoid Fever Statistics, Appendix A.

---

* *Water Supply of Cities*, Champaign, Ill., 1896.

CLASS I. — CONTAINING ALL CITIES SHOWING A TYPHOID FEVER DEATH RATE OF 10 OR LESS PER 100,000 OF POPULATION LIVING.

CLASS I.

City.	Source of Water Supply.	Population.	Typhoid Fever Death Rate.
Hague,	From sand dunes,	187,545	4.7
Rotterdam,	Filtered water from River Maas,	276.338	5.7
Munich,	Spring water from Mangfall Valley,	406,000	6.0
Dresden,	Filter wells and gallery by River Elbe,	342,340	6.2
Vienna,	Springs in the Schneeberg,	1,526,023	6.6
Berlin,	Filtered water from River Spree and Lake Tegel,	1,695,313	7.1
Copenhagen,	Filtered from wells and springs,	333,714	9.0

CLASS II.

City.	Source of Water Supply.	Population.	Typhoid Fever Death Rate.
Christiania,		182,856	10.6
Breslau,	Filtered from River Oder,	377,062	10.7
Amsterdam,	Haarlem dunes, and River Vecht, filtered,	489,496	11.9
Stockholm,	Lake and well water,	267,100	12.3
London,	Kent wells, and filtered water from Rivers Thames and Lea,	4,421,955	14.4
Trieste,		161,866	14.7
Edinburgh,	Impounded and filtered water from Pentland Hills,	276,514	16.4
Hamburg,	Filtered water from River Elbe,	625,552	17.7
Brooklyn,	Impounded water, and open and driven wells,	1,140,000	18.0
New York,	Impounded water from Croton and Bronx Rivers,	1,934,077	19.3

CLASS III.

City.	Source of Water Supply.	Population.	Typhoid Fever Death Rate.
Paris,	Rivers Seine, Marne, and Vanne, Ourcq Canal, artesian wells, and springs,	2,511,629	22.0
Sydney, N.S.W.	Impounded water from Upper Nepean River,	423,600	22.0
Glasgow,	Loch Katrine,	705,052	23.0
Buda-Pest,	Ground water from wells,	579,275	23.0

CLASS III. — *Continued.*

City.	Source of Water Supply.	Population.	Typhoid Fever Death Rate.
Brussels,		518,387	23.5
Manchester,	Lake Thirlmere,	530,000	25.7
New Orleans,	Drinking-water from tanks and cisterns,	275,000	25.9
Altona,	Filtered from River Elbe,	148,934	26.8
Davenport,	Mechanical filter, Mississippi River,	35,000	28.6
Venice,	Impounded water,	103,254	28.7
Milwaukee,	Lake Michigan,	257,500	29.3
Brisbane, Qu.		93,657	29.7

CLASS IV.

Date.	Source of Water Supply.	Population.	Typhoid Fever Death Rate.
Detroit,	Detroit River,	279,000	30.1
Boston,	Lake Cochituate and Sudbury River,	508,694	32.6
Buffalo,	Niagara River, at head,	350,000	34.3
Turin,		344,203	34.3
Rome,	Fontanadi Trevi, Aqua Felice, and Paoli,	473,296	35.7
Dayton,	Driven wells,	85,000	36.0
Liverpool,	Lake Vyrnwy (Wales),	632,000	36.3
Providence,	Pawtuxet River,	150,000	36.4
Covington,	Ohio River,	50,000	36.6
Newark,	Impounded water from Pequannock River,	230,000	38.1
San Francisco,	Impounded water from mountain springs,	330,000	38.4
St. Louis,	Mississippi River,	570,000	39.0

CLASS V.

City.	Source of Water Supply.	Population.	Typhoid Fever Death Rate.
Prague,		364,632	41.4
Baltimore,	Gunpowder River, Lake Roland,	507,398	43.6
Nashville,	Filter gallery, Cumberland River,	87,754	44.7
Philadelphia,	Schuylkill and Delaware Rivers,	1,188,793	45.0
Cleveland,	Lake Erie,	330,279	46.4
Denver,	South Platte River and Marston Lake,	150,000	47.2
Toronto,	Lake Ontario,	196,666	49.3
Cincinnati,	Ohio River,	341,000	49.4

CLASS VI.

City.	Source of Water Supply.	Population.	Typhoid Fever Death Rate.
Dublin,	River Vartry, impounded water, filtered,	349,594	52.3
Quincy,	Mechanical filters, Mississippi River,	42,000	53.6
Moscow,	Mytisch springs and ponds, Moscow and Yanza Rivers,	753,469	54.4
Newport,	Ohio River,	30,000	57.7
Knoxville (with suburbs),	Mechanical filters, Tennessee River,	45,000	59.7
Milan,		441,948	59.7

CLASS VII.

City.	Source of Water Supply.	Population.	Typhoid Fever Death Rate.
Indianapolis,	Driven wells, and White River,	165,000	64.5
Chattanooga,	Mechanical filters, Tennessee River,	40,000	68.2
Washington,	Potomac River,	278,150	71.1
Chicago,	Lake Michigan,	1,619,226	71.2
Jersey City,	Passaic and Pequannock Rivers,	187,098	72.5
Louisville,	Ohio River,	211,100	74.3
Lawrence, Mass.,	Filtered water from Merrimac River,	55,000	75.3
St. Petersburg,	Filtered water from River Neva,	954,400	77.2
Lowell, Mass.,	Merrimac River, driven wells,	85,700	77.6
Pittsburgh,	Alleghany River,	280,000	84.2
Atlanta,	Mechanical filters, Chattanooga River,	110,000	85.1
Alexandria, Egypt,	River Nile, by canal,	231,396	143.4
Cairo, Egypt,	River Nile, by canal,	374,838	168.3

CLASSIFICATION BASED ON LAST YEAR REPORTED (1896).

CLASS I.

City.	Population.	Rate.	City.	Population.	Rate.
Amsterdam,	489,496	3	Vienna,	1,526,623	5
Munich,	406,000	3	Hamburg,	625,552	6
Hague,	187,545	4	Stockholm,	267,100	6
Dresden,	342,340	4	Copenhagen,	333,714	7
Berlin,	1,695,313	5	Breslau,	377,002	8

CLASS II.

City.	Population.	Rate.	City.	Population.	Rate.
Paris,	2,511,629	11	Lawrence,	55,000	15
Rotterdam,	276,338	12	Edinburgh,	276,514	16
Altona,	148,934	13	New York,	1,934,077	16
Trieste,	161,886	13	Milwaukee,	257,500	18
London,	4,421,955	14	Brussels,	518,387	18
Brooklyn,	1,140,000	15	St. Louis,	570,000	19

CLASS III.

City.	Population.	Rate.	City.	Population.	Rate.
Buffalo,	350,000	20	Dayton,	85,000	25
Detroit,	279,000	20	Quincy,	42,000	26
Davenport,	35,000	20	Venice,	163,254	27
Sydney,	423,600	20	Providence,	150,000	27
Newark, N.J.,	230,000	21	Rome,	473,296	27
Glasgow,	705,052	23	Prague,	364,632	28
Manchester,	530,000	23	Toronto,	196,666	28.5
Turin;	344,203	24	Buda-Pest,	579,275	29

CLASS IV.

City.	Population.	Rate.	City.	Population.	Rate.
Chattanooga,	40,000	30	Liverpool,	632,000	32
San Francisco,	330,000	31	Christiania,	182,856	33
Boston,	508,694	32	New Orleans,	275,000	33
Covington,	50,000	32	Philadelphia,	1,188,793	34
Knoxville, (without suburbs),	37,000	32	Baltimore,	507,398	37

CLASS V.

City.	Population.	Rate.	City.	Population.	Rate.
Indianapolis,	165,000	41	Dublin,	349,594	45
Lowell, Mass.,	85,700	42	Chicago,	1,019,226	46
Cleveland,	330,279	43	Moscow,	753,469	46
Louisville,	211,100	45	Cincinnati,	341,000	48

CLASS VI.

City.	Population.	Rate.
Washington,	278,150	51
Nashville,	87,754	55
Milan,	441,948	55

CLASS VII.

City.	Population.	Rate.	City.	Population.	Rate.
Atlanta,	110,000	60	Newport, Ky.,	30,000	63.0
Brisbane,	93,657	60	Alexandria,	231,396	89
Pittsburg,	280,000	61	Cairo,	374,838	141
Denver,	150,000	61	St. Petersburg,	954,400	142
Jersey City,	187,098	61.5			

A review of the statistics furnished by the tables reveals some interesting facts : —

No city in the United States appears in the first class, and only two cities (Brooklyn and New York) appear in the second class. All other cities in these two classes are found abroad.

Considering that as an average for seven years, and for the last year, from seven to ten of the large cities of the world fall within the limit of the first class, it is painfully evident that a typhoid fever death rate of 10 per 100,000 of population living is easy of attainment when municipal corporations really desire to bring it about. Few people realize the relative standing of cities in the hygiene of their public water supplies ; and this classification will enable a comparison to be made, which should convince even the skeptical that in the matter of our public water supplies we are far behind the larger cities of Europe.

Referring to the cities of the first and second class, Rotterdam draws its water supply from the River Maas, one of the mouths of the Rhine, and passes it through sand filters before it is delivered to the consumers. Amsterdam* and The Hague draw their water supplies from the sand dunes, and afterwards subject it to careful filtration. Vienna and Munich depend upon water from large springs at high elevation in the Alps ; the former in the Schneeberg, 65 miles southwest of the capital, and the latter in the Mangfall valley, 37 miles from the city. Dresden is supplied from an infiltration well on the banks of the Elbe, which, according to Mr. B. Salbach,† intercepts an underground flow parallel to the river.

Berlin, the largest city in the first class, draws its water from

---

* This city takes a portion of its water supply from the River Vecht.

† *Transactions American Society of Civil Engineers,* vol. xxx., p. 293.

two sources, — the Stralau Works from Lake Tegel,* an expansion of the River Havel, and the Frederickshagen Works from Lake Müggel, an arm of the River Spree. At both stations the water is subjected to sand filtration before it is pumped to the distributing reservoirs or mains. Some of the most conscientious and complete investigations of sand filtration have been conducted with the filters of these works by Plagge, Proskauer, Piefke, and others.

Either spring water or filtered well and river waters constitute the sources for the cities in the first class.

London falls in the second class, and here the sources of supply are the Rivers Thames and Lea, and wells in the chalk or soft limestone. The enormous consumption of water by this city, now quite 200,000,000 imperial gallons per day, compels an abstraction at times of quite 30 per cent of the whole stream flow of the Thames, and even a larger proportion of the Lea.

The watersheds of these streams are heavily populated by urban and rural communities ; and in spite of precautions to prevent sewage contamination of the water, there is no doubt that, with a low stream flow and small dilution of sewage effluents, the pollution of the raw river waters at times is very great. A review of the history of the London sand filters and their operation further suggests that the same solicitude for water quality is not found here as in some of the Dutch and German cities, and to these facts may be ascribed the higher death rates from typhoid fever in London than in the cities grouped in the first class.

The natural conditions of the water supplies of Edinburgh, New York, and Brooklyn are in some respects alike, with the probability that the New York watershed is more completely protected from manifest sewage pollution than the watershed of Edinburgh in the Pentland Hills. Filtration of the water is occasionally resorted to by the latter city, according to Mr. J. P. Kirkwood, mainly to correct the turbidity ; and it is not known that any large improvement has taken place in the manner of operating the filters of late years. The hygiene of the water supply of Edinburgh should be like that of New York, and the typhoid fever rates support this view.

---

* The works at Stralau have not been operated for several years, but are kept in reserve. All water is now supplied from the Lake Müggel Works.

Hamburg, a city which for a period of seven years falls in the second class, but which since the introduction of filtered water is found in the first class, has had an unique experience. Prior to May, 1893 (the spring following the cholera epidemic), the water was drawn from the Elbe, and, apart from a limited sedimentation in reservoirs of small capacity, was sent to the consumers with no improvement in its quality. Since the date mentioned all water has been filtered under the supervision of Dr. Dunbar, director of the Hygienic Institute, and Mr. Rud Schröder, inspector of the Water-Works, with the result that the typhoid rates have been reduced quite 73.5 per cent. No other change has been made in the water supply than its filtration. The water of the Elbe, with its sewage pollution from all sources above the city, is used now as heretofore ; but none of it goes into the distributing mains until it is first passed through an elaborate system of plain sand filters.

Cities which depend upon water supplies from sources known to be sewage polluted, and of which no attempt is made at purification, very naturally suffer from high typhoid rates ; and an examination of the cities in classes four to seven shows that nearly all of them are in our own country.

The classification of cities for the last year of report (1896) enables Hamburg, Newark, Jersey City, and Lawrence to show what has been accomplished toward reduction of the typhoid rates by the substitution of good for bad water.

With reference to the use of public water supplies for dietetic purposes, in cities of Europe, the author, in a recent lecture upon the hygiene of water, published in the *Dietetic and Hygienic Gazette*, Philadelphia, October, 1896, says : —

" When comparisons are made of the typhoid death rates of cities in Europe with cities in this country, the claim is sometimes urged that the people of Europe, and especially of Germany, are not water drinkers, that beer is their usual beverage ; and upon the other hand, that the people of the United States are not beer drinkers, but water drinkers, and therefore more exposed to water-carried infections. When it is stated that The Hague has a typhoid death rate of 5 per 100,000 of population, this, according to some critics, is not to be taken as an evidence of the high quality of water supplied to the city, but as an indication that the people of The Hague generally do not drink water, and depend upon beer or some other manufactured beverage."

" This expression of doubt by some, that water may be so purified by artificial means, or may be naturally so pure as to largely diminish the probability of one contracting typhoid fever by drinking it, suggests inquiry along three lines : —

"1. Is the water supplied to certain foreign cities such as to reduce the typhoid fever rates or inhibit the disease, if it were generally used as a beverage ?

" 2. Is the water generally used for drinking in the larger cities of the United States such as to be the probable cause of our high typhoid fever rates ?

" 3. Is it true that the people of London, Berlin, Hamburg, and other European cities are largely beer drinkers, while the people of Boston, New York, Cincinnati, and other American cities are largely water drinkers ?

" It is not possible to answer the first question directly. Despite the great chemical and bacterial improvement by sedimentation and (or) filtration of certain polluted waters like that of the Elbe at Hamburg, and the Maas at Rotterdam, one cannot say positively that such waters, even after treatment, will not contain the typhoid bacillus, or be the carrier of infection to some ; and we are compelled to measure the improvement in quality of such waters by their influence upon the health of the people who use them.

" In regard to the quality of water supplied to the people of certain cities in Europe, it should be manifest, if this was not to be used as a drinking-water, that a very large annual expense could be avoided in those cities by pumping water direct into the reservoirs or street mains from any convenient source, without attempting in any manner an improvement in its quality before it is distributed to the consumers.

" Water of high hygienic quality is not required for the sprinkling of streets and lawns, for the extinguishment of fires, for the flushing of sanitary apparatus, for steam boilers, and many other uses; and if the water is not to be used for drinking and other dietetic purposes, great care and expense in the selection of a source of supply, or in efforts at improvement of the quality of water, are surely wasted.

" Considering that over ninety-eight per cent of the consumption of water by any large city is for purposes wholly unaffected by its hygienic quality, it would seem very singular indeed that a city like Berlin (for instance) should be at an extra expense of ten dollars per million gallons to fit the water for drinking purposes, before a gallon of it is permitted to go into the public mains. This great cost for purification of the water from Lakes Müggel and Tegel is not necessary if the water is to be used only for street sprinkling or other purposes apart from drinking and the requirements of the cuisine. Moreover, the water from Lake Müggel, after it has passed through the filters at Frederickshagen, as we have shown, is chemically and bacterially as pure as many natural spring or deep well waters which are known .to be altogether safe for drinking purposes, and chemically and bacterially pure or nearly pure waters

are not needed for any of the many uses of water, excepting for drinking, cooking, and the washing of uncooked articles of diet. No one would propose an elaborate and expensive treatment of a polluted water unless some portion of it was to be drunk.

"The water of the River Elbe, when it reaches Hamburg, is of sufficient purity for all ordinary purposes; but the most modern works upon a large scale for the improvement of polluted waters have recently been devised by that city, and these works are carefully operated to reduce the noxious properties of the Elbe water before it is distributed to the citizens. This work of purification is not intended to make the water better for the great majority of the uses to which it is applied, but to make it a water which the inhabitants can drink with the least risk of infection from typhoid fever and other water-carried diseases. If it were a fact, as some are disposed to think, that the people of Hamburg do not drink water, why should that city be at such great effort and expense to render the water of the Elbe fit to drink before it is permitted to go to the consumers?

" But the most pronounced efforts to procure a supply of public water which certainly shall not be the cause of infection is found at The Hague, where the water is first obtained from wells driven in the sand dunes and afterwards passed through filters of sand, the grade of which is finer than that of nearly every other city which has adopted sand filtration. The water of The Hague as it comes from the driven wells in the dunes very likely is equal to that of any of the driven well waters which we are accustomed to drink with a feeling of perfect security. But the officials of that city, not content with a water which at its source is far superior to nearly all of our public waters, set about to improve its hygienic quality by slow filtration through beds of fine sand, with the result that their city has had for many years nearly the lowest recorded typhoid fever death rate of any of the large cities of the world. Are we to ascribe this low typhoid rate to the drinking of beer, gin, or Schiedam schnapps by the people of The Hague, or shall we credit it to the drinking of this exceptionally pure water from the public mains?

" From such information as the author has been able to obtain, it is altogether probable that in the consumption of beverages other than water we are quite abreast of the people of this old Dutch city, and the only certain difference in the conditions surrounding the two cities which would affect the typhoid rates is found in the quality of their respective public water supplies.

" It is not difficult to answer the second question. Nearly all the water supplies of the large cities of this country are polluted with household sewage, and are the carriers of the typhoid bacillus from the sick to the well. Having knowledge of the fact that many of our large cities are daily drawing water for drinking and other purposes from sources of known sewage pollution, it is proper to look upon the typhoid rates of such cities as the natural result of this indifference to one of the first laws of health, viz., a pure drinking-water.

" In regard to the third line of inquiry the author is not able to state the per capita per annum consumption of beer by many of the larger cities of Europe; but the greatest consumption is accredited to Munich, which for one year used 125 gallons per capita.* An investigation of the probable consumption of beer by the larger cities of this country reveals the startling fact that even the city of Boston consumed 65 gallons of beer per capita during the year 1894, while Cincinnati indulged itself to the extent of 80 gallons per capita, and Milwaukee, for the same year, reached the respectable figure of 105 gallons per capita. Of the list of ten of the larger cities of the United States, the lowest per capita per annum consumption for the year 1894 was 46 gallons, and the highest 105 gallons. The amount of beer made and drunk in the United States for 1894 allows nearly 16 gallons for every man, woman, and child of the whole population. We all know that large quantities of beer (and other artificial beverages) are made and sold in this country, and we know that these are not substituted for the industrial and sanitary uses of water. From the limited information at command, I am sure it would be a mistake to assume that the people of Europe drink nothing but beer,† or that the people of this country drink nothing but water."

* *Encyclopædia Britannica*, ninth edition, vol. xvii., p. 32.

† The average daily consumption of water by Munich, 1895–1896, was 12,947,683 U. S. gallons, corresponding to a daily per capita consumption of 32.38 gallons.

CHAPTER VI.

PURE AND PURIFIED WATERS.

WATER supplies from sources of known purity undoubtedly are superior to purified water from polluted sources ; but these are very rare, and only a few cities peculiarly favored, like Vienna, Munich, and Dresden abroad, and some of the smaller cities and villages in this country, can make them available. The water from certain mountain springs and streams, and from some deep wells, from the standpoint of hygiene, may be considered " pure ; " while that supplied to cities where filtration or sedimentation in large reservoirs is practiced, may be regarded as " purified " water.

Viewed from a chemical and bacterial standpoint, there is no degree to pure water ; but from the hygienic point of view there may be, and apparently are, degrees of purity. The water of Vienna is said to be naturally pure, so is the water of Manchester (England) and New York ; but accepting the typhoid fever rates as an index of water quality, the water of Vienna is by far superior to that of either of the other two cities. Manchester and New York attempt to protect the drainage grounds of their sources, and preserve the water from direct sewage pollution, which efforts are only partially successful. Vienna, Munich, and a few other cities seek their water supplies in sources which apparently are beyond the reach of pollution.

Liverpool, like New York and Boston (new works), has sought its water supply in a district which is sparsely inhabited, and not exposed to the sewage from large organized communities ; and as an additional precaution in behalf of the public health, provision is made for filtration of this water before it reaches the city.

In considering sources of water supply in mountain springs at moderate distance from cities to be supplied, and sources in deep wells, it should not be overlooked that similar sources cannot be made available for all or even many cities. Nor should the fact be ignored, that the enormous per capita consumption in nearly every American city renders the problem of a "pure" or "purified" water supply for our cities much more difficult of solution than in the cities of Europe. Berlin, with about the same population as Chicago, uses less than one-fourth of the quantity of water per diem; London, with a population of over 5,000,000, probably uses no more water than Philadelphia; while Hamburg, with nearly twice the population of Cincinnati, uses less than three-fourths as much water. The consumption or rather the waste of water in many cities, is a serious impediment to improvement in works of public water supply; and the abuse of water privileges must be curbed, if we are to have water of the same quality as that of many of the cities of Europe.

Of the larger cities of the United States which derive their water supplies from driven wells, Brooklyn thus obtains from many sources, covering a large territory, about 32,000,000 gallons per day,* or over four-tenths of the daily supply. The maximum yield of the system of artesian wells at Memphis, Tenn., has been stated at 16,000,000 gallons per day.† The maximum capacity of the system of driven wells at Dayton, Ohio, is given as 6,750,000 gallons, and at Lowell, Mass., as 12,000,000 gallons per day.‡ Upon the same authority the average daily consumption of water from the system of driven wells at South Bend, Ind., is 1,900,000 gallons; and the maximum daily consumption from the artesian wells at Jacksonville, Fla., is given as 1,557,557 gallons. Many smaller cities have systems of artesian or non-flowing wells which yield from a few hundred thousand to one or two million gallons per day, and all such may be regarded as highly favored by nature in the matter of their public water supplies.

In Europe, especially in Germany, it is the policy to seek public water supplies in sources of natural purity, such as mountain springs and deep wells, where these are available, and to

---

* Mr. I. M. DeVarona, in *Report on the Future Extension of the Water Supply of the City of Brooklyn*, 1896, p. 26.

† *Report on Extension and Betterment of Cincinnati Water-Works*, 1896, p. 27.

‡ *Manual of American Water-Works*, 1897.

limit the consumption of water to the yield of such sources. When the yield, as at Dortmund for instance is relatively large, the allowance per capita per diem is correspondingly liberal ; while at Leipsic, where the yield of ground water is relatively small, the per capita consumption also is small.

In order to utilize to the fullest extent the natural sources of pure water for public supply, the people of Germany are willing to limit the use and waste of such water sometimes to very small ·per capita daily allowances, reasoning, doubtless, that the requirements of hygiene are better satisfied with small amounts of pure water than large volumes of polluted water.

Among the larger cities of Europe which depend partly or wholly upon ground waters may be mentioned London, the Kent Works of which during July, 1896, supplied from deep wells a daily average of 23,270,000 U. S. gallons to an estimated population of 583,436, allowing thus nearly 40 gallons per capita.

In the table on the following page are given the principal cities of Germany, etc., which depend in whole or part on ground water supplies.*

If the double system of water supply which prevails in parts of Paris (where the very excellent water of the Vanne is used for dietetic purposes) should be adopted by cities in this country, then it will in most instances become a comparatively easy task to secure the limited quantity of water required for drinking and culinary uses, either from sources of known purity or by very careful filtration.

The great advantage of water from a source not open to sewage or semi-sewage pollution, as, for instance, deep wells intercepting water which has been thoroughly purified in passing through the drift, over water purified by any process of filtration, is found in the fact that such water is at all times safe ; while safety to the public of purified water depends altogether upon the skill and care of the officials in charge of the filters. A lack of technical knowledge or vigilance upon their part may result in great damage to the health of the people supplied.

Naturally "pure" water is not available by the great majority

---

* *Statistische Zusammenstellung der Betriebs Ergebnisse von Wasserwerken*, Munich, 1895.

of cities. To supply a so-called pure water to London from sources in Wales, nearly \$200,000,000 will be required; and even in that instance it is proposed by the County Council to filter the

GERMAN CITIES SUPPLIED WITH GROUND WATER.

CITIES.	DATE OF REPORT.	POPULATION.	DAILY YIELD OF WELLS. U. S. GALS.	PER CAPITA DAILY ALLOWANCE. U. S. GALS.	PROPORTION OF WATER FROM WELLS.
Schalke,	1893	280,000	11,429,790	40.8	All.
Dortmund,	1893–4	170,000	9,617,260	56.6	"
Cologne,	1893–4	286,000	8,425,535	29.5	"
Dresden,	1893	309,000	6,912,000	22.4	"
Bochum,	1893–4	148,500	6,764,100	45.5	"
Leipsic,	1893	391,000	6,131,170	15.7	"
Stockholm,	1893	251,000	6,045,850	24.	"
Copenhagen,	1893	337,500	5,990,789	17.8 *	. . .
Essen,	1893–4	135,000	4,869,495	. 36.	All.
Barmen,	1893–4	125,000	4,380,533	35.	"
Augsburg,	1893	80,000	4,253,900	53.2	"
Düsseldorf,	1893–4	157,000	4,204,468	27.	"
Charlottenburg,	1892–3	255,000	4,204,087	15.8	"
Elberfeld,	1893–4	144,000.	3,906,663	27.1	"
Mülheim, Ruhr,	1893–4	67,000	3,729,280	55.7	"
Hannover,	1893–4	221,000	3,477,132	15.7	"
Freiberg,	1893	51,000	3,157,980	62.	"
Frankfort,	1893	198,800	3,057,138	. . .	40%
Duisburg,	1893–4	73,875	2,793,280	37.8	All.
Carlsruhe,	1893	80,000	. 2,763,514	34.5	"
Halle,	1893–4	123,000	2,605,294	21.1	"
Crefeld,	1893–4	106,000	2,301,588	22.0	"
Witten,	1893–4	45,000	2,195,849	48.8	"
Strasburg,	1893–4	95,000	1,964,511	. 20.6	"
Vienna,	1893	998,000	1,877,795	. . .	10%

water before it is delivered to the consumers. Upon this aspect of the water question Dr. Leffman † says : —

"When propositions for filtration are made, it is usual for some persons to suggest that a pure water supply should be selected. . . . Surface water is so liable to pollution that the word 'pure' has, in regard to it, only a comparative sense; and in establishing an elaborate water supply, we should establish systems of storage and filtration, no matter how excellent may be the district in which the water is collected and through which it flows."

* Springs and wells, proportion not given.   † *Public Health*, 1897, p. 118.

Changes may occur in the quality of water from natural sources by subsequent pollution of the tributary watersheds. Large watersheds constituting the sources of supply for cities are more exposed than small watersheds used by villages, and absolute security in either case is to be had only by complete control of the effective drainage grounds.

The water of deep wells may become polluted by sewage from improvements which encroach on their drainage area; and the area drained by such wells should be free from habitation, and such commercial operations as are calculated to contaminate the soil and pollute the rainfall which percolates through the soil to the wells.

A proposition by the author (1894) to sterilize by distillation, and distribute through a separate system of mains, that portion of a city water supply which was used for drinking and dietetic purposes, developed much adverse criticism. Partly, as alleged, because such water, when deprived of the minerals in solution, would not be so favorable to the animal system as are natural waters; partly because of the difficulty of educating people to the use of sterilized water when other water was less expensive and more convenient to obtain; and partly because of the expense of a duplicate system of mains to distribute such water to the consumers.

The first objection is the only one worthy of serious consideration. If it is true that sterilized water exerts a prejudicial influence on digestion or any of the animal functions, then it should not be recommended; but observation among people who are regularly using distilled water does not bear out the assertion sometimes made, that such water is less beneficial for dietetic uses than clean cistern or pure well water. Neither is the author aware that systematic experiments have ever been conducted to ascertain the real influence of sterilized water on the human system, unless it may be held that the favorable results of the use of distilled water in the United States navy and on ocean steamships furnishes the desired data. If the salts and minerals lost by distillation are really essential to a perfect drinking-water, it would seem to be much safer to add these in proper proportions to distilled water, than to assume the risk to health which accompanies the indiscriminate use of natural waters for drinking.

If it were true that a distilled water, lacking in lime, soda, potash, etc., was unfitted for the manufacture of teeth and bone in young children, this fact should be manifest in the children of suburban and other villages, which depend almost entirely for drinking upon cistern water. The author's observation for many years along this line furnishes no proof that cistern water, if clean and free from objectionable organic matter and bacteria, is not a perfectly safe and satisfactory drinking-water. In fact, rain-water falling in suburban districts, caught on clean slate roofs, and collected in clean cisterns, should furnish the purest and best of natural waters. Underground cisterns intended for the collection and storage of drinking-waters should be tight, and not subject to contamination through the soil from neighboring cesspools and vaults; otherwise, pollution may occur, and such cistern water would be quite as objectionable in a hygienic view as any other sewage-polluted water.

Certain spring and well waters may be quite free from organic matter and bacteria, and still be dangerous to health by reason of minerals in solution. Lead, arsenic, copper, etc., and iron in excess, are objectionable ingredients of drinking-waters; and petroleum above one part in two millions, it has been stated, unfits water for drinking.[*] Some of these substances may be in waters which, when tested by bacteriological methods and the microscope, would be found very pure. Chemistry, however, can reveal and measure them.

While certain surface waters can be carried in large, deep reservoirs with an improvement in quality, water from ground sources cannot be stored in open shallow reservoirs without developing a growth of vegetable and animal matter, the luxuriance of which depends upon the climate and sunlight, and to some extent upon the mineral constituents of the water. Tall tanks and stand-pipes, the depth of which is usually greater than that of earthen reservoirs, and the water area small in relation to capacity, may be used to store ground waters without apparent change in quality; but in these the quantity of water stored is always small when compared with the daily consumption.

---

[*] *Water Supply, Chemical and Sanitary,* Wm. Ripley Nichols, New York, 1883, p. 75.

The investigations of Mr. G. C. Whipple, of the Massachusetts State Board of Health,* show very conclusively that sunlight is the controlling factor in the development of algous growths in stored waters, which suggests that the light should always be rigorously excluded from reservoirs and large tanks intended for the reception of ground waters. It has been the author's usual practice to cover steel tanks and towers for the storage of ground waters, but he is not aware of any trouble or complaint arising from the storage of ground waters in the few open tanks of works with which he has been associated.

According to Professor Mason,† "to keep a ground water in good condition it is necessary to cover the reservoir. Such waters are usually charged with mineral matter suitable for plant food, and the higher organisms will be likely to grow therein unless light be excluded."

The rapid development, during the summer, of vegetable growths in shallow open reservoirs carrying ground waters, is well known ; and the growth and (or) decay of some of these organisms have produced unpleasant tastes and odors in stored waters, but no proof is at hand that they have been the specific cause of disease. Numerous investigations have shown that *asterionella, nostoc, oscillaria,* and other of the green *algæ, crenothrix* (fungi) and *uroglena* (infusoria), have each at times imparted peculiar tastes or odors to stored waters ; and it is altogether likely that other of the microscopic organisms in water may be concerned in producing effects which justify objections to the use of such waters from an æsthetic standpoint, even if not positively injurious to health.

Assuming that the development of vegetable organisms in stored waters depends principally upon the penetration of light, it is obvious why turbid river and surface waters can be stored in large, deep reservoirs for great lengths of time without injury, and, as a rule, with positive improvement in their quality. During the early days of storage the color is so strong, and the water so nearly opaque, that there is no penetration of light ; and upon subsidence of the heavier matters in suspension many of the vegetable organ-

---

* *Journal of New England Water Works Association*, September, 1896.

† *Water Supply*, by William P. Mason, New York, 1896, p. 261.

isms, including the bacteria, are carried down, and deposited on the bottom and slopes of the reservoirs.   Upon the other hand, the usual properties of ground water, viz., —

(1) Limpidity and lack of color,

(2) Small or no organic matters in suspension,

(3) Large amounts of dissolved salts readily assimilable by plant life, — are favorable to the growth of cryptogams.

Add to these light and heat by exposure in open reservoirs, and all the conditions are present essential to the rapid growth of algæ.   The Vanne water, which is used for dietetic purposes in portions of Paris, is obtained from springs; and to preserve it without change of quality it is conducted to the city in a closed conduit, received in distributing reservoirs from which the light is carefully excluded, and reaches the consumer quite as pure as it was upon issuing from its mountain source.

The smaller cities and villages often are peculiarly favored in sources of satisfactory public water supply; while larger cities, where the consumption of water per capita and in the aggregate is greatly in excess of that of the smaller communities, are compelled to procure the required daily volumes of water, in many instances, from sources utterly unfit for domestic uses.   A mountain spring or system of driven wells, which will furnish an abundance of pure water to some small municipality, would be too insignificant for consideration as a source of water supply to a city ; and intelligent people are prone to neglect the fact that a water source which may meet the requirements of a village of a few thousand population would be inadequate to supply even the drinking and culinary water of a large city.

Referring to present sources of city water supply, it can be said that Vienna, Munich, Dresden, Stockholm, Copenhagen, a portion of Paris and other cities abroad, together with several of the smaller cities and many villages in this country, have water supplies which are naturally pure ; while London (omitting the Kent Works), Berlin, Hamburg, Liverpool, and many smaller cities in Europe, Lawrence, Mass., and several other cities in this country, have purified water supplies.

In this connection it is difficult to discuss the water supplies of cities in America using mechanical filters. The typhoid fever rates of these cities are considerably higher than the rates of cities in Europe which use plain sand filtration for the purification of polluted waters ; and inquiry among the manufacturers of the filters, and the officials of the water-works using them, reveals the startling information that (in instances at least) the filtered water is not generally used by the people of such cities. This is also true of certain cities and villages which have very excellent water supplies from natural sources.

In a certain city of Ohio, where the public water supply is from a system of driven wells and of very excellent quality, it is said that less than one-fourth of the population draw their water supply from the city mains. The remainder, after nearly thirty years' experience with a public system of water-works, still depend for domestic purposes upon the water from wells and cisterns. In the interest of the public health, and where the public water supply is unexceptional, the use of wells and cisterns for drinking-water should be prohibited (as they are in Vienna), and the use of the public water be made compulsory. Of what avail is it to secure water of high quality if the people are permitted afterwards to take their drinking and dietetic water from sources of doubtful value, and, as is well known to many sanitary officers, from sources exposed to sewage pollution ?

It is a strange anomaly that in the larger cities (many of which are supplied with sewage-polluted waters) all the people are by the force of circumstances compelled to take their water from the public mains, while in the small cities and villages, in which the public water is often of most excellent quality, the use of the better water is altogether optional with the people.

It is impossible to tell how much physical suffering might be traced to water supplies, which are regarded by municipal corporations and water companies as fit for domestic uses, and to the continuous use by cities of waters of known sewage pollution. Certain it is that typhoid fever, cholera (in the Orient), and other intestinal disorders, annually claim thousands of victims, which would be saved if all people were equally and sincerely interested in having drinking and dietetic waters of the highest attainable purity.

In the mountains, where the population is sparse, water of satisfactory quality and in abundance is often found. But at lower elevations, along the rivers and lakes, and at tide water, where the people are collected in large numbers, mountain sources of water supply are rarely available. Doubtless "there is enough wholesome water on the face of the earth to supply all the inhabitants thereof," but the conditions clearly demonstrate that this is not well distributed.

Cities have been located, not according to the rules of hygiene, but according to the requirements of commerce. Revenue has been the dominating factor ; and upon the sanitarian has fallen the burden of rectifying evils which have followed the total disregard in so many cases of the fundamental laws of health.

In the introduction to this work a statement is made that "water is an essential of human existence ; " and this is true, not only as it is used in connection with the body needs, but in connection with the fruits of the soil, in tempering the atmosphere and heat of the earth's crust, and in many other ways. Restricted to our animal requirements, it may be said that "pure water" is "an essential of health," while "impure water" involves hazards to life and health which we have no right to incur.

It is feasible for a small percentage of the world's population to procure water supplies from natural sources which will satisfy the most advanced requirements of hygiene, but for the great majority of the people satisfactory water supplies are obtainable only by works of artificial purification.

CHAPTER VII.

CITATIONS ON TYPHOID FEVER EPIDEMICS.

PRACTICAL illustrations, so far as they are available, concerning the causes of typhoid fever epidemics, are especially valuable in supporting the theory that a sewage-polluted water, or a water carrying the germs of typhoid fever, will produce infection of the same disease in persons who may drink such water, or who in some way may have ingested food which has been in contact with such water. In this connection it is not necessary that a line should be drawn between the colon bacillus and the typhoid bacillus as found in the human spleen ; either or both may be going into the sewers of cities, and from the sewers into rivers, lakes, and other sources of public water supply. It is sufficient and prudent to assume that the dejections of a typhoid patient may contain the specific organism which is the cause of this disease, and in the instances noted in this chapter the evidence is at times overwhelmingly in support of this view.

LAUSEN, SWITZERLAND.

The typhoid epidemic which occurred in this village during the latter part of 1872 has been mentioned so frequently and with so much respect as to make it a classic in the epidemiology of this disease. The circumstances were briefly as follows : A few cases of typhoid fever, occurring at a distance of one or two miles from the village, were supposed to have caused a contamination of the water of the village well, from which an infection of 130 persons, with 8 fatalities, in due time followed. From the official report of the epidemic by the health officer of Basle, it appears that a brook, passing near the premises where the original cases of typhoid occurred, was used for the washing of the linen of the patients, and at the same time as a channel for the disposal of the typhoid dejections. The course of this brook caused it to join another stream which passed through Lausen at a considerable distance below the village ; but for some time it had been suspected that an underground connection existed between the brook at a place below the original location of the fever and the village well, although from surface indications, any sewage discharged into the brook would pass into the larger stream below the village, and not be the cause of pollution to the village water or create an offense to its population.

After the epidemic, an investigation showed that the brook did have an underground connection with the village well ; and notwithstanding the percolation of the water through a mile or more of pervious material, typhoid germs, which came into the brook from the source of the original infection, were carried into the public well, and spread the disease in the village at such an alarming rate that one in every six of the whole population was attacked. The original case of typhoid fever was held to have been imported into the neighborhood of Lausen.

A *résumé* of the simple facts in this instance shows : —

1. No typhoid fever had been known of in Lausen for sixty years, and the general health of the people was exceptionally good.
2. During the summer of 1872, several cases of typhoid had occurred outside of the village, at a distance of a mile or more.
3. The Furlen Brook was used as a channel of discharge for the dejections of the original patients, and for the washing of their linen.
4. Salt, thrown into the brook below the original location of the disease, in due time appeared in the water of the Lausen public well.
5. The infection was limited to those who drank of the water of the public well, while families which abstained from the use of the water of this well were not affected.

The Lausen circumstance has been so well described in certain books and reports upon the subject, that it is here introduced principally to show that natural filtration so-called, through the pervious materials of the drift, while it may render water very fair to look upon, cannot be accepted as a safeguard against typhoid infection, if the cause of infection should exist in the locality of a source of ground water supply such as was had in Lausen.

CATERHAM, ENGLAND.

The outbreak of typhoid fever at Caterham occurred in the early part of 1879, and was reported on early in April of that year. In this instance there were upward of 100 attacks of the disease, of which 19 were fatal. It was proved beyond doubt (according to Mr. Edward Easton, Chairman of the Caterham Water Company), that the origin of the epidemic was due to the evacuations of one workman accidentally contaminating the water of the well. This workman, although suffering with a " walking" case of typhoid fever, was employed in the tunnels connecting the wells which constituted the source of water supply for Caterham and Redhill. While so employed, his frequent dejections were collected in a bucket, and from time to time hoisted out of the well. During one trip of the bucket an accident occurred, causing a portion of its contents to be spilled into the water ; and from this in due time grew an epidemic of typhoid fever, alarming in proportion to the population of the district supplied from this source.

Of this unfortunate occurrence, Dr. Thorne Thorne, who conducted the investigation,* says : —

" The water supply of Redhill and Caterham was derived from deep wells in the chalk and lower greensand. It was discovered that a workman employed in excavating an adit between two of the wells had previously contracted enteric (typhoid) fever at Croydon, and had been overtaken by diarrhœa on several occasions while working in the well. There appeared no doubt that the poison of the excreta was conveyed to the drinkers of the well water, and communicated the disease."

The circumstances of the affair are revolting in the extreme ; and how a person suffering with the early symptoms of typhoid could be permitted to follow his occupation immediately in the

* " Report Royal Commission on Metropolitan Water Supply," Appendices to *Minutes of Evidence*, p. 533.

presence of the water from which a small population drew its daily supply, is beyond comprehension.

Aside from a specific cause of disease which may be traced to this lapse of moral responsibility upon the part of some one, it is disgusting to know that a man would be so far lost to the sense of decency as to continue his labors under conditions like these. Here was a system of wells from which a large number of people were daily drawing water for drinking and other purposes, in which some repairs or improvements were being conducted while the water was being pumped out of them for domestic consumption, and a workman known to be suffering with diarrhea, if nothing worse, was permitted to follow his labors in the wells, and dispose of his dejections in a manner which was offensive to sentiment, even if proper precautions had been observed to prevent contamination of the water. But such precautions were not observed ; and in due time the bucket was tipped, some of its contents went into the water, and upwards of 100 persons were made to suffer as a consequence of a proceeding which was little short of a crime.

In the exhaustive examination conducted by the Royal Commission on Water Supply for London (1893), this Caterham occurrence is mentioned several times by the witnesses ; and the principal deduction drawn from it by the Commission was, that if the dejections of this workman had been tipped into the River Thames instead of the Caterham wells, it would have been so largely diluted as to have had no effect on the health of the people who take their water from the Thames companies.

Stripping the matter of all verbiage, it appears that 100 cases of typhoid fever with 19 deaths were traced to the contamination of this Caterham water, by the accidental discharge of a portion of the dejecta from a mild case of typhoid fever.

PLYMOUTH, PA.

The town of Plymouth, Pa., in the spring of 1885 was visited by a severe epidemic of typhoid fever, which had its origin in the pollution of the public water supply by the dejections of a single isolated patient.

The water of the town is impounded in a reservoir at an elevation sufficient to maintain a supply by gravity; and upon the drainage ground of this reservoir, at the time of and before the epidemic, lived a family, a member of which was temporarily located in Philadelphia. This member came home ill with typhoid fever during the winter of 1884–1885; and to avoid infection of the family vault, his dejections were thrown upon the snow or ice-covered ground some distance from the residence. When the warm rains of late winter set in, the snow and ice about the premises melted, and ran into the reservoir. Within two or three weeks an epidemic of typhoid fever occurred in Plymouth; and out of a population of about 8,000, over 1,100 were stricken with the disease, of which 114 were fatal cases.

In the Lausen epidemic, the typhoid germs went into the water of the Furlen brook; the water of the brook, or a portion of it, went into the village well. Result, an epidemic of typhoid fever in a little village which for more than two generations had been wholly exempt from this disease.

In the Caterham and Redhill epidemic the dejections of a typhoid patient were mixed with the water of a well which constituted the source of supply for a small population; this water was pumped to the patrons of the water company, and an epidemic of typhoid fever followed.

In the Plymouth epidemic, the typhoid fever dejections were thrown upon the frozen soil; rains followed, and the runoff of rainfall and melted ice carried these into the reservoir which constituted the water supply for the city. Result, a typhoid epidemic which at the time attracted the attention of the whole country.

In connection with the epidemic at Plymouth, Pa., the following from the *Engineering Record*, July 18, 1896, will be of interest:—

"The report was made public last week of Dr. Chas. P. Knapp, County Inspector of the Pennsylvania State Board of Health, of Wyoming, Pa., who in April last investigated the water supply of Plymouth, Pa., where typhoid fever has been prevalent for some time past. Dr. Knapp reported that the water of Plymouth is subject to contamination from a dairy farm on the head waters of the stream from which the supply is taken. This is the same farmhouse and stream to which was traced in 1885 the typhoid epidemic in Plymouth, when there were 1,500 cases and 150 deaths."*

* The cases and deaths from this epidemic have been differently reported by different authorities.

ZURICH, SWITZERLAND.

" In the spring of 1884, Zurich was visited by a virulent outbreak of typhoid fever, which, beginning in the month of March, reached its maximum intensity in April, and practically disappeared by the end of June, fully two per cent of the population having been attacked and nine per cent of the cases proving fatal. The Commission appointed to inquire into the cause of this epidemic arrived at the conclusion that the infection could not be traced to abnormal meteorological or sanitary conditions; but that the filtered Limmat water, although clear and chemically satisfactory, contained an abnormal quantity of bacteria. It was subsequently discovered that, owing to the dredging operations in connection with the new quay-works, the impure matter deposited at the bottom of the river had been stirred up, and, not being effectually retained by the submerged filter-bed, had found its way into the concrete main, which was by no means water-tight, and had been damaged during the blasting and removal of an erratic block from the bed of the Limmat. The reason why the defective condition of both filter-bed and conduit did not arouse suspicion until after the outbreak of the epidemic was twofold, — first, the Limmat water was generally so clear and chemically pure that filtration was considered of altogether secondary importance ; and, secondly, the permeability of the concrete, laid at 2 to 3 meters depth below the river bed, was regarded as an advantage rather than a defect, inasmuch as the sand in which the conduit was imbedded was supposed to act as a filtering medium. The bacteriological investigations, in conjunction with the proved percolation of impure matter through the filter and conduit, stamped the Limmat water as the vehicle of infection. . . . Hence, at Zurich, the necessity was promptly recognized of providing an entirely new water supply for the town and suburbs."*

(The submerged filter mentioned above has been experimented with by several cities in this country. It is a filter constructed in the bed of the river, of such materials as may be convenient, with no provisions for cleaning or renewal of the filtering materials. Such filters, wherever used within the author's knowledge, have been failures as sanitary devices.)

SPRING WATER, N.Y.

Spring Water in 1889 was a village of 600 population, situated two and one-half miles south of Hemlock Lake, which constitutes the source of water supply for Rochester, N.Y. This village was on the watershed of the lake, and typhoid fever occurring there

---

* Preller on the *Zurich Water Works*, London, 1892, p. 7.

was a menace to the health of the larger community. The water supply of the village was obtained from open and driven wells sunk a short distance into the drift.

A so-called endemic of typhoid fever, which occurred in this village during October and November of that year, was made the subject of careful investigation by Mr. George W. Rafter (then assistant engineer of the Rochester Water-Works) and Dr. M. L. Mallory. The following information is taken from the Report of these gentlemen to the chief engineer of the water-works : —

"The earliest clearly defined case of typhoid fever we found to be that of . . . a boy thirteen years of age, who, when taken sick with the disease on Sept. 29, was employed at Snyder's Hotel. . . . Not only is the well at this place in close proximity to the privy (thirty feet away), but half-way between the well and the privy we found a board slop drain, which undoubtedly discharges into the well a considerable portion of its contents. The family claimed, however, that the water of this well had been considered bad for a year and a half, and none of it had been used for domestic purposes during that time ; the water so used having been all obtained from the well on the adjoining premises. . . . We found the pump in working order, with pail beneath the spout partly filled with water, and with a dipper in the pail. On questioning the servant girl, it appeared very evident that the water was sometimes used. . . .

"Our view as to the origin of these cases of typhoid fever in the village . . . is therefore as follows : The hotel was certainly an original center of infection as . . . four persons living there were taken sick with the disease ; and while we are unable to establish the fact definitely, we consider it very probable that some 'walking' case of typhoid fever stopped at the hotel, and . . . inoculated the hotel privy with germs of typhoid contained in the dejections. The chemical analyses of the water of the hotel well, . . . and the bacteriological examinations, both show the water to be exceedingly bad, unfitted for domestic use, and the environment such as to lead, with the certainty of a mathematical demonstration, to the conclusion that there is gross pollution from the privy and slop drain."

The village of Spring Water at the time of this outbreak had a population of 600, of which 20 were attacked with typhoid fever. "The soil upon which the village stands is of an open, pervious character for a depth of 10 to 20 feet," while the wells (open and driven) had a depth of 10 to 18 feet. Previous to this attack of typhoid fever the village had a record of being an unusually healthful locality.

It is stated in the report that the Eberth bacillus (*b. typhosus*) was found, upon examination by Dr. H. C. Ernst of Harvard University, in a sample of water from one of the wells supposed to have been concerned in spreading the infection.

The admixture of filth and drinking-water, which was assumed to have been the secondary cause of this epidemic, is going on on a very large scale all over the land, with this difference, however, that in Spring Water the mixing was done right on the premises of the citizens, while the plan usually pursued is to pollute the water supply of one city with the sewage of another. Will a time arrive when there will be a law on the Federal statute book which will give the Engineer Corps of the War Department full power to prevent the sewage pollution of all navigable streams and bodies of water under its control, and when all water craft will be compelled to dispose of their sewage and garbage in some other manner than by dumping it *ad libitum* into these rivers and lakes, which constitute the sources of water supply for so many populous cities and towns?

LOWELL, MASS.

During the autumn and winter of 1890–1891, the city of Lowell, Mass., was visited with a severe epidemic of typhoid fever, which had its origin in two or three cases of typhoid fever in a small manufacturing village (North Chelmsford) situated on Stony Brook, a small stream which flowed into the Merrimac River about three miles above the Lowell Water-Works intake. Within due time after typhoid developed at Lowell, the city of Lawrence, on the Merrimac River about nine miles below Lowell, was also stricken with typhoid fever. The city of Lowell discharges its sewage into the river below the city, while the city of Lawrence below draws its water supply from the river after it has been polluted by the Lowell sewage.

Thus from Stony Brook the disease was traced to Lowell, and from Lowell to Lawrence. Stony Brook was inoculated through the use of wooden privies overhanging and discharging the fecal matter into the stream, which in turn carried the bacillus of typhoid into the Merrimac River, from which it was pumped into the Lowell reservoir, and distributed to the citizens through the public water mains. The fecal discharges of the typhoid patients at Lowell went into the sewers; these in turn inoculated the river below that city, and furnished the infection to the sister city of Lawrence, which pumped the typhoid-infected water to its reservoir, and like Lowell, supplied it to its citizens through the public water mains.

Very careful investigations, conducted by Professor W. T. Sedgwick, biologist to the State Board of Health of Massachusetts, clearly established the origin of the epidemic among the people living on Stony Brook, and its carriage to the cities of Lowell and Lawrence through the medium of the public water supply.*

SAULT STE. MARIE, MICH.

"The city of Sault Ste. Marie takes its water supply above the rapids, and ordinarily it is very pure water. In the fall of 1890, owing to a break in the lock, more than two hundred boats were detained for two days above the lock and in the immediate vicinity of the intake. Some ten days later typhoid fever appeared, and the deaths were reported to be not less than thirty. All the cases appeared within a few weeks, and sample (analysis below) was taken at this time." †

ANALYSIS OF WATER FROM SAULT STE. MARIE.

SOURCE. — LAKE MICHIGAN.

PARTS PER 100,000.			BACTERIA. PER C. C.	KIND OF BACTERIA FOUND.
Free Ammonia.	Albuminoid.	Chlorine.		
0.0224	0.0168	0.33	2,000	*B. Venenosus.*

This water was regarded as the cause of typhoid fever; and *b. venenosus*, according to Dr. Vaughan, is classed as a pathogenic organism. "One drachm of a bouillon culture, twenty-four hours old, injected into the abdominal cavity of a rat, produced death."

ST. LOUIS, MO.

During the year 1892–1893, the city of St. Louis, Mo., U.S.A., had an unusual case and death rate from typhoid fever, the annual mortality from this disease rising from 34 to 103 per 100,000 of population living.

---

* *Report Massachusetts State Board of Health*, 1892, p. 668.

† *A Bacteriological Study of Drinking Water*, by Victor C. Vaughan, Ph.D., M.D., Ann Arbor, Mich., 1892, pp. 8–12.

A careful investigation by the public health department revealed the fact that in those districts of the city where the water from the public mains was not generally used for drinking-purposes, the citizens were almost wholly exempt from the infection, and that with few exceptions the cases were all confined to a district the people of which drew all or part of their drinking-water from the public mains.* The water supply of St. Louis is obtained by pumping from the Mississippi River, and the only purification attempted is to allow 24 to 36 hours for sedimentation in several low-level reservoirs.

ELMIRA, N.Y.

This city was visited by an epidemic of typhoid fever during January and February of 1896, the cause of which was carefully inquired into by Professor Olin H. Landreth of Schenectady, N.Y. From his very complete report the following facts are gleaned : —

Elmira is situated on the Chemung River, with a population at the time of the epidemic of 37,500. In the cities and villages above Elmira, on the river and its tributaries, and within a reach of 50 miles, an aggregate population of 40,000 is found, among less than three-fourths of which 70 cases of typhoid fever were reported to have occurred prior to the outbreak or increase in the typhoid rates at Elmira.

Of this number six cases were on premises which sewered to the river, and "a larger number with less definite but equally direct connection with the river." According to the report, the time required for the passage of sewage from the most remote point, where previous cases of typhoid had been recorded, to the water-works intake at Elmira, would be but a few hours.

During December (1895), there had been fifteen days of continuous cold weather, followed late in the month by heavy rains which caused a freshet in the river, and carried down with the run-off of rainfall considerable polluting matter collected on the frozen ground.

The epidemic of typhoid in Elmira followed the flood in the Chemung River.

---

* *Annual Report of Health Commissioner*, 1892–93, p. 120.

Samples of water from the river at the intake of the Elmira Water-Works, sixteen miles below the nearest point of sewage pollution, taken Dec. 28, 1895, and Jan. 21, 1896, gave from 45,000 to 1,080 bacteria per cubic centimeter, *among which was found the colon bacillus.* The larger number of bacteria per cubic centimeter of water was found while the river was in flood or directly after; a condition often noticed in connection with rivers subject to a wide range of flow. Aside from the very large number of bacteria found at the earlier date of examination, there were other unmistakable evidences of sewage pollution of the water.

Search for the typhoid bacillus failed to reveal its presence in the water; but this is not surprising, for we fail to find it even under much more favorable conditions, and the failure to find it is only negative evidence that it is not in the water.

After a careful review of all the facts bearing upon the epidemic, Professor Landreth reached the following conclusions:—

1. The milk supply was in no way responsible for the epidemic.

2. The city water supply was unquestionably the means by which the infection was introduced and the epidemic originated.

3. The city water supply was, in all probability, infected by the typhoid bacillus from the Chemung River from cases occurring up-stream during the summer or fall of 1895.

4. The city water supply as now taken from the collecting gallery is quite probably liable to infection at any time from the occurrence of typhoid fever cases near the gallery, in unsewered premises, through the medium of the ground water, and may already have suffered such infection.

5. A number of cases of fever during the latter stages of the epidemic are due to secondary infection from adjacent previous cases, largely through the medium of wells infected from vaults and cesspools.

6. Well water should be very thoroughly boiled before being considered safe for use. It is now more liable to infection than river water.

PARIS, FRANCE.

In *Popular Science* for December, 1895, Mr. Stoddard Dewey
is authority for the following statement : —

" In the French army stationed at Paris in 1888, there were 824 cases of
typhoid fever, and in 1889, 1,179 cases of typhoid fever. During this time the
army had been drinking the sewage-polluted water of the River Seine. In
1889 the water of the River Vanne was substituted for that of the Seine,
when the number of cases for the next four years, 1890–1893 inclusive, was
reduced to 299, 276, 293, and 258. Through an accident the water of the
Vanne became contaminated, and for the next three months the cases rose to
436. The Vanne again became comparatively free from contamination; and
for the next four months of 1895, but *eight* cases in all occurred, and these
were charged to some *other water* than that of the River Vanne."

SAN FRANCISCO, CAL.

The investigation of the public water supply of this city in its
relation to typhoid fever, by Dr. M. J. Rosenau, has been mentioned in a previous chapter ; and in order to appreciate the full
force of the facts disclosed, the following brief description of the
sources of supply is quoted from the official report to the Super-
vising Surgeon-General, U. S. M. H. S.

" The Spring Valley Water Company furnishes San Francisco most of its
water. Its principal source is from three catch basins, made by damming
conveniently shaped valleys, between 12 and 20 miles from the city, in San
Mateo County. These three reservoirs are known, respectively, as Crystal
Springs, San Andreas, and Pilarcitos. From each a pipe-line leads to the
city, thus making three water districts. These districts are irregularly shaped,
and discontinuous, owing to engineering difficulties. These three systems are
connected in such a manner that the water from any one reservoir may be
pumped to either of the other two districts. This fact negatives the importance of regarding the districts as separate, from a sanitary standpoint. Smaller
reservoirs in the city are used more for the purpose of storage in case of sudden increased demand, by fire, or from accident, than for obtaining pressure.
The flow is continuous.

" The Visitacion Water Company supplies about 600 consumers in the
southern section of the city. The source of this water is from eight wells sunk
in Bay View Valley, on the outskirts of the city. Six of these wells are 150 feet
deep, one is 180, the other 130 feet through sand and gravel. The wells do not
flow spontaneously, and are fitted with deep-well pumps. They are known as

artesian wells; but as they do not pass through an impervious stratum, they do not comply with the original meaning of that term.

" *Wells.* — From the best information at my command, there are very few private wells for drinking and household purposes in the city."

The usual methods for collecting and planting water samples were followed, the samples being taken from taps in houses. All water was collected by Dr. Rosenau, with the usual precautions to insure a proper sample, and to avoid the introduction of adventitious organisms. " Special care was exercised to select a tap that led directly from the mains." Fermenting organisms were isolated by the fermentation tube, according to the method proposed by Dr. Theobald Smith.

" In several instances the colon bacillus was isolated by planting ½ cubic centimeter of the suspected water directly upon Wurtz milk-sugar litmus agar, and growing the plants at 41°.5–42° C. This slight modification of Smith's method has proven useful, not only for isolating suspicious organisms, but it is believed it may be used to give a proximate idea of their number to the cubic centimeter.

" In case the above methods failed to find fermenting organisms, the water was further studied upon gelatin and glycerin agar, with the result that, in seven samples, eight suspicious organisms were found. These all proved to be forms belonging to the group of proteus, and resembling *b. proteus vulgaris.* They all grew well at room temperature, also at 37°, but not at 41°.5 C."

Thirty-six samples of water collected from widely separated points were examined between Dec. 4, 1895, and Feb. 7, 1896.

" Fermenting organisms were isolated from 14 of the 36 samples; 8 of these 14 contained proteus, and the remaining 6 the colon bacillus. . . . In the San Andreas water, both the colon bacillus and proteus were found. In the Pilarcitos water also, both proteus and the colon organisms were isolated. In the Crystal Springs water, only an occasional proteus was met with. The greater freedom from fermenting organisms enjoyed by this water is in accord with the control of the watershed, and indicates what may be accomplished in preventing contamination of the water by excluding all habitation from the water basin. *The Visitacion (deep well) water was found to contain the colon bacillus.*"

Concerning the colon bacillus, the Report quotes a paragraph from Dr. Abbott * which is worthy of reproduction here.

---

* *The Principles of Bacteriology,* by A. C. Abbott, M.D., Philadelphia, 1894, p. 422.

" In the normal intestinal tract of all human beings and many other mammals, as well as associated with the specific disease producing bacterium in the intestines of typhoid fever patients, is an organism that is frequently found in polluted drinking-waters, and whose presence is proof positive of pollution by either normal or diseased intestinal contents; and though efforts may result in failure to detect the specific bacillus of .typhoid fever, the finding of the other organism, the bacterium *coli communis*, justifies one in expressing the opinion that the water under consideration has been polluted by intestinal evacuations from either human beings or animals. Waters so located as to be liable to such pollution can never be considered as other than a continuous source of danger to those using them."

To which Dr. Rosenau adds, "This organism was found in samples from San Andreas, Pilarcitos, and Visitacion."

" The fact that the colon bacillus was more readily isolated from the water after the heavy rains, and that fermentation was also more frequent after the heavy rains than before, would indicate soil-washings as one of the sources of this organism in the water; but that its presence in the water is not alone the result of soil-washings of pasture lands is indicated by a study of the typhoid fever records. Typhoid fever is a constant factor in San Francisco, and a study of (the relation of) the death rate from this disease to (the) rainfall shows a striking coincidence in several years; i.e., a marked rise in deaths following the first heavy rains."

In a table covering the period July, 1882, to June, 1895, inclusive, Dr. Rosenau has given in parallel columns the total monthly rainfall and deaths from typhoid fever, from which the diagram on the opposite page has been drawn.

Referring to the diagram, which gives the totals of rainfall and deaths from typhoid fever for fourteen years, it does not appear that the higher typhoid rates are always coincident with the higher rates of rainfall. In fact, the death rate fourth in magnitude for this interval of time occurred during the month of least rainfall (August). Generally, however, the curve of typhoid fever deaths declines with the curve of rainfall, and rises before the period of high precipitation begins.

DENVER, COL.

During the past year (1896), the typhoid rates being higher than usual, an investigation of the probable causes was instituted by the health commissioner, with the result that the public water supply was held accountable for the increase of the case and death rates for this disease.*

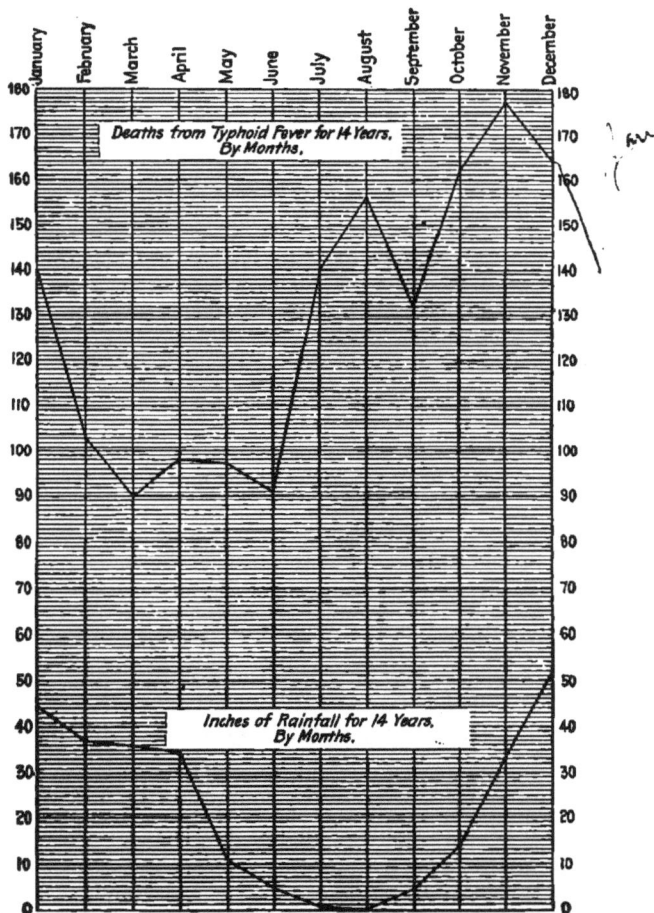

Fig. 2. Totals of Rainfall and Deaths from Typhoid Fever, for a Period of 14 Years, San Francisco, Cal., from January, 1882, to December, 1895.

(*From Notes in Dr. Rosenau's Report on City Water Supply.*)

The Report contains a table of the deaths from typhoid fever for the years 1892 to 1896 inclusive, for the months of June to

* Preliminary Report of the Health Commissioner to the Mayor, Denver, Oct. 12, 1896.

September, from which the months of July, August, and September, are reproduced below : —

DEATHS FROM TYPHOID FEVER.

YEAR,	1892.	1893.	1894.	1895.	1896.
July,	2	8	3	2	0
August,	12	4	8	5	13
September,	9	5	8	8	28
Total,	23	17	19	15	47

Commenting upon this the health commissioner says : —

" Is it to be wondered at that such an increase of typhoid fever prevalence in a few weeks should have called attention to the water supply? Investigation of the location of the cases showed that they were fairly well distributed throughout the city; and so far as could. be determined there was no local cause operative in any part of the city to cause this disease, nor was there any one. possible cause of infection common to all those affected except the water they drank. . . ."

" We know that when a certain small percentage of cases due to local infection of milk or other food, or contracted by nurses, is eliminated, the great bulk of cases of typhoid fever in all epidemics is due to the one common cause, — an infected water supply. When the probable sources of that infection are discovered, it is the plain duty of those upon whom the responsibility lies to suggest the remedies. Failure to adopt the remedial measures that are necessary, means deliberate acceptance of responsibility for the resultant loss of human life."

The city of Denver has two distinct sources of water supply, — one from the Platte River, and the other from an artificial reservoir called Marston Lake, the latter source being fed from mountain streams. Both sources were found by the health officials to be exposed to sewage pollution ; and although it was claimed that the water of the river and lake was filtered before it was delivered to the consumers, the Report indicates that this was wholly ineffectual, and not calculated to improve its quality.

MIDDLETOWN, CONN.

This was an epidemic of typhoid caused by oysters which had been fattened in Quinepiac River, near the mouth of a private drain or sewer, from premises where, during the time the oysters were planted, two cases of typhoid fever had occurred. The epidemic followed a banquet or supper given in the autumn of 1894 by two of the societies of Wesleyan College, at which some of the students indulged in the oysters raw, while the others ate only cooked oysters. The students who ate raw oysters were the only ones affected.

The oysters had been taken from distant beds, and replanted in this little stream for the purpose of " plumping " them by having a current of fresh water run over them during ebb tides. The current of fresh water in this case was probably charged with the germs of typhoid fever from the two cases mentioned above. The reports on the epidemic indicate that the oysters had not been planted at the mouth of the sewer for any great length of time before they were taken up for sale ; but, considering the oyster as a natural scavenger of the organic matter in sewage, this time was altogether sufficient for the absorption of some of the sewage and disease germs from the sewer which discharged into the river just above the oyster-bed.

The students who ate only cooked oysters escaped infection, the cooking being sufficient to sterilize the oysters and such liquid as was contained in the shells.

In this instance the dejections of the original typhoid patients were thrown into the sewer, and the sewer discharged into the river about three hundred feet above the oyster-bed. The typhoid germs were absorbed by the oysters, and the oysters were absorbed by the students, with the usual result in such cases, that typhoid fever reappeared among the students who ate the unsterilized oysters.

STAMFORD, CONN.

" There has been considerable alarm at Stamford, Conn., over an epidemic of typhoid fever. Over 160 cases appeared in a short time, and the investigation of the State Board of Health showed that all were on the route of one milk-seller. The investigators came to the conclusion that impure milk was the source of the disease. The milkman bought his milk from farmers about Stamford ; but as these farmers also sold their milk to other persons who were not reported ill, it was evident that the germs entered the milk after it came into the possession of the retailer.

" It was found that the milkman washed his cans in water from a well on his premises, which, upon being analyzed, proved to be totally unfitted for drinking-purposes, and dangerous to use. This case, like the Montclair epidemic, . . . shows that an infected milk supply may be answerable for many typhoid outbreaks which are not chargeable to a water supply." *

The mass of evidence on the cause of typhoid fever abroad and in this country is to the effect that it is a water-carried disease ; and even in those epidemics where (as at Stamford, Conn., April, 1895, and Montclair, N.J., April, 1894) milk was the immediate distributer of the germ, water used in connection with the dairy operations has been the carrier of the typhoid bacillus. From which it follows, that if the typhoid organism is kept out of our water supplies, typhoid fever would cease to exist as a scourge of the youth and promise of our land.†

ELIZABETH, N. J.

" Typhoid fever has become epidemic here, over fifty cases having been reported ; and a joint investigation by the Local and State Boards of Health is probable. To the use of polluted water is attributed the outbreak." ‡

" There is a marked increase in the number of typhoid fever cases in this city. Not less than forty cases are now being treated by the doctors, and four deaths have occurred, all the victims being adults." §

" E—— M——, aged thirteen, died to-day of typhoid fever at the Alexian Hospital. It is the fifth fatal case during the epidemic. His home was on Rahway Avenue, where the disease prevails, and where polluted wells were discovered. Nine cases are in the Elizabeth General Hospital, and House Physician Whitehead is ill, with symptoms of typhoid." ‖

EVANSVILLE, IND.

" Dr. Metcalf, of the Indiana State Board of Health, has been in Evansville to examine into the cause for the prevalence of typhoid fever. There are one hundred cases of this disease reported by the local physicians. Dr. Metcalf accepted the opinion shared by the physicians that impure water, more than anything else, was at fault. Two of the largest sewers empty into the Ohio River, from which the water supply is taken near the city water-works." **

---

* *Engineering Record*, May 11, 1895.
† *Fire and Water*, Sept. 22, 1894.
‡ *New York Times*, Aug. 20, 1894.
§ *New York Times*, Aug. 21, 1894.
‖ *New York Times*, Sept. 2, 1894.
** *Fire and Water*, May 11, 1895.

Thirty-five thousand deaths a year in the large cities of the United States are said to be due to typhoid fever alone, a disease the causes of which are fully understood, and which sanitarians declare is entirely preventable. The mischief-making germ is usually taken into the system in drinking-water, which has been contaminated with dejecta from other victims residing many miles away. In some cases when there is a typhoid epidemic, the outbreak is traceable to the use of water from a well located near cesspools ; in others to the common supply of a town, either a river or a lake. To guard against pollution, cities should obtain control of the land around the source of their water supply, and by rigid regulations insure such purity as sensibly to reduce the death rate. But where such a stream as the Mississippi, or such a lake as Michigan, is the reliance of any great center of population, precautions of this sort are obviously impracticable. Hence, measures must be taken either by individual consumers or municipal authorities to sterilize the water supply whenever there is occasion for suspicion.*

The difficulty of impressing upon some people the dangers of a polluted water supply is due to the fact that the drinking of such water is not followed by instant death.† But where is the substantial difference between death from an instant cause, and after two or three or more weeks of wasting fever ? The former would be preferred by most men. Because the drinking of a polluted water does not kill at once, like a dose of active poison, it is none the less a poison to some susceptible systems ; and any corporation which, after the fact of pollution is known, refuses to supply a safe water when a safe water can be had, or refuses to so deal with the present water as to render it innocuous to health, is deserving of the just censure of a suffering public.‡

The following quotation would seem to indicate that this view of the matter is sometimes taken : —

"Warren, Ohio, won a great victory over the Warren Water Company. The judgment for $7,621.35, obtained by the company against the city in the lower court recently, was canceled by the Circuit Court, which held that the company had not furnished pure water, as bound to do under its contract."§

* *New York Weekly Tribune*, Oct. 3, 1894.   ‡ See Appendix C.
† *Fire and Water*, Sept. 22, 1894.   § *New York Tribune*, Nov. 18, 1894.

CHAPTER VIII.

SEDIMENTATION OF POLLUTED WATERS.

EXPERIMENTAL information upon the influence of sedimentation on the quality of water supplies is rather meager; although the fact is well known that sedimentation for even a few hours, with certain waters, has a marked effect on their appearance, while sedimentation for great lengths of time, according to Miquel, has wholly eliminated the evidences of organic matter and bacteria in the water of the River Seine. It is reasonable to suppose that in due time all organic matter in a polluted water, contained in a subsiding or impounding reservoir, would be appropriated by the bacteria of putrefaction and converted into ammonia compounds; and these, then acted upon by the nitrifying organisms, and converted into nitrous and nitric acids, which uniting with the bases, such as lime, magnesia, soda, potash, etc., in the water, will be precipitated as insoluble harmless compounds.

Such sedimentation as is really effective in connection with works of public water supply is probably limited to the precipitation by gravity alone of the suspended matters which give color to the water, such as sand, clay, and the complex combination of inorganic and organic matter called "silt." Some chemical and biologic changes occur in the water during this precipitation of suspended matter by gravity; but when the sedimentation is limited to a few hours or a few days, it is doubtful if any marked improvement in the quality has taken place.

Some improvement in color of turbid waters will usually take place within a few hours, unless the color is due to finely divided peaty substances, but no change in the organic matter or bacterial contents and species will in most instances occur.

Sedimentation of a character which will really affect the hygiene of water requires great length of time, and should be conducted in very large deep reservoirs, which precludes an attempt at purification of polluted waters by sedimentation alone by most cities.

The following table contains the counts and percentages of reduction of bacteria, in the water of the Ohio River, for an interval of time not exceeding thirty-two days. The Cincinnati tap water, although pumped to a distributing reservoir, really has no time for sedimentation before it leaves this reservoir and is used by the consumers; while the Covington, Ky., reservoirs are of such capacity in relation to the daily consumption, that usually there is about one month's time allowed for subsidence before the water passes from the reservoirs to the consumers.

REDUCTION OF BACTERIA BY SUBSIDENCE.[*]

DATE OF INOCULATION.	DAYS OF GROWTH ON GELATIN.	BACTERIA PER C. C. OF WATER.		PERCENTAGE OF BACTERIA IN COVINGTON WATER.	REDUCTION BY SEDIMENTATION. PER CENT.
		Cincinnati.	Covington.		
1896					
Jan. 17,	5	1,472	272	18.50	81.50
" 23,	4	1,599	194	12.13	87.87
" 28,	4	5,062	172	3.39	96.61
" 28,	4¾	. . .	182	3.59	96.41
Feb. 4,	4¾	1,656	53	3.20	96.80
" 4,	6	2,042	56	2.74	97.26
" 8,	7½	1,561	63	4.04	95.96
" 11,	4½	1,526	75	4.95	95.05
" 17,	7	684	20	2.92	97.08
" 21,	4	329	26	7.90	92.10
" 21,	7	1,232	112	9.09	90.91
" 26,	3¾	1,144	84	7.34	92.66
" 26,	5	1,436	102	7.10	92.90

The numbers of bacteria and percentage of reduction in the Covington water were at times very gratifying, and indicate what may be expected in situations where the water can be carried in a quiescent state in large reservoirs for several months before it is drawn off for use.

According to Professor Percy Frankland, the average number of bacteria in the two streams which discharge into the Loch Linthrathen, the source of water supply of Dundee, was 1,240, while

* *Report of Engineer Commission on Extension and Betterment of Cincinnati Water Works*, 1896, p. 15.

the average number of bacteria in the water issuing from the lake was 30, showing a reduction in bacterial contents of the water by subsidence of 97.6 per cent.

The same authority gives the following results from samples of water from the West Middlesex Works for 1892 : —

	BACTERIA PER C. C. OF WATER.
Thames water at Hampton,	1,437
Same water after passing two storage reservoirs,	177

Showing a reduction of 87.7 per cent in the bacteria by a few days' subsidence.

In the report of bacterial examinations of the river waters supplied to London for 1895, Dr. E. Frankland gives the following data : —

AVERAGE FOR TWELVE MONTHS.

SOURCE OF WATER.	BACTERIA PER C. C.	PERCENTAGE OF REDUCTION.
Thames at Hampton,	· 13,646	. . .
Chelsea reservoirs, 13 days' storage,	3,177	76.7
West Middlesex reservoir, 6.3 days' storage,	971	92.9
Lambeth reservoir, 6.4 days' storage,	3,520	74.0
Grand Junction reservoir, short storage,	917	94.0
River Lea, Angel Road,	14,075	. . .
East London reservoirs, 15 days' storage,	6,280	55.4

The reductions above are obtained from natural subsidence, without the aid of chemicals. The author's experiments with potash alum and slaked lime, on the suspended matter in the Ohio River water have given the following results : —

TAP WATER TREATED WITH POTASH ALUM AND SLAKED LIME; SUSPENDED MATTER ALLOWED TO SUBSIDE DURING 24 HOURS IN ICE-CHEST.

DATE.	KIND OF WATER.	DAYS OF GROWTH ON GELATIN.	COLONIES PER C. C. OF WATER.
Dec. 11, 1896,	Plain tap water,	4	11,021
" " "	Treated with 2.57 gr. of alum per gal.,	3	1,674–1,803
" " "	Treated with 3.74 gr. of slaked lime per gal.,	4	55– 59

Reduction by alum (without filtration) per cent,   84.22
Reduction by lime (without filtration) per cent,   99.48

Another test of the same water, treated with two and a half milligrams of potash alum to two ounces of water, kept in ice-chest for forty-eight hours, sample taken without disturbing sediment in bottle, cultivated on gelatin, gave the following results : —

Date.	Days of Growth.	Colonies per C. C. of Water.
December 13, 1896,	4	1,866–2,315
Reduction by alum (without filtration) per cent,		81.04

Hard water from the Colne Valley Water-Works, according to Professor Percy Frankland, contains 322 bacteria per cubic centimeter, and after treatment for reduction of hardness by the Clark process, with two days' subsidence, contains 4 bacteria per cubic centimeter, indicating a reduction of the bacterial contents, by the lime process and two days' sedimentation, of nearly 99 per cent.

Another experiment by the same authority, using the Clark process in combination with a mechanical separator in which only two hours were allowed for deposition of the lime, gave the following results : —

Artesian well water (London) contained 182 bacteria per cubic centimeter, while the treated water issuing from the mechanical separator contained 4 bacteria per cubic centimeter, showing a reduction of nearly 98 per cent in the bacterial contents of the water.

The following experiments upon assisted subsidence of the bacteria in water are given by Professor E. Ray Lankester, in his evidence before the Royal Commission on Metropolitan Water Supply : * —

EXPERIMENTS SHOWING EFFECT OF SUBSIDENCE OF MUD AND CLAY ON THE NUMBER OF BACTERIA IN SUSPENSION IN WATER.

1. Three jars, A, B, C, each holding one liter of Oxford tap water, were taken on June 27, 1892. To A were added and well stirred in, 25 grams of sterilized kaolin ; to B, similarly 12 grams of sterilized kaolin ; C was untouched. After 15 hours the kaolin had completely subsided, and plate cultures were made from each

* Appendix C, p. 456.

jar in order to determine the relative number of bacteria *now* in suspension in the water.

> From A, 1,200 colonies per c. c. were obtained.
> "   B, 2,790   "   "   "   "
> "   C, 7,040   "   "   "   "

Repetitions of the experiment yielded similar results, showing that as much as five-sixths of the bacteria present were carried down by the subsiding kaolin, when added in proper quantity.

2. On July 7 river mud sterilized by heat (80 degrees C.) was substituted for kaolin. To one liter jar of Oxford tap water 30 grams of the river mud were added and stirred in, while a second liter jar of the same water was kept for comparison. The jars stood undisturbed for 20 hours. The river mud having now completely subsided, plate cultures of the water in the two jars were made. That to which nothing had been added showed 55,000 colonies per cubic centimeter, while that to which the river mud had been added showed only 15,400 colonies.

The experiment with sterilized river mud was repeated on July 26 and 27 with similar results; viz., a reduction of the bacteria by subsidence of the mud to the extent of nearly three-fourths.

(These experiments have importance not only for the history of bacteria in the river normally, but especially for the question of the storage of flood water. The subsidence of the mud suspended in such flood water would largely tend to purify the water from any excess of bacteria.)

3. Experiments on addition of lime to river water. June 18, 1892, two liter jars of river water (Thames, Oxford) were taken; to one, 6½ grams of slaked lime were added. After two days, plate cultivations were made from the water in each jar; that to which no lime had been added showed 5,000 colonies; that to which the lime had been added showed only 280 colonies per cubic centimeter.

Reduction by lime 94.4 per cent.

A similar experiment with tap water on June 20 gave 120 colonies without lime as against 15 colonies where the lime had been added.

Reduction by lime 87.50 per cent.

Alum has a still more remarkable effect than lime on the bacteria in river water. On the 17th of September two liters of tap water were taken for comparison. To one (liter) ¼ gram of alum was added. After subsidence (i.e., 24 hours) the untouched water gave (1) 15,130 colonies, while the water to which the alum had been added gave none at all. On the 26th of September a similar experiment gave (2) 2,380 colonies in the untouched water, and 8 in that to which alum had been added.

Reduction by alum (1) = 100.00 per cent.

Reduction by alum (2) = 99.66 per cent.

The alum used by Professor Lankester amounted to 14.60 grains per gallon, which at 1.6 cents per pound would make the cost of treatment per million U. S. gallons $33.32 for chemicals alone. No mention is made of the presence of undecomposed alum in the water, but it cannot be doubted that with such a proportion of alum a considerable astringency must have been imparted to the water.

EXPERIMENTS ON THE PRECIPITATION OF THE SUSPENDED MATTER IN OHIO RIVER WATER.

The data detailed in the table below were collected by Mr. Edward Flad, C.E., in connection with certain experiments on sedimentation for the city of Cincinnati, 1889, and indicate that sedimentation for an interval as short as 40 hours will reduce the suspended matter by weight nearly 80 per cent.

EXPERIMENTS ON THE PRECIPITATION OF THE SUSPENDED MATTER IN OHIO RIVER WATER AT CINCINNATI, OHIO.

No. of Sample.	Date, 1889.	Hours of Settling.	Silt Held in Suspension Parts by Weight per 1,000.		Percentage of Silt Removed by Settling.
			Before Settling.	After Settling.	
4	Jan. 7	42.2	0.3635	0.1225	66.3
2	9	47.0	0.3610	0.1135	68.5
5	11	46.3	0.2350	0.1435	38.9
7	13	48.0	0.1005	0.0490	51.2
8	15	47.1	0.0920	0.0330	64.1
14	17	47.3	0.3900	0.1305	66.5
13	19	46.5	0.1590	. . .	. . .
17	21	48.2	0.2011	0.0932	53.6
26	23	41.5	0.0865	0.0246	71.5

EXPERIMENTS ON PRECIPITATION. — *Continued.*

No. of Sample	Date, 1889.	Hours of Settling.	SILT HELD IN SUSPENSION Parts by Weight per 1,000.		PERCENTAGE of Silt Removed by Settling.
			Before Settling.	After Settling.	
24	Jan. 25	30.4	0.0405	0.0540	. . .
19	26	40.4	0.0955	0.0220	75.9
29	29	5.3	0.1640	0.0720	56.1
30	29	40.3	0.2235	0.0580	74.0
31	31	30.3	0.2225	0.1098	50.6
33	Feb. 1	41.2	0.3095	0.0720	76.8
34	3	31.5	0.2760	0.0910	67.0
38	4	42.0	0.1000	0.0445	76.5
40	6	28.2	0.1615	0.0615	61.0
43	7	40.3	0.1548	0.0560	63.8
61	9	30.3	0.0555	0.0325	39.6
60	10	40.4	0.0450	0.0220	51.1
44	12	30.6	0.0415	0.0360	13.2
62	13	41.1	0.0462	0.0188	59.3
67	15	30.2	0.0665	0.0125	81.2
69	16	39.4	0.2635	0.0330	85.8
77	18	31.0	0.5425	0.1287	76.3
74	19	40.5	0.5900	0.1085	81.6
75	21	31.5	0.5623	0.1628	71.1
78	22	41.2	0.3780	0.0945	75.0
80	24	29.6	0.3455	0.0855	75.3
83	25	40.3	0.3811	0.0930	75.6
84	27	47.1	0.2940	0.0765	74.0

A review of the data in the table indicates that the greatest percentage of reduction of the silt accompanies the greatest turbidity of the river water.

Experiments by the author upon the rate of reduction of the suspended matter in the Ohio River water have given the following results : —

SEDIMENTATION OF SUSPENDED MATTER IN OHIO RIVER WATER, DECEMBER, 1896.

	Parts per 100,000.
Original amount of matter in suspension,	54.00
Matter in suspension at end of two days,	15.00
Matter in suspension at end of four days,	13.50
Matter in suspension at end of six days,	12.00

Showing a reduction of 72 per cent of the suspended matter in two days, 75 per cent in four days, and 77.8 per cent in six days.

The rate of subsidence will depend upon the specific gravity of the matter in suspension, and the quiescence of the water under-going sedimentation. When the specific gravity of the suspended matter is considerably in excess of one, and the water altogether at a state of rest, the precipitation will be rapid. Conversely, with a specific gravity of the suspended matter not much above that of water, and the water in a state of agitation, the sedimentation will be slow, and under unfavorable conditions there may be no precipitation by subsidence at all.

The reduction of organic matter in water by subsidence is due partly to precipitation of matters heavier than water, and partly to destruction of organic matter in suspension by bacterial action; while the reduction of the bacterial contents of water by sedimentation is accomplished partly by precipitation of the bacteria in contact with the suspended matter, and partly by the natural decay of the less hardy species of the water bacteria. In the biologic action which occurs in large bodies of water, the weaker species of the bacteria, as organic matter, are absorbed by or become food for the stronger species; and this process of the destruction of the weaker by the stronger forms goes on until all food supply is exhausted, whereupon the strongest species perish, and in a manner still to be explained are converted into the harmless nitrogenous compounds, and as such are precipitated along with the inorganic matters in suspension in all surface waters.

REDUCTION OF HARDNESS AND BACTERIAL CONTENTS BY ADDITION OF LIME.

Experiments conducted by Mr. Dibdin,* on the water of the New River Company furnished the following results : —

DATE.	BEFORE TREATMENT.		AFTER TREATMENT.		PERCENTAGE OF REDUCTION.	
	Hardness.	Bacteria.	Hardness.	Bacteria.	Hardness.	Bacteria.
Dec. 16, 1895.	17.4	96	5.4	12	68.4	87.5
Dec. 18, "	17.4	110	5.0	6	71.3	94.5
Dec. 20, "	17.4	60	8.5	16	51.2	73.4

* *Analytical Investigations of London Water Supply*, London County Council, January, 1896.

The lime treatment reduced the red color in the water, by Lovibond's tintometer, 100 per cent, and the yellow color 35 per cent. No change was noticed in the "free ammonia" after and before treatment, while the albuminoid ammonia was reduced 23 per cent. The chlorine was unaffected by the treatment, while the oxygen absorbed on a four-hour test before and after treatment was reduced 25 per cent.

The total solids were reduced from an average of 24.3 parts per 100,000 parts of water before treatment to 11.8 parts after treatment. In all the tests the water was dosed with 9.4 per cent of a saturated lime-water. Of these tests Mr. Dibdin says, "It would therefore seem that by the adoption of the system of softening, the present supply, in respect to its chemical quality and bacteria, would be improved to a degree comparable with that of the Welsh sources." *

Such experience as has been had along the line of reduction of hardness in water for city supply has revealed the interesting fact, that the addition of lime to a hard (polluted) water is effective in the purification of the water, as well as in the reduction of the hardness, as indicated by the experiments previously noted.

Elaborate appliances for the lime treatment of water are now being built by several companies abroad, and the author is informed that the Jewell Filter Company of Chicago has built some apparatus for this purpose for cities in this country.

With reference to the cost of water softening on a very large scale, the following information is abstracted from Reports by Mr. W. J. Dibdin, chemist, and Sir Alex. R. Binnie, engineer, to the London County Council, on the London Water Supply for 1895.

Considering, according to Mr. Dibdin, the cost of lime alone for a daily treatment of 200,000,000 imperial gallons, this will amount to £35,000 or $175,000 per year. Considering the cost

---

* It is not within the province of this work to discuss projects of water supply; but it may be of interest to mention that the Welsh sources with which Mr. Dibdin compares the lime-treated London water are ably and elaborately presented in a Report by Sir Alexander R. Binnie to the London County Council, entitled, *Available Sources of Water Supply for London, June,* 1894.

The development of these sources in Wales will provide a daily supply of 415,000,000 imperial gallons, at an estimated cost of nearly $200,000,000, the water to be conducted to the metropolis through two aqueducts 150 and 176 miles long.

of lime and all labor, Mr. Binnie puts this at £300 to £310 per million imperial gallons treated daily per year, while the cost of apparatus and buildings for lime treatment, he estimates at £3,500 to £4,500 or $20,000 per million imperial gallons treated daily. For the present daily consumption of water by London (200,000,000 imperial gallons), Mr. Binnie puts the annual cost at £60,000 or $300,000.

Reducing these figures to our measures and values, the annual cost for 1,000,000 U. S. gallons treated per day, for a reduction from a hardness of 17 degrees by Clark's scale to about 5 degrees for lime alone, according to Mr. Dibdin, becomes $708.00 ; and the whole cost of lime and labor, according to Mr. Binnie, will be $1,270.32, or about $\frac{44}{100}$ cent per 1,000 gallons of water treated. These figures are based upon the treatment of 240,000,000 U. S. gallons per day, and this cost would naturally not be applicable to small quantities of water per diem.

CHAPTER IX.

STERILIZATION OF DRINKING-WATER.*

SEVERAL years ago, in discussing the hygiene of public water supply, the author took the ground, that, as the proportion of water used for drinking-purposes was one-half per cent or less of the whole quantity consumed by the takers from a public source, the better plan was not to attempt to secure the whole supply of potable quality, but to render any water available fit for drinking-purposes by domestic filtration.   Later experience satisfies him that this plan will not answer for several reasons : —

1. All consumers of a public water supply cannot, or will not, use domestic filters.

2. There is no domestic filter which is absolutely proof against the dangers of polluted water.

3. Even if a satisfactory filter was obtainable, it is doubtful if the average householder would give this the attention it requires to keep it at all times in condition to act as a safeguard.

In view of which the conclusion has been reached, that if the consumer is to have a safe drinking-water, it must come to him in this condition through the public water mains.   In other words, the matter of purity must be looked after by the municipal corporation or the water company.   The prevalence of typhoid fever in any city or town having a public water supply is evidence that the water now generally furnished to consumers is unpotable, and that municipal corporations and water companies are delivering to their consumers water containing the specific organism of typhoid fever.

* A portion of this chapter is abstracted from a paper by the author, read at the Eighth International Congress of Hygiene and Demography, Buda-Pest, Austria, September, 1894.

It is common for physicians in case of doubt of the purity of a water supply, to recommend that water for drinking-purposes be boiled ; but the boiling of water renders it insipid and unpalatable, and it is claimed by some of the manufacturers of filters that water deprived of certain of its natural gases and solids in solution (as it will be by boiling) is not as wholesome as natural waters. The author has been unable to obtain any reliable information of the influence on the human system of the salts and gases in solution in natural waters, and is uncertain whether the continuous use of boiled water as a beverage will be deleterious. Considering that filtered and boiled water will be limpid and sterile and deprived of all toxic properties, and assuming that such water will not be in- jurious to the system, may not the problem of an absolutely safe drinking-water finally be solved by combined filtration and distilla- tion ? If carried out to its legitimate conclusion this would mean the treatment of a sufficient quantity of water by the municipal corporation for drinking and culinary purposes, and the delivery of this to consumers through an independent system of comparatively small mains. But the expensive apparatus for distillation ; the cost of duplicating the street mains, even with pipes of small diameter ; and especially the large annual expense of operation, — might at first sight seem to prohibit any attempt by this process to purify water on a large scale.

For the purpose of estimating the probable cost of this method of water purification for city use, let us take an American city with a population of 400,000, and allow a daily consumption of water for all purposes of 40,000,000 U. S. gallons, or 100 gallons per head of population ; of which quantity it will be assumed that $2\frac{1}{2}$ per cent, or 1,000,000 gallons per day, is used exclu- sively for drinking and cooking purposes, including water for the washing of culinary vessels and apparatus. To sterilize by heat 1,000,000 U. S. gallons of water per day of 24 hours will require an hourly distillation of 347,100 pounds ; and assuming the average temperature of the filtered water (or feed water) to the boilers to be 60° Fahr., and the pressure of distillation to be six pounds above the atmosphere, then the total heat to be added to each pound of water will be 1,124 B. T. U.

If the steam in going from the boilers to the surface condensers be made to pass through suitable closed heaters, through which also the cold water to the boilers is being pumped, then a part of the heat of the steam will be given up to the feed water, and a smaller amount of heat will be required from the coal or other fuel to sterilize a given amount of water, and a smaller capacity of boilers and surface condensers will be required. Since the cold water from the filters will be pumped under full boiler pressure through these closed heaters, it will be possible (if such heaters are of sufficient capacity) to supply to the water not only the sensible heat, but a part of the latent heat from the heat in the steam before it is finally condensed in the surface condensers ; or of the heat in the sterilized water a large percentage can be recovered and utilized in heating the filtered water to the boilers, with a corresponding saving of fuel.

The cost of fuel being the *bête noir* in the problem of sterilizing by heat the drinking-water for a city, it is desirable that the facts in connection with the expenditure of fuel be carefully and fully considered. The rate at which the feed water is pumped to the boilers being the same as the rate of flow of steam through the heaters to the condensers, it follows, that, if the heaters were large enough and sufficient time allowed for the passage of the steam through them, and there were no losses of heat by radiation, etc., one-half of the heat of the steam would be transferred to the water on its way to the boilers ; or of the 1,124 heat units added per pound of water in the boilers, 562 units would be carried back in the feed water. But the recovery of 50 per cent of the heat assumes an efficiency beyond the reach of ordinary heating apparatus ; and some allowance must be made for the losses by conduction and radiation, and by contact of air, which can safely be put at 10 per cent ; and considering the very slow rate of transfer of heat when the temperature of the steam (partially condensed) and that of the feed water approximate each other, it will be safe to allow another 10 per cent loss upon account of time ; from which, as a practical proposition, it is estimated that of the heat carried off from the boilers by the steam, 30 per cent may be recovered in the feed-water heaters, leaving

70 per cent to be taken up by the cooling water in the surface condensers.

It will therefore be necessary to supply to each pound of water pumped into the boilers $1,124 \times .7 = 787$ heat units; and with coal and boilers showing an efficiency of 11,250 heat units per pound of fuel, each pound of coal will distill 14.3 pounds of water at 6 pounds pressure above the atmosphere; and for the distillation or sterilization of 347,100 pounds per hour (1,000,000 U. S. gallons per day), there will be required 291 tons (2,000 pounds) of coal, or an annual consumption of 106,215 tons.

The boiler capacity to distill this amount of water daily has been estimated as follows : An ordinary return tubular boiler supplied with water at 60° Fahr., and working at six pounds pressure above atmosphere, will easily evaporate 3.5 pounds per hour per square foot of heating surface; and if the heat required per pound of water be 787 instead of 1,124 thermal units, then each superficial foot of heating surface can be expected to evaporate 5 pounds of water per hour; and for the evaporation of 347,100 pounds per hour, there will be required $\frac{347,100}{5} = 69,420$ square feet of heating surface. Allowing 2,000 square feet to each boiler, there will be required 35 boilers, each 6 feet 6 inches diameter by 18 feet long, with the proper complement of tubes. The feed-water heaters to heat the filtered water and partially condense the steam from the boilers have been estimated in the following manner : —

Each square foot of surface, taking the tube in the heater as $\frac{3}{16}$ inch or less in thickness, will readily transfer 4,000 thermal units per hour, equivalent to the heating through 337° Fahr. of 12 pounds of water; and to heat $\frac{347,100}{12}$ pounds will require 29,000 square feet of heating (or cooling) surface in the heaters; or with an allowance of 1,000 square feet of surface to each heater, there will be required 29 heaters to deal with 1,000,000 gallons of water per day.

Surface condensers constructed with thin brass tubes can be estimated to condense 15 pounds of steam per square foot of cooling surface per hour; and if these also are of 1,000 square feet each, there will be required, to deal with 1,000,000 gallons of water in 24 hours, 23 such condensers.

The apparatus, therefore, which we have outlined for the sterilization by heat of 1,000,000 U. S. gallons of water per day, consists in detail of a duplicate filter plant, each half of 1,000,000 gallons daily capacity; pumping machinery in duplicate of 1,000,000 gallons daily capacity to take the filtered water and supply it to the boilers; steam-boilers to evaporate the water under low pressure; closed feed-water heaters to cool the steam and heat the feed water; surface condensers to condense the steam; and pumping machinery to take the condensed steam and sterilized water, and pump it into the mains for distribution to the consumers. The filters, heaters, and steam-boilers will require buildings for their protection from the weather, while the condensers may be exposed to the weather without detriment to their operation or durability. In addition to the apparatus mentioned, for a city of the population we have assumed, there will be required about 350 miles of mains of small diameter, to distribute the sterilized water to the various premises to be supplied.

We are now ready to estimate the cost of constructing and operating such a plant for water purification : —

COST OF CONSTRUCTION.

Two filter plants, each of 1,000,000 gallons daily capacity,	$15,000.00
Filter-house,	4,000.00
Thirty-five steam-boilers, complete,	63,000.00
Twenty-nine feed-water heaters, complete,	29,000.00
Twenty-three surface condensers, complete,	34,500.00
Boiler-house,	30,000.00
Two sets of pumping machinery, each set of 1,000,000 gallons daily capacity, to supply the filtered water to the boilers,	9,000.00
Two sets of pumping machinery, each set of 1,000,000 gallons daily capacity, to pump the sterilized water into the mains,	12,000.00
Pumping-station,	12,000.00
Add for pipes, valves, etc., at sterilizing-station,	20,000.00
350 miles of mains at an average cost of $4,500 per mile,	1,575,000.00
Total,	$1,803,500.00

Cost per capita of population, $4.50.

FIXED ANNUAL CHARGES.

Interest on cost of construction at 5%,	$90,175.00
Annual payment to sinking-fund to redeem construction bonds invested at 4% for 40 years,	18,972.82
Total,	$109,147.82

OPERATING EXPENSES.

106,215 tons of coal at $2,	$212,430.00
Forty-five men at $2 per day, and five men at $3 per day,	38,325.00
Total annual cost,	$359,902.82
Annual cost of operating, and fixed charges per capita,	$0.90

Or for filtration and sterilization of the drinking-water for a city of 400,000 population, the cost per capita per annum cannot be in excess of $1. Are we prepared to pay this for absolute immunity from typhoid fever and other water-borne diseases?

The Yaryan Company of New York has kindly furnished the author an estimate of cost and operation for a water-sterilizing plant upon its system, which will be more economical of fuel and labor than the simple apparatus described. Adopting in our estimate the figures supplied by this company, the costs are as follows : —

COST OF CONSTRUCTION.

Filters and filter-house,	$ 19,000.00
Yaryan quadruple effect sterilizer,	225,000.00
Boiler-house,	30,000.00
Pumping machinery and station,	33,000.00
Distributing mains,	1,575,000.00
Total,	$1,882,000.00

FIXED ANNUAL CHARGES.

Interest and sinking-fund,	$113,898.64

OPERATING EXPENSES.

100 tons of coal per day, at $2, for one year,	$73,000.00
15 men at $2 per day, and 4 men at $3 per day,	15,330.00
Total annual cost,	$202,228.64
Annual cost of operating and fixed charges per capita,	$0.50
Or $.0554 per 1,000 gallons, sterilized and delivered.	

This scheme for water purification involves, as shown, a separate system of small mains to convey the sterilized and filtered water from the works to the consumers, and requires a separate service pipe from these mains to bring the water into each premises, after which, as a measure of hygiene, the use of such water for drinking and cooking purposes should, if found necessary, be made compulsory.

It will be noticed that no allowance has been made in the cost of operating for the cooling water to the surface condensers, because the 97–98 per cent (or as much of it as may be required) of unsterilized water supplied to the city may be made to pass through the condensers as cooling water without extra cost.

In regard to the figures heretofore given, it is not the purpose to state with precision all the details of cost of this method of water purification, but rather to lay down a principle, and let it be worked out for each particular case. Doubtless in some cities the cost of construction and operation will be less than has been shown, while in others, for local reasons, it may be greater. But it is reasonable to claim that sterilized and filtered water can be obtained in our larger cities within the cost given, or at about one-tenth cent per gallon; and the purpose of the approximate figures stated on the previous page is to show that the cost per unit of volume, or per capita of population, for absolutely sterile water, is not so great as to prohibit its use if demanded by the people.

Water such as this process of purification will furnish can neither be the habitat nor carrier of any kind of bacteria (nor of the toxalbumins which these may develop); and if any organisms came into it adventitiously, they would perish for lack of food.

One great difficulty in the way of introducing a process for the sterilization of drinking-water on a large scale in the United States, lies in the well-known fact that the construction of public works of any magnitude in most cities is seized upon as a political advantage by the dominant party; and the average tax-payer, upon whom the burden of cost falls, usually views with alarm any proposition to inaugurate an improvement requiring a large outlay of money, in spite of the fact, perhaps, that his health or that of his family, and possibly their lives, may depend upon the construction of such works. In cities, however, like Berlin, Vienna, and St. Petersburg, which are under imperial control, no difficulty should be experienced in establishing a process for the sterilization and

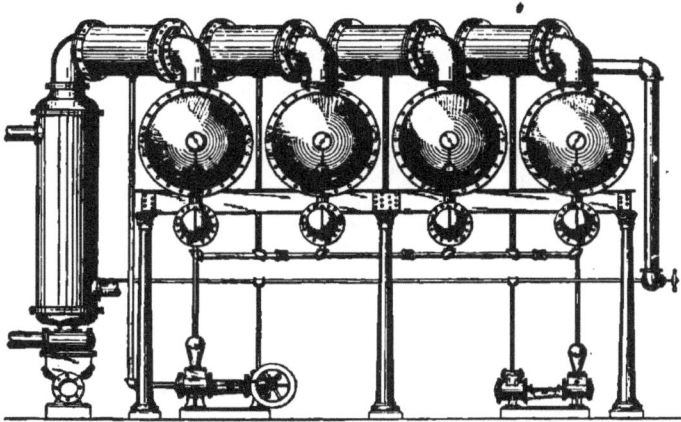

Front Elevation.
Fig. 3.

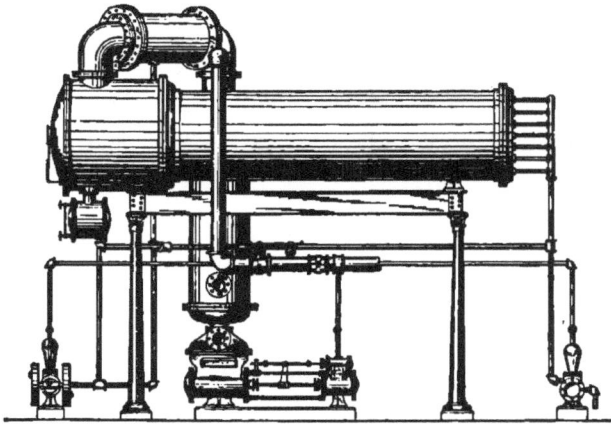

Side Elevation.
Fig. 4.

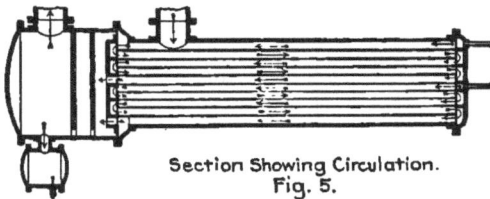

Section Showing Circulation.
Fig. 5.

Figs. 3, 4, and 5.   Yaryan Apparatus for Sterilizing Water.   Quadruple Effect.

special distribution of the small percentage of water used for drinking and culinary purposes whenever the health boards are ready to recommend it.   When this shall be done by these or any other cities, and the sterilized water is used by all the citizens, then such cities will be absolutely free from typhoid fever and other water-borne diseases so far as these may be chargeable to the local water supply.   But no amount of care upon the part of any city to defend its water supply from pollution, or render it safe to health as a drinking-water after pollution, can prevent the importation of typhoid fever from some other locality, where the hygienic regulations for the drinking-water are less rigid, and where the water contains the typhoid germ.   From which we reason that a system or process for the purification of drinking-water, to be wholly effective, must be universal in its application ; but no sanitary improvement, however essential it may be to health, has been, or ever will be, applied everywhere at one and the same time.   It must have its origin in some city, the efficacious results must be shown and published ; whereupon other cities, towns, and localities will speedily adopt it, and in due time the benefits of such improvement will be enjoyed by all the civilized people of the earth.

During the World's Fair at Chicago, 1893, all the employees, numbering nearly 15,000, used sterilized drinking-water, with the result that so long as this water only was used, no diarrheal troubles were reported among the men.   Upon the few occasions when for short intervals of time the sterilized drinking-water was discontinued, intestinal disorders arose ; and where typhoid fever occurred, it was traced to a disregard of the rules of the Exposition with reference to drinking-water.*

The sterilization of the water was effected by passing it through an ordinary feed-water heater, where it was raised to 212° Fahr., and kept at this temperature for a short time.   Analysis of the water revealed no bacterial life.

According to Surgeon-General Tryon of the United States Navy,† "It may be stated that the medical officers of the navy

---

* *Proceedings Fourteenth Annual Meeting A. W. W. Association*, pp. 22–24.
† *Water Supply, Chemical and Sanitary*, Wm. P. Mason, New York, 1896, p. 156.

recognize the great value of distilled water in the improvement in health that has followed its introduction, particularly in certain foreign stations."

No one will venture to deny that water properly sterilized by heat in an ordinary steam-boiler will be absolutely safe for drinking-purposes. All the bacteria or organic matter (in solution) originally in such water will be wholly destroyed or precipitated by evaporation under atmospheric pressure in a closed generator ; and if we accept the proof that water is the carrier or original cause of typhoid fever, then we are compelled to admit that water properly sterilized cannot foster or carry the bacillus. With such water universally used for drinking and cooking purposes, the typhoid bacillus would perish, and typhoid fever cease to-exist.

With few exceptions, it is vain to look for water wholly safe for drinking-purposes at its source. Few cities enjoy such water to-day, otherwise among their inhabitants who use the water exclusively typhoid fever would be unknown ; and doubtless in any city where the water is of such quality that analysts have pronounced it safe for drinking-purposes, it is being drunk to the exclusion of any other available water.

The principal objections which have been offered to a double water supply, whether the water of better quality is improved by sterilization or filtration, or is naturally of high quality, are : —

1. The better water will not always be used for drinking and dietetic purposes. Some people will forget the danger of drinking the unpurified water, and resort to that which is most convenient, thereby defeating the very purpose of a double supply.
2. It is urged that many of the poorer people cannot afford to introduce two kinds of public water into their houses.
3. In many instances the better water will be used for other than dietetic purposes.

The first of these objections can be overcome by proper education and example. The instinct of self-preservation must be wrought upon, and the natural tendency to take the better of two things equally attainable may be expected to encourage the use of the better water for drinking and culinary purposes. The second objection can be overcome by gentle compulsion, in the same manner that other sanitary improvements are carried out by municipal corporations at the cost of the property benefited. The third objection can readily be overcome by metering the purer water supply, and in cases where such water is freely used about the premises the cost thereof will be paid by the consumer.

It is probable that now a system of double water supply is rather too refined for most municipal corporations, but it is possible that such may be demanded by future generations. Many physicians and hygienists at the present time favor the dual system, through one branch of which water of the highest quality is to be delivered for drinking and culinary purposes, while through the other, water for the coarser uses is supplied to the consumers.

NOTE. — Referring to the Yaryan Apparatus for the sterilization of drinking-water (p. 125), quite extensive plants on this system have been in operation for several years at Perim and Kosseir, on the Red Sea, and at Troon, Scotland; converting from 6,000 to 12,000 gallons of sea-water into fresh water per day of 24 hours, with an expenditure of about $\frac{1}{4}$ pound of coal per gallon of water distilled, including the water for the boilers, and the fuel for operating the necessary pumping-machinery.

CHAPTER X.

FILTRATION OF WATER SUPPLIES.

THE purpose of this chapter is the discussion of devices and plans for the purification of large volumes of water for city use, and is not intended to touch upon the subject of domestic filters. The author believes that domestic filters, however well designed, are, in the hands of the users, a delusion and a snare ; and instead of being a safeguard against water-borne diseases, they really encourage the growth of the water bacteria, among which at times may be pathogenic organisms.

The tests noted in Chapter III., on Bacterial Contents of Various Waters, is therefore the only reference to domestic filters ; and these have been included among others of water in and about the city of Cincinnati.

Continuous sand filtration as practiced in Europe has gone through an experience of nearly fifty years, and one would suppose that this length of time should be sufficient to remove the matter from the domain of experiment and establish it in the domain of fact. Still, curiously enough, there are some who discuss sand filtration as practiced abroad very much as they do the subject of air navigation and the *mobile perpetuum,* — things very interesting in themselves, but quite impossible of any practical results. This indifference to the wonderful performance of sand filters in European cities is a bar to the development of works of water purification in this country, and is the cause of a large continuous loss of valuable lives and much physical suffering, eighty to ninety per cent of which might be averted if artificial works of water purification were as largely used in this country as they are abroad.

Some writers in their enthusiasm have declared that sand filters properly constructed and operated will furnish pure water. This is a mistake. No filter operated upon a practical basis has ever furnished pure water ; but the so-called purified water is so much superior to the unfiltered water that it will meet the practical requirements of cities and communities to-day, and when the time is reached that people demand absolutely pure water, methods for furnishing it will doubtless be forthcoming. For the present, and as a practical method of water purification, filtration may be regarded as entitled to full credit at the hands of city officials and water-works managers.

Filtration, as the term is defined and generally understood, consists of an interception or straining out from a fluid such suspended matter as is larger in some dimension than the pores of the filtering medium. The action is supposed to be purely mechanical, and the efficiency of a filter will be measured by the fineness or coarseness of the filtering material. The filtration of water, however, demonstrates that the fineness of the filtering material (sand) is not exactly a measure of the efficiency, and the finest or smallest grain of sand does not always give the best results.

This fact, then, would naturally suggest that the straining action is only a part of the work accomplished by the filter; and in addition to the interception of certain suspended matters at the surface of the sand-bed, some other forces are at work to reduce the suspended matter, including the bacteria, in the water. One of these forces is now known to be the action of the bacteria on the organic matter. This is called the biologic action of the filter.

All the common species of bacteria found in water are *saprophytes*, and depend for subsistence on dead organic matter. In fact, the bacteria are chiefly concerned in the destruction of this organic matter, and its conversion into harmless nitrates. The action of certain well-known forms of water bacteria upon sloped agar, is seen to be the production of a film, or expansion so-called, of its products of vital activity over the surface, and, if possessed of anaërobic properties, in the body of the agar. This expansion is indicative of the effect and propagation of the bacteria on the food material.

The bulk of the suspended matter, including the bacteria in water, will be intercepted at the surface of the sand. Here the process of splitting up the organic matter into its nitrogenous and carbonaceous elements is continually going on ; the carbons going off as carbon dioxides and other gases, and the nitrogenous matters being converted into nitrous and nitric acids, which in turn unite with the bases in the water, forming nitrites and nitrates, in themselves harmless products of bacterial action.

This biologic action of a filter is, after all, its most important function. The simple straining process of a bed of sand or of other filtering material, while competent to render turbid water clear, could have but little effect upon the bacteria, because many of these are so small in some dimension as to grow through a sand-bed of almost any practicable fineness. The action of the organisms in the water on the organic matter results in the production of a thin semi-gelatinous film over and around the grains of sand in the upper layers of a bed, which in due time becomes so dense as to clog it, and require a high head to force the desired amount of water through the sand ; whereupon such sand-bed is temporarily taken out of service, the water drawn down some distance below the surface, and the upper fraction of an inch of the sand removed. With the new surface of sand exposed, the filter is ready for service again.

When the water is drawn off a filter for renewal of the surface of the sand-bed, two important events occur. One consists of the paring off of a thin layer of the clogged sand mentioned above ; and the other of a complete or partial aëration of the sand-bed, by means of which the nitrifying bacteria in the bed are supplied with air (oxygen), without which, according to the authorities who have especially studied these organisms,* the nitrifying bacteria would soon perish, and their functions in the reduction of nitrogenous organic matter to nitrous and nitric acids be lost.

All sand filters are therefore intermittent filters. None work continuously. Each time the water is drawn down below the surface of the sand-bed, there is a partial aëration of the sand; and when the water is drawn off entirely, during the operation of paring away the upper one-half ($\frac{1}{2}$) inch or so of dirty sand, the bed is rested, as it were, and complete aëration occurs.

* Winogradsky, Warington, Percy Frankland, Dr. E. O. Jordan, and Mrs. Ellen H. Richards.

This upper dirty layer of sand, which contains inorganic matter intercepted from the water, and the products of vital activity of the water bacteria, is called the "Schmutzdecke" by Mr. Piefke, who, the author believes, was the first to point out the manner in which the semi-gelatinous film was formed, and how it consisted of intercepted matter in suspension, and organic matter in process of destruction by bacterial agency.

To one untutored in bacteriologic work, it may be difficult to understand the action of the bacteria on nutrient matter in water ; but to bacteriological students it is sufficient to state that in a filter the action of the bacteria upon suitable food material found in the water will be like that of bacteria cultivated in sterilized artificial media. The materials found in water may be more or less suitable for some of the water bacteria ; and those which find the organic matter fitted to their needs will flourish on the surface of a sand-bed, and appropriate to their support such matter as may be found in suspension or intercepted at or near the surface of the sand.

It is abundantly proven that the bacteria do not penetrate the sand-bed to any great depth,* and the surface of the sand where the interception of suspended matter must occur is also the principal seat of operations of the bacteria and other organisms in the water. The bacteria are not the only forms of life in water, and some allowance must be made for the destructive action of the infusoria and other forms of aquatic life upon the organic matter of which all these forms are themselves a part.

The following diagram and description showing the rate at which the bacteria grow in the sand-bed from the surface downward, is taken from Mr. Gill's paper on the filters at the Frederickshagen Station of the Berlin Water-Works.

" It has been stated above that the number of bacteria colonies is greatest at the surface of the sand, and decreases very rapidly in successive layers beneath. In Fig. 6, 0, x, z, y, represents the 2-foot deep sand-layer of a filter. If with 0 as origin, and distances along 0, x, representing depths of sand-layer, and those along 0, y, numbers of bacteria colonies per kilogram of sand, the

* *The Filtration of the Müggel Lake Water Supply, Berlin,* by Henry Gill, M.I.C.E., London, 1895, p. 12.

60,000,000 bacteria colonies per kilogram of the ripe sand be plotted at each of the depths 0, 4, 8, 12, and 24 inches, the line h, m, parallel to 0, x is arrived at. The hatched strip 0, x, m, h, then represents the ripe condition of filter sand after long use, in which condition a powerful water current and attrition of the grains against each other fail to free them from the bacteria. If now, with the same abscissæ, the 734, 190, 150, 92, and 60 millions be plotted as ordinates, the curve m, p, q, r, is arrived at. This curve exhibits pictorially the density of the bacteria colonies in the various layers of a sand filter at the close of a period of service when it gives the best results."

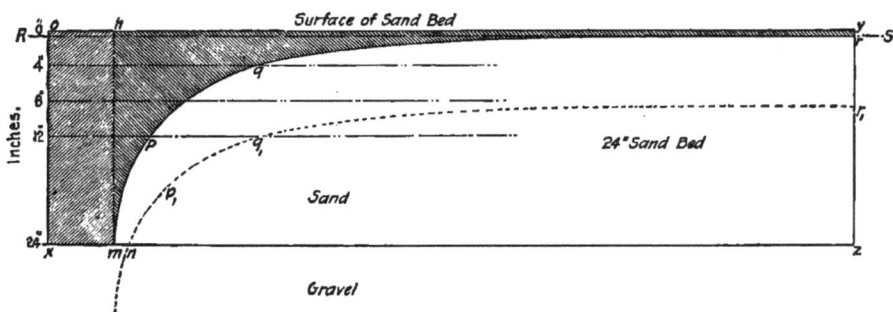

Fig. 6. Diagram Showing Accumulation of Bacteria in Sand-Bed.

The "Schmutzdecke," or film of intercepted suspended matter and products of bacterial action, is a delicate membrane lacking in consistency, and easily broken by too rapid changes of pressure (head) on the sand-bed; and when broken bad results are liable to follow. The author cannot do better than quote again from Mr. Gill upon this feature of sand filtration.*

"Since the bacteria are liable to be washed downwards by a stream of greater force than that which prevailed when they came into contact with the sand grains, it is of the utmost importance to avoid an increase of speed, especially a sudden increase. Mechanical arrangements must be adopted to prevent this, and it must be impossible that any filter in action can in any way affect the yield of the neighboring filter. The chief cleansing action takes place in the mud deposit on the surface of the sand, and in the sand immediately at the surface. In this region the coating of deposit is soft, and with its dense population requires careful and tender treatment to avoid squeezing out the bacteria by undue pressure. It is obvious that as soon as an appreciable

* *The Filtration of the Müggel Lake Water Supply, Berlin,* by Henry Gill, M.I.C.E., London, 1895, p. 12.

deposit has taken place on the sand ·surface, any increase of 'head' must be chiefly caused by the layer of this deposit.   If the sand beneath is not absolutely homogeneous, as it cannot be, any increase of pressure may cause a depression and a tearing of the mud-skin on the less dense parts of the surface of the sand.   Through such a rupture the bacteria are at once washed by the increased local current which ensues into the sand beneath, and may be carried through the entire layer.   Yet a gradual increase of pressure must of necessity take place, when the yield is to be constant, in order to overcome the increasing friction of the passage of the water through the filtering medium, in proportion as its insterstices become gradually closed by the deposit.   Nor is such increase, if gradual, injurious, provided certain limits be not exceeded.

Mr. Gill states that the maximum " head " for the Müggel Lake filter is 2 feet, but this has been increased in other instances to 5 or 6 feet without an apparent breaking of the surface film on the sand-bed.

After a filter has been scraped, and refilled with filtered water from below to the surface of the sand, water should be drawn from the settling-basin onto the filter to the full depth of high-water mark, and allowed to stand several hours before any flow occurs from the filter.   This interval of rest will be in continuation of the subsidence of the suspended matter in the water, and will assist in the formation of a coat of slime over the sand-bed before the flow is started.   After the water has remained at rest for a few hours over the sand-bed, the flow should be started cautiously, at a low rate, and gradually increased until the maximum allowable rate has been attained.

ACTION OF THE INTERMITTENT SAND FILTER.

In the continuous sand filter substantially the whole work of purification is accomplished at or near the surface of the sand-bed. The " Schmutzdecke," or dirty cover, which is regarded by foreign engineers as an essential of proper sand filtration, is not considered of special importance in the intermittent filter.   In this it is assumed that the organic matter in the water is reduced by the action of the bacteria in the bed of sand to nitrous and nitric acids, which unite with the bases in the water, forming insoluble and harmless nitrites and nitrates.   This work is chiefly accomplished by the nitrifying bacteria, discovered by Winogradsky in the soil at Zurich, and by Dr. Jordan and Mrs. Richards in the sewage at Lawrence, Mass.; but the ordinary water bacteria are also useful in breaking up the organic matter in water before it is acted upon by the nitrifiers.

The intermittent filter receives the water for a number of hours or days, and then rests for a number of hours or days, until the water held in the sand-bed has drained away, and the interstitial spaces are filled with air, when the filter is supplied with water as before.

Thus, while the action is intermittent from day to day, it otherwise is continuous in operation, the scraping and cleaning of the sand being only such as can readily be done during the short intervals of rest.

In the intermittent sand filter the bed of sand for the whole depth is supposed to act in the work of water purification, while the upper one-half inch or less of sand is known in the continuous filter to be concerned in the reduction of the bacterial contents as well as of other matters held in suspension by the water. The operation of the Lawrence, Mass., filter, since it was put in regular service, suggests that there has been some departure from the original method of use, and that in the days of continual service, and the resting and scraping of the sand-bed, it conforms more nearly than was intended to the method of operation pursued with sand filters abroad.

By the thorough and frequent aëration of the sand-bed, it is held by the designer (Mr. Mills) that there will be a "burning up" of the organic matter intercepted at the surface and in the depth of the filter, and by proportioning properly the duration of service and rest, with a complete draining of the bed each time it is rested, all organic matter will be consumed. The aëration of the sand-bed is intended to maintain the vitality of the nitrifying bacteria, which are the organisms concerned in the final destruction of the organic matter, and its conversion into nitrites and nitrates.

It is the theory that the intermittent filter is capable of continuous renewal by the forces within itself, and the large periodical expense required to restore the sand-bed of the continuous filter to its normal condition will be materially reduced. Enough experience has not been had with this system of filtration to express an opinion upon its adaptability to other waters than that of the Merrimac River; but both in the bacterial results and typhoid rates of Lawrence, since it was put in service four years ago, it seems not to have attained the high standard of efficiency reached by the continuous sand filters of Europe.

Any statement heretofore made upon the operation of sand filters is assumed to be the natural action without the aid of extraneous materials to assist in the precipitation of suspended matters, or in the formation of a coagulum at the surface of the sand. Aside from the use of particles of iron in a revolving cylinder (Anderson process), it is not known that any artificial agency is relied upon to insure the successful operation of sand filters in Europe.

From a knowledge of natural filtration as it occurs in the drift, it is easy to perceive that artificial sand filtration may be made to accomplish results far superior to natural filtration as it sometimes occurs. Thus the size and uniformity of the sand-grains, the effective head, and rate of flow through the sand-bed, may be so proportioned that the resultant filtrate is equal in purity to spring or deep well water. And this result can be obtained, not seldom, but at all times, and without regard to the original condition of the water. Assuming that the typhoid fever death rate is a correct index of the quality of a public water supply, then it appears that filtration can produce a water which will rival the purest of natural waters.

The water of Vienna and Munich is mountain spring water, not surpassed by any, and equaled by that of few cities of the world. The typhoid rates by the author's scale (Chapter V.) for these cities since 1890 have been : —

DEATH RATES FROM TYPHOID FEVER PER 100,000 OF POPULATION LIVING.

YEARS,	1890.	1891.	1892.	1893.	1894.	1895.	1896.	AVERAGE.
Vienna,	9	6	8	7	5	6	5	6.55
Munich,	8	7	3	15	2.5	3	3	5.94

Omitting the rate for 1893 for Munich, when there appears to have been an unwarranted increase in the typhoid rates, the average for the other six years becomes 4.4.

The water of Rotterdam and Berlin is filtered, the first from the River Maas, and the second from the Rivers Spree and Havel, both of which have received sewage and surface drainage from urban and rural territory before the water reaches the intakes of these works.

DEATH RATES FROM TYPHOID FEVER PER 100,000 OF POPULATION LIVING.

Years.	1890.	1891.	1892.	1893.	1894.	1895.	1896.	Average.
Rotterdam,	6	4	6	5	4.8	2	12	5.7
Berlin,	0	10	8	9	4	5	5	7.14

Note the fact that the death rate for Rotterdam is lower than for either Vienna or Munich. Note also that the comparison is not between cities of one country where the consumption of beer and other beverages is high, and of another country where from modesty, if for no other reason, we must claim that the consumption of beverages other than water is low.

Aside from the fact of equal quality as shown by comparison of spring and filtered waters, the theory of sand filtration, properly studied, leads to the conclusion that water of more uniform quality can be had from artificial filters than from irregular and scattered sand-beds as found in the drift, in some of which the size and irregularity of sand-grain and position of the sand-bed are not calculated for proper filtration. Spring water and well water may be pure, but we cannot state with assurance how it has been made pure ; while with filtered water we know how purity, so-called, has been obtained, and by repeating the process of purification we can reproduce the quality of filtrate.

The insufficiency of natural filtration through the drift is well recognized by those who have given the matter serious consideration. Dr. Drown, in the *Report of the Massachusetts State Board of Health for 1891*, p. 355, says :—

" Although water badly contaminated with sewage or the wastes of human life may be purified by thorough filtration so as to be free from organic matter and bacteria, yet in cases of ground waters of this origin and character we seldom feel complete security that the conditions of perfect filtration will always exist. A long-continued rainfall, for instance, may result in more rapid filtration, and consequently less perfect purification ; or the creation of new sources of contamination nearer the spring may result in its dangerous pollution.

" It is for such reasons that a certain suspicion always attaches to ground waters which have at any time in their history been seriously polluted. The use of ground waters, whether springs or wells, in built-up communities, should therefore be avoided ; for we have no control over the conditions of filtration, and have no means of knowing (except by constant vigilance in the examination of the water) when a water hitherto well purified may become injuriously impure. The danger from the use of ground waters in populous regions increases with the increase of population, and with the nearness of the sources of pollution to the spring or well."

The methods of water purification which have given such excellent results in cities of Europe are generally sedimentation for a few days in large reservoirs, combined with slow filtration through beds of sand ; and in some situations, like that of Berlin at Lake Müggel, where there is usually but little turbidity to the water, it is at times pumped direct from the lake to the filters.

Sedimentation is accomplished in reservoirs which will hold from a day to several days' supply. While at a state of rest in these reservoirs, much of the suspended matter which imparts color to the water will be precipitated, and form layers of mud on the bottom and sides of the basin.

While a few days' subsidence of turbid polluted water may have no large influence upon its quality, it will remove much of the suspended matter which otherwise will clog a sand filter, and reduce its term and efficiency of service.

Careful study of the subject of sand filtration has led to the opinion that it is possible to have the sand so fine and the rate of filtration so slow that, theoretically, all suspended matter, including the bacteria will be arrested on or in the sand-bed. But this would require enormous areas of filter surface, with limited commercial efficiency, and the cost of water so obtained would be prohibitory on a large scale.

In order, however, to approach as nearly as practicable the ideal condition of filtrate at a reasonable cost, it is desirable that all the heavier matter should be removed by subsidence before the water is put on the filters. Hence the use, in the water-works of London, Hamburg, and other foreign cities, of subsiding reservoirs in which the water is stored for several hours or days before the process of filtration begins.

It is not possible to make a sewage-polluted water fit for drinking-purposes by subsidence alone, excepting the water is permitted to remain in a wholly quiescent state in large, deep reservoirs for many months or years; a condition altogether impracticable for most cities; while subsidence for a few hours or days will reduce the suspended matter and silt in most turbid waters to a state which will admit of the use of comparatively fine sand in the filters, and rates of delivery higher than the average of European practice. The Engineer Commission on the Improvement of the Water-Works of the city of Cincinnati, proposed a rest of the Ohio-river water in subsiding reservoirs for four days before it was drawn off to the filters.

The time allowed for sedimentation before the water is thrown on the filters varies in different cities, and sometimes is controlled by financial rather than hygienic considerations. The following table contains the data upon this subject, from a few of the works abroad which combine subsidence with filtration : —

TIME ALLOWED FOR SEDIMENTATION.

LONDON,	Chelsea Works,	12.0	days.
	West Middlesex,	5.6	"
	Southwark,	4.1	"
	Grand Junction,	3.3	"
	Lambeth,	6.0	"
	New River,	4.4	"
	East London,	15.0	"
HAMBURG,		19–30	hours.
ROTTERDAM,		24	"
BERLIN,	Frederickshagen Works,	24	"

The views of English engineers at present distinctly favor sedimentation of surface waters previous to filtration ; and the new works proposed by Sir A. R. Binnie for the supply of London, notwithstanding the water impounded from the Welsh sources is naturally of very high quality, contemplates filtration of this water before it is distributed to the consumers.

In his report on the new sources of supply proposed for London, Mr. Binnie says : —

> "Although it will be seen from the chemist's analyses of the water of the Usk, the Yrfon, the Towy, the Wye, etc., that the waters in their natural state are of greater purity and contain less solid matter than the London water after filtration, and although these waters will be stored and be subjected to subsidence in the large reservoirs which I have described, and in some cases will be decanted or drawn off from one reservoir into another, yet I consider that when all precautions are taken, the water should be filtered before delivering to the consumer."

According to certain principles formulated by the Imperial Board of Health, Berlin (1893), the rate of filtration should not exceed 4 inches vertical per hour, or 8 feet per day, which corresponds to a daily rate per acre of 2,606,630 U. S. gallons. From some experiments by the late Mr. W. Kümmel, engineer of the Altona, Germany, Water-Works,* at rates of filtration of 4, 8, and 16 feet vertical per day, he obtained the best bacterial results from the higher rates, as indicated by the following table : —

1,303,315 U. S. gallons per acre per day	= 11 to 97 colonies per c. c.			
2,606,630 " " "	= 5 to 79 " "
5,213,260 " " "	= 7 to 72 " "

Mr. Kümmel did not regard 8 feet per day as "beyond doubt the maximum of safe filtration;" he thought though, that "the danger of a trespassing pathogenic organism is much more unlikely at the lower than at the higher rates, and that the best velocity was not the same for all waters." He felt confident "that the difference in the mineral, vegetable, and animal admixtures is of high importance in this question," and that we should endeavor to ascertain the best rate for each separate water and water-works.

From the latest published *Annual Report of the Massachusetts State Board of Health* (1895), the following notes from the experimental filters at the Lawrence station are taken : —

* *Transactions American Society of Civil Engineers*, vol. xxx., p. 333.

INTERMITTENT SAND FILTERS.

RATE OF FILTRATION. GALLONS PER ACRE PER DAY.	AVERAGE BACTERIA PER C. C. IN RIVER WATER.	AVERAGE BACTERIA PER C. C. IN FILTRATE.	PERCENTAGE OF BACTERIA REMOVED.
2,000,000	11,600	29	99.75
2,500,000 to 5,000,000	16,300	137	99.16
5,000,000 to 7,000,000	11,600	72	99.38

CONTINUOUS SAND FILTERS.

RATE OF FILTRATION. GALLONS PER ACRE PER DAY.	AVERAGE BACTERIA PER C. C. IN RIVER WATER.	AVERAGE BACTERIA PER C. C. IN FILTRATE.	PERCENTAGE OF BACTERIA REMOVED.
1,000,000 to 2,500,000	13,950	72	99.49
2,500,000 to 5,000,000	18,220	273	98.56
5,000,000 to 7,000,000	11,600	73	99.37
7,000,000 to 10,000,000	16,500	130	99.22

The average results given in the table were obtained with sands varying in "effective size" from 0.14 to 0.48 mm., and "uniformity coefficient" from 1.6 to 3.7, while the thickness of sand-bed varied from 60 to 7 inches. Considering the efficiencies of the filters with sand-beds not less than 48 inches in thickness, the 5 intermittent filters for rates of filtration from 2,000,000 to 6,600,-000 gallons per acre per day gave an average bacterial reduction of 99.32 per cent, while the 8 continuous filters for rates of filtration from 2,000,000 gallons to 8,200,000 gallons per acre per day gave an average bacterial reduction of 99.32 per cent.[*]

The influence of rate of filtration on the organic matter and bacterial contents of the Zurich filtered water is shown by Dr. A. Bertschinger of the Municipal Laboratory of Zurich, in the following table : —

CHEMICAL QUANTITIES IN PARTS PER 100,000 OF FILTERED WATER.	RATE OF FILTRATION PER ACRE PER DAY IN U. S. GALLONS.				
	4,356,000.	5,227,200.	8,712,000.	16,262,400.	21,489,600.
Organic matter,	1.65	1.69	1.70	1.70	2.02
Free ammonia,	0.0007	0.0008	0.0004	0.0004	0.0006
Albuminoid ammonia,	0.0028	0.0027	0.0027	0.0027	0.0037
Bacteria per c. c. in filtrate,	20	31	22	15	18

* *Twenty-seventh Annual Report Massachusetts State Board of Health*, p. 505.

Commenting on these results, Mr. Preller * says (adapting his figures to U. S. gallons and rates per acre per day) : —

"These results show, therefore, that, provided the filter-beds are in efficient working order, neither the chemical nor the bacteriological purity of the filtered water is impaired by increasing the rate of percolation from 5,953,200 to 16,262,400 U. S. gallons per acre per day, a fact which is at variance with the view advanced elsewhere, that the mean rate of percolation for sand-filters should be limited to 3,194,400 U. S. gallons per acre per day."

According to Mr. Schröder, the number of bacteria in the unfiltered Elbe water at Hamburg ranges from 800 to 3,000, while the filtered water seldom contains above 30 colonies per cubic centimeter, and at times is as low as 20 colonies per cubic centimeter, showing a reduction of 97.5 to 99.0 per cent in the bacterial contents of the raw water.

The following tables from Dr. E. Frankland's † bacterial analysis of the water supplied by the London companies from the Rivers Thames and Lea, are very interesting when viewed from the standpoint of artificial water purification upon a large scale.

COMPANIES WHICH TAKE WATER FROM THE RIVER THAMES.

CHELSEA WATER COMPANY.

BACTERIA PER C. C. OF WATER.

Month.	Unfiltered Water.	After 12 Days' Storage.	After Filtration.
January,	11,560	1,360	20
February,	26,800	460	44
March,	18,000	240	28
April,	7,520	Lost.	4
May,	2,060	140	24
June,	6,760	1,150	178
July,	2,220	420	20
August,	1,740	200	18
September,	4,300	140	2
October,	39,760	340	8
November,	8,560	280	12
December,	160,000	854	55
Average,	24,107	508	34

Average percentage of reduction by subsidence, 97.85
Average percentage of reduction by subsidence and filtration, 99.86

* *Zurich Water Works*, C. P. Du R. Preller, London, 1892, p. 26.
† *Annual Summary of Vital Statistics*, London, 1896, p. lxxiv., *et seq.*

WEST MIDDLESEX COMPANY.

BACTERIA PER C. C. OF WATER.

MONTH.	UNFILTERED WATER.	AFTER 5.6 DAYS' STORAGE.	AFTER FILTRATION.
January,	11,560	3,460	44
February,	20,800	1,820	16
March,	18,000	2,340	24
April,	7,520	720	20
May,	2,060	280	4
June,	6,760	1,000	301
July,	2,220	680	8
August,	1,740	300	6
September,	4,300	120	14
October,	39,700	740	30
November,	8,560	5,520	25
December,	160,000	26,760	120
Average,	24,107	3,605	51

Average percentage of reduction by subsidence,   85.05
Average percentage of reduction by subsidence and filtration,   99.79

SOUTHWARK AND VAUXHALL COMPANY.

BACTERIA PER C. C. OF WATER.

MONTH.	UNFILTERED WATER.	AFTER 4.1 DAYS' STORAGE.	AFTER FILTRATION.
January,	11,560	. .	32
February,	20,800	. .	234
March,	18,000	. .	102
April,	7,520	. .	1,116
May,	2,060	. .	36
June,	6,760	. .	24
July,	2,220	. .	188
August,	1,740	. .	12
September,	4,300	. .	68
October,	39,760	. .	16
November,	8,560	. .	142
December,	160,000	920	8,020
Average,	24,107		832.5

Average percentage of reduction by filtration alone,   96.55

GRAND JUNCTION COMPANY.

BACTERIA PER C. C. OF WATER.

MONTH.	UNFILTERED WATER.	AFTER 3.3 DAYS' STORAGE.	AFTER FILTRATION.
January,	11,560	290	28
February,	26,800	400	83
March,	18,000	380	97
April,	7,520	1,110	112
May,	2,060	540	56
June,	6,760	567	376
July,	2,220	410	32
August,	1,740	510	21
September,	4,300	360	63
October,	39,760	740	49
November,	8,560	1,580	110
December,	160.000	38,000	1,106
Average,	24,107	3,741	178

Average percentage of reduction by subsidence,   84.48
Average percentage of reduction by subsidence and filtration,   99.26

LAMBETH COMPANY.

BACTERIA PER C. C. OF WATER.

MONTH.	UNFILTERED WATER.	AFTER 6.0 DAYS' STORAGE.	AFTER FILTRATION.
January,	11,560	6,560	56
February,	26,800	13,380	56
March,	18,000	5,120	40
April,	7,520	5,340	12
May,	2,060	1,080	8
June,	6,760	1,280	130
July,	2,220	1,340	20
August,	1,740	600	60
September,	4,300	1,080	30
October,	39,760	4,660	12
November,	8,560	2,920	24
December,	160,000	56,000	116
Average,	24,107	8,280	47

Average percentage of reduction by subsidence,   65.65
Average percentage of reduction by subsidence and filtration,   99.81

COMPANIES WHICH TAKE WATER FROM THE RIVER LEA.

NEW RIVER COMPANY.

BACTERIA PER C. C. OF WATER.

Month.	Unfiltered Water.	After 4.4 Days' Storage.	After Filtration.
January,	2,510	1,040	31
February,	2,080	1,580	31
March,	4,240	1,820	11
April,	1,340	500	4
May,	1,340	300	7
June,	1,640	420	17
July,	1,500	480	12
August,	840	340	67
September,	2,540	660	16
October,	4,400	820	7
November,	3,200	4,880	69
December,	14,540	7,480	266
Average,	3,347	1,693	45

Average percentage of reduction by subsidence,   49.42
Average percentage of reduction by subsidence and filtration,   98.65

EAST LONDON COMPANY.

BACTERIA PER C. C. OF WATER.

Month.	Unfiltered Water.	After 15 Days' Storage.	After Filtration.
January,	6,720	3,140	68
February,	7,880	1,600	69
March,	20,640	1,460	49
April,	Lost.	Lost.	52
May,	8,180	1,180	81
June,	11,720	2,340	208
July,	2,680	1,520	43
August,	6,020	2,140	68
September,	32,000	2,160	41
October,	12,220	1,460	53
November,	10,880	3,200	62
December,	80,000	13,420	145
Average,	18,085	3,056	78

Average percentage of reduction by subsidence,   83.10
Average percentage of reduction by subsidence and filtration,   99.56

PERCENTAGE OF BACTERIA REMOVED.

WATER COMPANY.	No. of Days of Subsidence.	By Subsidence.	By Subsidence and Filtration.
Grand Junction,	3.3	84.48	99.26
New River,	4.4	49.42	98.65
West Middlesex,	5.6	85.05	99.79
Lambeth,	6.0	65.65	99.81
Chelsea,	12.0	97.85	99.86
East London,	15.0	83.10	99.56
Southwark and Vauxhall,	Percentage of Bacteria removed by Filtration without Subsidence.		96.55

The preceding tables have been given in some detail in order to discuss the numbers of bacteria in the water after filtration. The first observation which one will naturally make is the extreme variation of results for different months by the same company, and for the same months by the different companies. Keeping in view the London standard of bacterial contents of potable water, — i.e., 100 colonies per cubic centimeter, — it appears that all of the companies complied with the standard for the month of January. Only one of the seven companies (Southwark) failed to comply with the required standard for February; and only one company, the Southwark again, failed to bring the bacterial contents of the filtrate within the prescribed limit for the month of March.

The record of the Southwark Company indicates very bad work for several months, and as an average for the year, and is to be accounted for only upon the ground of insufficient filter capacity, or gross negligence in the manipulation of the filters. Once only did the Chelsea and New River Companies, and twice only during the year did the West Middlesex, Lambeth, and East London Companies pass the bacterial limit, while the work of the Southwark and Grand Junction Companies for the year was generally very poor.

With the exception of the Chelsea Company, the work of the filters for December was not up to the standard of London water. Referring to the Chelsea Company, and omitting the bad work of the filters for June, the average for the other eleven months was

21.4 bacteria per cubic centimeter, of filtered water, at times falling so low as 2 and never exceeding 55. Neglecting the bad work of the West Middlesex filters for the months of June and December, the average for the other ten months was 19.1, the lowest count being 4, and the highest count 44 bacteria per cubic centimeter.

An examination of all the tables reveals the fact that four of the companies at times brought the bacterial condition of the water down to 8 or less per cubic centimeter of the filtrate, and since these very encouraging exhibits do not always occur simultaneously by months, it must be credited to management of the filters or favorable company conditions, rather than to conditions prevailing in the unfiltered waters.

It is apparent from the tables that the performance of the filters of the London works for the winter months is in some instances very unsatisfactory, and this must be due to a cause which is susceptible of remedy. If it is chargeable to uncovered filters, then covering should be resorted to. But the Hamburg authorities assure the author that they have been able with uncovered filters, and by an ingenious device for scraping the sand under the ice-cake (see Fig. 26) which forms in their climate, to keep the bacteria in the filtered water down to 30 per cubic centimeter. It is well known that the winters are more rigorous in Hamburg than in London ; and if it be possible to satisfy the hygienic requirements in Hamburg during the winter, it surely should be possible to do so in London.

It will also be noticed that the low bacterial counts in the filtrate do not always follow the lower counts in the unfiltered river water ; thus, the Chelsea filters were successful in reducing the number of bacteria in the water to 4 per cubic centimeter with 7,520, and to 2 per cubic centimeter with 4,300 in the applied water ; when with only 1,740 and 2,220 colonies in the river water, the bacteria in the filtrate rose to 18 and 20 per cubic centimeter.

For the West Middlesex Company the conditions seem to change somewhat, the lower counts of bacteria in the river water being followed by lower counts in the filtrate. This is not always true, even for this company : for with 26,800 bacteria per cubic centimeter in the river water, the bacteria in the filtrate were as low as 16 per cubic centimeter ; while with only 4,300 in the river water, the bacteria in the filtrate were 14 per cubic centimeter of the water.   The cause of these variations and apparent vagaries may be found in the relative condition of the filters in service during the respective months.   If the bacterial examinations happened shortly after one or more filters had been cleaned, the counts in the filtrates might be relatively high ; while if the examination had just preceded the cleaning of a filter, the count might be relatively low.

Aside from the poor work accomplished at times by the London filters, it is manifest that filtration, properly conducted, can produce remarkable changes in the bacterial contents and quality of sewage-polluted waters.   The general results as shown by the tables indicate marvelous possibilities which can be attained by filtration under a rigorous discipline upon the part of the health authorities, and a proper accountability upon the part of the water companies.

Failure to attain a low bacterial condition of the filtrate, as we have seen, is not due to the weather, nor to the bacterial contents of the unfiltered water, but to causes which an inflexible regimen would speedily remove.   A review of the seven waterworks of London which take their supply from rivers would be unfair if it failed to state the fact that these companies were hard pressed at times to secure the required quantity of water ; and it is doubtless true, that if the supply of water from the Thames and River Lea was at all times ample, and not a matter of grave concern, the English engineers would undertake to supply a filtrate which should never exceed the prescribed standard of bacterial contents, and usually be lower than that of average spring waters.

The diagram on page 151 contains, to uniform scale, (1) the depth or thickness of finer sand-bed ; (2) the rate in imperial gallons per acre per day ; and (3) the percentage of bacteria in the applied water removed by filtration, — for each of the seven London companies which filter their water supplies.   The solid black

surfaces show the thickness of sand-beds; the finely hatched surfaces show the rate of filtration per acre per day; and the coarsely

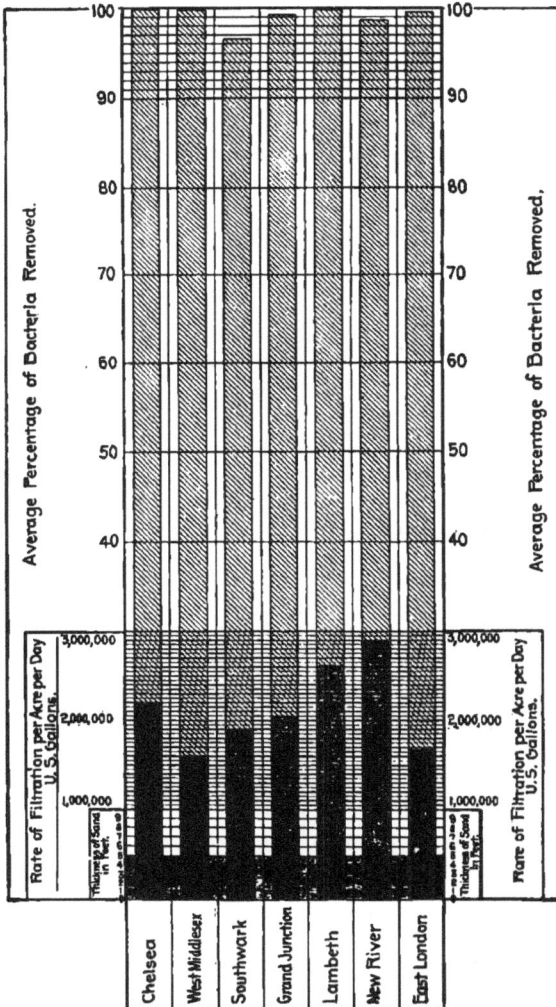

Fig. 7. Diagram Showing Operation of London Filters, 1890.

hatched surfaces the percentage of bacterial efficiency. The ordinates originate at a common zero plane.

The following very interesting table is taken from Mr. F. A. Meyer's paper * on the Hamburg Water-Works (p. 23) : —

NO. OF BACTERIA PER C. C. OF WATER AT VARIOUS POINTS OF THE HAMBURG WATER-WORKS.

SOURCE OF SAMPLE.	BACTERIA PER C. C. OF WATER.	
	Dec. 23, 1893	Jan. 17, 1894
New intake from River Elbe, Billwarder Island,	1,665	1,953
From settling-basins, " "	674	1,031
From main conduit to filters, " "	909	1,053
Unfiltered water from Filter No. 1, Kalte Hofe,	818	. .
" " " No. 3, "	. .	1,094
" " " No. 19, "	782	. .
" " " No. 20, "	. .	1,061
Filtered water from Filter No. 1, "	18	. .
" " " No. 2, "	. .	33
" " " No. 3, "	. .	31
" " " No. 4, "	8	. .
" " " No. 5, "	18	. .
" " " No. 6, "	. .	21
" " " No. 7, "	7	. .
" " " No. 8, "	. .	35
" " " No. 11, "	33	28
" " " No. 12, "	45	30
" " " No. 15, "	. .	. .
" " " No. 16, "	24	16
" " " No. 17, "	29	14
" " " No. 18, "	7	4
" " " No. 19, "	11	9
" " " No. 20, "	. .	18
" " " No. 21, "	. .	. .
" " " No. 22,† "	. .	. .
From the new main collecting channel, "	19	17
" " old " " " "	23	26
From siphons to the clear-water basin, Rothenburgsort,	25	23
From clear-water basin, "	31	24
From pumping-well, "	28	40
From tap in the Hygienic Institute, Hamburg,	97	85
From tap at No. 25 Gunther Street, "	94	69

NOTE. — Where no numbers of bacteria are given, the filters were not in service on the day the test was made.

* Chapter XIII.

† The plan of the works at Hamburg contemplates twenty-two filters, of which Filters Nos. 9, 10, 13, and 14 are to be constructed.

The average for the 10 filters in service Dec. 23, 1893, was 20 bacteria per cubic centimeter, while for the 11 filters in service Jan. 17, 1894, the average was 22 bacteria per cubic centimeter in the filtered water, a reduction of 98.8 to 98.9 per cent of the bacteria in the river water.

The increase in numbers from the filters to the taps at the Institute of Hygiene, and on Gunther Street in the city, is not in accord with the experience at Lawrence, Mass.,* where the numbers of bacteria are generally found to be less as the water passes from the clear-well of the filter to the service taps in the city.

LAWRENCE, MASS. CITY FILTER.

BACTERIA PER C. C. AVERAGES FOR 1895.

MERRIMAC RIVER WATER.	EFFLUENT FROM FILTER.	OUTLET OF DISTRIBUTING RESERVOIR.	TAP AT CITY HALL.	TAP AT EXPERIMENT STATION.
10,666	122	122	84	77

From daily bacterial examinations for the six months ending April 30, 1896, the following averages are given : † —

LAWRENCE, MASS. CITY FILTER.

BACTERIA PER C. C. OF WATER.

MERRIMAC RIVER WATER.	EFFLUENT FROM FILTER.	OUTLET OF DISTRIBUTING RESERVOIR.	TAP AT CITY HALL.	TAP AT EXPERIMENT STATION.
7,533	134	119	86	85

The Hamburg filters were started in operation five months before the Lawrence filter, and the influence of the better water on the bacteria in the street mains should be no less in the former than in the latter city. Such information as has come to the author on this subject indicates that within a period of three months or less, the regimen of the purified water is fully established in the street mains and service pipes, and neglecting the influence of a possible higher temperature of the water in the service pipes than in the clear-well of the filters, the former should show fewer bacteria than the freshly filtered water. The Law-

---

* *Twenty-seventh Annual Report Massachusetts State Board of Health*, p. 573, *et seq.*
† *Ibid.*, p. 581.

rence experience is in accord with this theory, and the author's ·
investigations along this line generally indicate that with filtered
water in pipes, and therefore not exposed to light and air, nor to
increased temperature, the bacteria diminish in numbers per cubic
centimeter after the water leaves the filters.

DOUBLE FILTRATION.

During the investigation by the Royal Commission on Metropolitan Water Supply, it was suggested by Dr. E. Frankland,[*]
that the quality of the London river waters might be improved by
a second or double filtration.   At first sight this proposition looks
very favorable, and if the operation of a sand filter was the same
as that of a fine strainer it would doubtless improve the quality
of the water by passing it successively through two or more filters
of diminishing sizes of sand ; but considering the action of a filter
in the removal of bacteria from water as a biological process, then
double filtration might yield a poorer filtrate than single filtration.

The formation of the gelatinous film on the surface of the
sand, and the closing of the pores, is hastened by, and, in fact, is
partly due to the deposition of the suspended organic matter in
the water.   In the process of double filtration this organic matter
would be almost wholly arrested upon the first filter, leaving a
small amount of material in the water from which to form the
film on the second filter, and the partially purified water would in
all probability pass through the latter with little improvement in
quality.   A preliminary filtration through a thin bed of coarse
sand, which would intercept the larger and heavier suspended
matters, might be of advantage in some instances, but as a rule,
double filtration cannot be regarded as the proper remedy for
unsatisfactory single filtration.

The biologic work of a plain sand filter has been so well
established that any proposition which inferentially rejects this
theory of action should be very carefully considered before it is
adopted in practice.

The film at the surface of the sand-bed consists partly of the

* *Minutes of Evidence*, p. 482, *et seq.*

intercepted suspended matters, and partly of the products of bacterial action on the suspended organic matter in the water, and this film in due time becomes in itself a very fine strainer, retaining thus at the top of the sand-bed the food for support of bacterial life ; and double filtration, to be successful, must contemplate a free passage of much of the food material and bacteria through the sand-bed of the first filter, to form the film on the sand of the second filter.

The author would gauge the performance of a filter by its practical results, and practical results are to be found in the influence of the water upon the typhoid fever rates of the city supplied from such filter. It matters not how much the bacteria are reduced in percentage of the applied water, or how far nitrogenous organic matter has been advanced towards nitrous and nitric acids, if the typhoid fever rates have not been lowered. But with a reduction of the bacteria, and conversion of organic matter into harmless compounds, there ought to be a reduction in the typhoid fever rates. That it should be so none will deny. But since the reduction of the typhoid fever rates is what we are aiming at, why not make this the measure of efficiency, and let the standard of operation of filters be based upon the percentage reduction of case and death rates, — or better still, let the contracts and performance be based upon a given death rate from typhoid fever, which shall follow the use of such filtered water?

This is the practical result which cities desire, and for which, when men are found with sufficient confidence, combined with knowledge, to pledge such results, the author believes they are willing to pay. It is all very well to point to a reduction of 99.9 per cent of the bacterial contents, and to the great chemical changes which have taken place in the water while passing through the filter ; but these are only steps in the journey, the end being the reduction of the typhoid rates.

If the register of vital statistics shows a reduction by the use of filtered water from 40 to 8 per 100,000 of population, or a percentage reduction of 80 in the typhoid rates, what need we care about the degree of bacterial and chemical changes ? Here we have something tangible, something that the people, as well as the bacteriologist and chemist, can grasp, and appreciate at its full value.

With reference to the time which water may be carried in storage after filtration, this will depend to some extent upon the original source of the water.   Surface waters always exposed to light will be less affected by the growths of flora and fauna than ground waters.   No water, whether pure or purified, will be so destitute of organic matter and bacteria as to no longer furnish the material for further algous and bacterial development.   But if, among the forms of bacterial life in stored waters, there are none of the pathogenic species, and in the organic matter in process of destruction there are no ptomains, no objection from the standpoint of hygiene can possibly be raised to the processes which may be going on in stored water.

The experience abroad universally favors the covering of storage or service reservoirs for filtered water.   Whether this precaution is absolutely necessary in all cases has not been shown as the result of carefully conducted investigations, and it is possible that certain waters can be filtered and carried without injury to quality in open reservoirs for many days.   Iron, lime, sulphur, and other salts in solution in waters, favor the growth of some species of vegetable life ; and the nature of the dissolved mineral substances in water doubtless has a strong influence on its quality, if carried in storage after filtration.

It is stated in connection with the Anderson Iron Purifiers at Paris, that the water from these is carried for nearly three weeks in covered reservoirs without change in bacterial contents, color, taste, or odor.   Upon the contrary, the water from the Lawrence, Mass., filter is pumped to an open distributing reservoir ; and the only cause of complaint which the author has noticed in the Annual Reports since the filter was started in service has been the formation of ice on the reservoir and filter.   The reservoir, when filled to a depth of 25 feet, has a water surface 694 by 375 feet, contains 40,000,000 gallons, and represents about 13 days'

storage. It consists of two equal compartments, and the water is delivered to either or both divisions of the reservoir at will.

The experience at Quincy, Ill., with stored filtered water, is very different from that at Lawrence, Mass. At the former place, since filtration has been practiced, during the summer months "there is a vegetable growth of a mossy character which some seasons imparts a fishy or woody taste to the water and other seasons does not." At Quincy mechanical filtration with alum is resorted to, while Lawrence depends upon plain sand filtration. (The author is not aware of any investigations upon the influence of undecomposed alum in water on certain species of plant life, and it is possible when these are made, they may show that plants having a strong affinity for potash or sulphur, will flourish in water purified with alum.) The reservoir at Quincy has an available water depth of 22 feet, a water surface of 350 by 250 feet, and contains 18,000,000 gallons. The average daily consumption during 1896 was 1,261,900 gallons, and the reservoir contains at the present time about 14 days' supply.

By Act of Parliament, 1855, the water companies of London were required to cover all distributing reservoirs which received filtered water within a radius of five miles from St. Paul's; and according to the statistics of the London works for 1893, the aggregate capacity of these reservoirs represented about four-fifths of the average daily consumption, or 20 hours' supply. At Berlin, Hamburg, and other cities of continental Europe, which, like London, use filtered waters, the distributing reservoirs are of small relative dimensions, and not intended for storage, but to compensate for the varying rates of consumption during the day.

CHAPTER XI.

TYPES OF SAND FILTERS.

SAND FILTERS may be classed as of four types : —

1. The so-called continuous filters of European practice, as designed by Mr. James Simpson of the Chelsea and Lambeth Water-Works.
2. The intermittent filter, as designed by Mr. Hiram F. Mills, C. E., for the water-works of Lawrence, Mass.
3. Natural filtration into collecting galleries, as illustrated in the water-works of Lyons and Angers, France, and in some cities of this country.
4. Mechanical filters, in which the sand-bed is restored to its normal condition by washing, without removal from the filter.

In situations where artificial filters are to be covered, there will be a saving in space by constructing the walls of masonry backed by puddle, as shown by Fig. 8 ; but with open filters, such as are used in London and Hamburg, certain advantages are to be had from the sloped walls, as shown by Fig. 13 (Chapter XIII.). Where filters are liable to be covered with an ice-cake, and the method of sand cleaning under the ice as practiced at Hamburg is adopted (Fig. 26), then a sloped inside wall is absolutely essential to the proper operation of this apparatus. The continuous filter is usually rectangular in plan ; but this is varied to suit the location, some of the London filters being circular. So far as form affects filtration, the beds may take any of the regular shapes in plan ; but for convenience of scraping and removing the sand, the rectangular form is to be preferred. Regulating devices to limit the head on a filter are regarded now as essential features of such works, in order to remove as far as possible from the attendants the power to seriously interfere with the regularity of operation of a filter. These regulating devices generally consist of floats which rise and

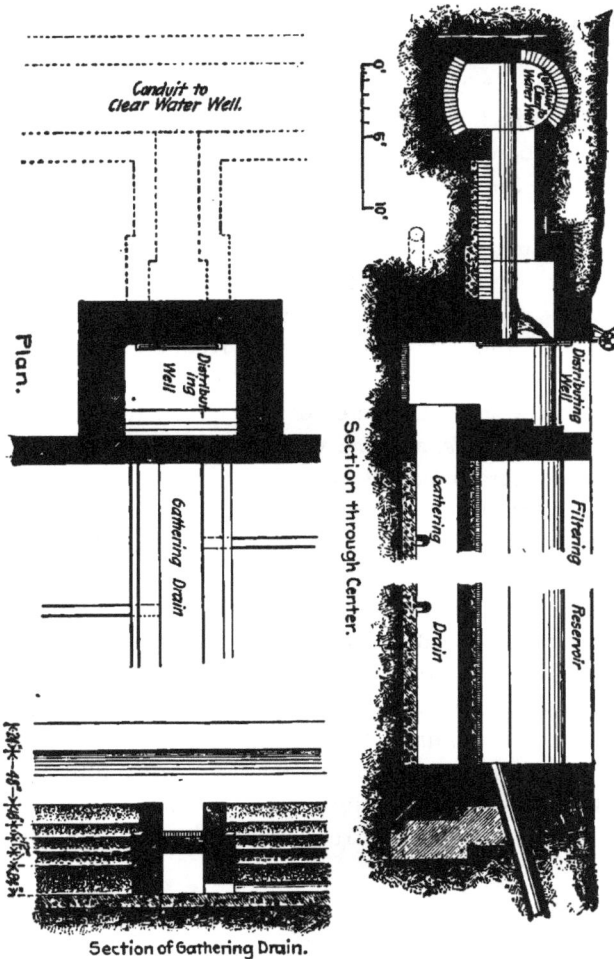

Conduit to Clear Water Well.

Plan.

Distributing Well

Gathering Drain

Section through Center.

Distributing Well

Gathering

Filtering

Drain

Reservoir

Section of Gathering Drain.

Fig. 8. St. Louis Water-Works. Details of Filters.

fall with the water in the inlet and outlet wells, actuating large balanced valves which are automatically raised and lowered to admit more or less water through the passages.

In cases where automatic regulators are lacking, sliding weirs and valves or gates, adjustable by hand, under intelligent supervision, will accomplish the same results.   In order that the effective head on the filter and rate of filtration might be conveniently regulated, Mr. Kirkwood proposed the device shown by Fig. 8, consisting of a weir which could be raised or lowered in guides by means of the winch shown at the ground level.   With this device the draught upon the clear-well, and the raising and lowering of the water-level therein, can have no effect upon the rate of delivery of the filter.

The continuous sand filter of European practice consists of a shallow reservoir with inclined or sloping sides when made with earthen walls, or with vertical sides if made of masonry.*   The surface area of these reservoirs ranges from an acre or less to as much as two acres.   The depth of the reservoir is 10 or 12 feet, according to the local character of the water, the materials available for the filter-beds, and the views of the designer.

The two general methods of construction of the basin part of plain sand filters is clearly shown by Fig. 8, which is a section of the filter proposed by Mr. Kirkwood for the city of St. Louis (1866), and by Fig. 15 (Chapter XIII.), which is a plan and section of the filters of Hamburg.   When the walls are vertical, as shown by Mr. Kirkwood's plan, these must be of masonry, backed with puddle or an impervious clay.   When made with slopes inside, the slope should be of water-tight materials, or puddled, and faced with a pavement or lining of concrete, asphalt, brick, or stone set in mortar.   Should ice form on the water in the filter, the thrust of the cake is less liable to injure the sloped sides than the vertical walls, while the cost of construction favors the basin with sloped walls.

In the bottom of this reservoir is placed a system of lateral parallel drains, which collect the water from all parts of the filter, and conduct it to one or more main central drains, by which it is removed from the filter to the clear-well, and from this it is pumped to distributing reservoirs, or direct into the distributing mains.

Over the drains in the bottom of the filter is laid a course of

---

* "Hygiene of Water," by the author, *Dietetic and Hygienic Gazette*, 1896, p. 599.

broken stone or large gravel about 12 or 15 inches thick ; over this a layer of small gravel 6 inches thick ; over this a layer of coarse sand 6 to 12 inches thick; and on top of the coarse sand is placed a layer of graded sand from 24 to 36 inches thick. This upper layer of sand is the real filtering material, the layers of sand and gravel below simply being beds for the support of this finer bed of graded sand at the top of the filter.

The capacity of a filter is stated as the average number of gallons which it will deliver per acre per day during the time it is in service. When the filter is new and the sand surface clean, the rate of delivery will be quite up to the average rate, even with a few inches difference of water level over the sand and in the effluent chamber ; but as the sand becomes clogged with the suspended matters in the water, and by the products of bacterial action upon the organic matter, the effective head of water on the sand-bed must be gradually increased, to filter the water at or near the standard rate, until in due time the limiting head is reached, and the rate of delivery of the filter diminishes until it is no longer profitable to operate it, when the water is shut off from it altogether, and the filter taken temporarily out of service.

The upper layer of graded sand is then carefully scraped for a depth of about one-half inch, the dirty sand removed and washed by mechanical apparatus devised for the purpose, and stored in the sand-house preparatory to putting it back on the filter whenever the successive scrapings have reduced the thickness of the upper sand-bed to 15 or 20 inches. The thickness of the upper layer of sand is seldom reduced to less than 15 inches, and the lower layers of sand and gravel are not disturbed or renewed at all unless some radical overhauling of a filter is shown to be necessary by the bacterial analyses of the water.

During the time of service of such a filter, it is acting continuously without interruption, day and night ; and the rate of delivery is maintained either by manual labor or automatic regulating devices as near to an established standard as possible.

The rate of delivery will depend (1) upon the grade of sand in the upper layer, (2) the effective head of water on the sand-bed, and (3) the condition of the water when it comes to the filter.

Neglecting the grade of sand and head, which are subject to control, it can generally be said that the rate of operation will depend upon the condition of the water.   Therefore, when filters are operated in connection with subsiding reservoirs, i.e., where the work of purification is a process of filtration combined with sedimentation, the larger the amount of work done in the subsiding reservoirs, the finer may be the grade of sand used, and the higher the rates of delivery of the filters per unit of sand surface.   The smaller size of sand-grain within certain limits will insure an improved quality of filtrate, and the higher rate of delivery will effect a reduced cost of treatment per million gallons of water.

Grading of Filter Materials. — In order that a filter shall give satisfactory results, both in rate of operation and quality of filtrate, it is necessary that the filtering materials, especially the bed of sand, shall be selected with regard to the size of its grains, and the relation to each other by weight of these several sizes in a bed of mixed sand.   In practice, wherever much experience has been had with sand filters, the materials are classified as boulders (or broken stone), gravel, and sand, the gravel being used frequently of two sizes, and denominated as coarse and fine gravel, and the sand of two general grades, a coarser grade above the small gravel, and the finer filtering-sand at the top of the filter-bed.

Filtering materials, as used at the experiment station of the Massachusetts State Board of Health, are examined as to "size" and "uniformity" of size of grains or particles, and graded to suit the particular work to which they are applied.   Chemical and bacterial analyses are also made of the matter attached to the sand grains, which it appears, even after repeated washings, is not entirely removed.*

The larger materials can readily be graded by hand picking; sands not less than 0.10 mm. mean diameter are separated and graded into commercial sizes by a series of sieves of brass wire, set in metal rims and shaken in a machine, for a time sufficient to secure the passage through the sieves of all but the particles larger than the mesh of the wire cloth, while particles of sand smaller than 0.10 mm. in any diameter are graded by water elutriation.

---

* *Müggel Lake Water Supply*, by Henry Gill, p. 11.

The method of separation of a mixed sand into its several sizes by means of sieves is obvious, and requires no explanation. Water elutriation of sand consists in adding to a volume of distilled water, measured in a beaker, a definite weight of clean, dry sand ; and after a thorough mixing of the sand and water by means of a strong current of air passed through a glass tube, a given time is allowed for the precipitation by gravity of the sand to the bottom of the beaker. It is well known that after the mixing of solids in a fluid, the larger and heavier particles settle first, and an experiment will demonstrate that all grains of sand of not less than a given diameter will be precipitated within a given time. By allowing more time, grains of smaller size and weight will settle out of the water ; and by allowing sufficient time, all the grains, however small they may be, will have been precipitated to the bottom of the beaker, and the distilled water above will be free from all suspended sand.

Adopting the results of sand measurement by the Massachusetts State Board of Health (with 230 cubic centimeters of water and 5 grams of sand), after a thorough mixing of the sand in the water, all grains which are precipitated to the bottom of the beaker within 15 seconds are considered as of not less than 0.08 mm. diameter. Similarly, all grains, which upon mixing and allowing one minute for subsidence are collected at the bottom of the beaker, are regarded as of not less than 0.04 mm. diameter, and all grains which remain suspended in the water at the end of one minute are regarded as of less than 0.04 mm. diameter. The weight of the smallest particles in a mixture of sand, the largest grains of which are less than 0.10 mm. diameter, is obtained by deducting from the whole mass (5 grams) the added weight of the grains larger than 0.08 mm. diameter, and the grains less than 0.08 mm. but larger than 0.04 mm. diameter. The difference is held to be the weight of the grains less in diameter than 0.04 mm. ; i.e., sizes from 0.10 mm. down to 0.08 mm., and from 0.08 mm. to 0.04 mm., are determined by water elutriation, while smaller sizes are held to be the difference between the whole weight and the sum of the weights of the two larger sizes.

In stating the dimensions used for comparison of sand-grains in a mass of sand constituting a filter-bed, two terms have been proposed by the Massachusetts State Board of Health* which are convenient for general use.

Effective Size of Sand-Grain. — This is that diameter of grain in a mass of sand of which 10 per cent of the mass by weight is smaller, and 90 per cent is larger in size. Thus, if upon physical analysis of a body of sand by sieves or any convenient method, it is found that the largest diameter for the 10 per cent by weight of the smaller grains is 0.50 mm., and 90 per cent is of diameter larger than 0.50 mm., then 0.50 mm. would be regarded as the "effective size." Or, assuming the mass of sand to be regularly graded from the finest to the coarsest particles, then the "effective size" will be that size of which 10 per cent of the whole mass by weight is smaller in diameter.

Uniformity Coefficient. — This is the ratio of the diameter of the sand-grain of which by weight 60 per cent is finer than itself, to the diameter or size of which 10 per cent is finer than itself. If by weight 60 per cent of a sample of sand is less than 0.50 mm., and 10 per cent is less than 0.25 mm., the "uniformity coefficient" is $\frac{.50}{.25} = 2$; or the diameter of grains of which 60 per cent is finer than itself, divided by the "effective size," gives the "uniformity coefficient."

The lower the "uniformity coefficient," i.e., the more regular in size are the grains of sand in any mass, the larger will be the water space or voids. With a high "uniformity coefficient," i.e., with great irregularity of size in the sand-grains, the smaller will be the water space or voids.

The influence on the bacterial efficiency of filters of the "effective size" of sand-grains, with widely different rates of filtration, is shown by the table on the following page.

The term "effective size" must not be confounded with the average size of sand-grain in a sample. The average size in a mass of mixed sand being always larger in diameter than the "effective size." The results obtained at Lawrence indicate that the finer 10 per cent of sand has as much influence on filtration as the coarser 90 per cent.

---

* *Twenty-fourth Annual Report Massachusetts State Board of Health*, p. 541.

EXPERIMENTAL FILTERS, LAWRENCE, MASS., 1895.

Type of Filter.	Rate of Filtration. Gallons per Acre per Day.	Effective Size of Sand-Grains. Millimeters.	Uniformity Coefficient.	Bacterial Efficiency.
Continuous,	1,980,000	0.14	2.2	99.49
"	3,576,000	0.23	2.3	99.73
"	6,780,000	0.29	2.7	99.37
"	4,280,000	0.38	3.5	99.51
"	4,680,000	0.48	2.4	99.45
Intermittent,	1,900,000	0.14	2.2	99.75
"	3,096,000	0.23	2.3	99.16
"	6,600,000	0.29	2.4	99.38
"	4,500,000	0.48	2.4	99.57

Sterilization of Filter Sand. — The sterilization of the sand-bed of the mechanical filter used in the Providence, R.I., tests [*] was shown by Mr. Weston to have no influence upon the bacterial efficiency of the filter; boiling of the sand in water for "one hour and fifty minutes" did not improve its capacity to restrain the passage of bacteria. Piefke, of the Berlin Water-Works,[†] previously had experimented with sterilized sand in a small filter, with the result that "more organisms were found in the filtrate than in the unfiltered water."

The same result has repeatedly been shown during the experiments of the Massachusetts State Board of Health at Lawrence.[‡] "Heating the sand and pouring the boiling water through it caused 100 times as many bacteria to pass through it with sewage for three months as passed through a similar filter whose sand and first water had not been heated."

Experience has amply demonstrated that the proper treatment of sand for use in water filters is a thorough washing, finally, with filtered water, until all detachable matter is removed from the grains, and in this condition the sand placed in the filter. The improved chemical and bacterial results of washed over sterilized sand suggests that the bacteria, which find a suitable nidus in a

---

[*] *Report on Results Obtained with Experimental Filters, Providence, R.I.,* p. 119.
[†] 1887.
[‡] H. F. Mills, *Transactions American Society Civil Engineers,* vol. xxx., p. 359.

sand-bed after the sand has been washed, are useful in the destruction of organic matter and of some species of water bacteria.

This filter is the outgrowth of two forces : (1) the abnormally high typhoid fever rates of the city of Lawrence ; and (2) the labors of the State Board of Health along the line of water purification. It consists of a single filter with a sand area of 2.50 acres ; and instead of a horizontal surface, like the European filters, the bed of sand is furrowed or channeled from side to side to provide a uniform thickness of sand through which the water from all points is compelled to percolate to the collecting drains at the bottom of the filter.

The mean elevation of the surface of the sand-bed is 2 feet below low water in the Merrimac River, and the filter is flooded for this depth from the river. The tank in which the filter is constructed consists of an excavation in the bank of the river, with a bottom elevation averaging 7 feet below low-water mark.

The general dimensions of this filter, as given in the Report of the Massachusetts State Board of Health for 1893, are as follows : —

Width of filter,	150 feet.
Length of filter,	750 "
Effective area of sand surface,	2.50 acres.
Depth of filtering-sand,	5.00 feet.
Effective size of sand,	0.25 mm.

The underdrains were placed 30 feet apart. On the line of each drain the excavation is carried down to elevation 8 feet below low-water mark in the river, for a width of 5 feet ; and the crests of the ridges midway between the underdrains are at elevation 6 feet below low-water mark, and 5 feet wide. From the crest down to the channel for the underdrains, the bottom is sloped at the rate of 5 feet horizontal to 1 foot vertical.

Over the ridges the depth of filtering-sand was made 3 feet for a width of 5 feet, and over the line of underdrains the depth of sand was made 6 feet for a width of 5 feet, the surface slope of the sand from the ridges to the crests being 10 feet horizontal to 1 foot vertical.

The section given in Fig. 9 indicates the manner in which the bottom of filter and surface of sand-bed were furrowed.

From the description in the report, it appears that each furrow or channel with its underdrain and superimposed filtering material is complete in itself, the underdrain terminating in a 10-inch pipe which passes through the masonry wall of an old filter gallery (lying parallel to the new filter). This filter gallery became, upon completion of the new intermittent filter, the clear-water reservoir from which the pumps take water. Assuming each 30 feet, then, a complete section of the filter, there are 25 such sections in the whole bed.

The underdrains consist partly of broken stone, and partly of glazed sewer pipe from 4 to 10 inches diameter, the larger pipe going through the wall of the former filter gallery. Considering an underdrain 150 feet long (width of filter), the broken stone and pipe are placed as follows: —

Broken stone,	90 feet.
Four-inch sewer pipe,	6 "
Six-inch sewer pipe,	50 "
Eight-inch sewer pipe,	4 "
Total,	150 feet.

The general slope or grade of the drain is given as 1 foot fall in 100 feet of length.

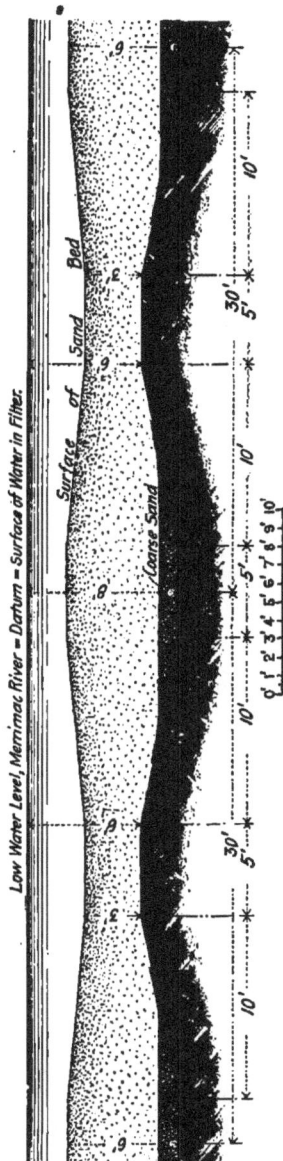

Fig. 9.
Longitudinal Section of Lawrence
(Mass.) Filter.

The water is brought from the river through a 24-inch iron pipe, which discharges into an open conduit, at one side of the filter, from which channels of concrete are extended to within 32 feet of the farther side of the sand-bed.   This conduit, together with the lateral channels, are intended to secure a uniform distribution of the water over the surface of the filter bed.

In the construction of this filter, the bottom (as is customary to prevent entrance and mixing of ground water with the filtered water) was not made water-tight, neither was the filter covered as the climate seems to require, for the reason as given by Mr. Hazen.*

"It was no easy matter to secure the consent of the city government to the expenditure of even the sum used; there was much skepticism as to the process of filtration in general, and it was said that mechanical filters could be put in for about the same cost.   Insisting upon the more complete and expensive form might have resulted either in an indefinite postponement of action, or in the adoption of an inferior and entirely inadequate process.   Still, I feel strongly that in the end the greater expense would have proved an excellent investment in securing softer water, and in the greater facility and security of operating the filter in winter."

The filter was proportioned for a daily rate of 2,000,000 gallons per acre, assuming that it would be in service for 16 hours and at rest for 8 hours, which would make the actual rate 3,000,000 gallons per acre per day while in service.   According to the report for 1895, the rate was 1,200,000 gallons per acre per day, as an average for the year.

During the year 1895, 1,096,000,000 gallons of water were passed through the filter,† and the total expense for maintenance was $7,400, or $6.75 per million gallons of water filtered.

For scraping and replacing the sand,	$3,477
For removing ice,	2,903
For washing 1,500 cubic yards of sand,	1,020
Total,	$7,400

(Laborers paid $2.00 per day.)

Omitting cost of removing ice, which would be unnecessary in milder climates, the cost per million gallons of water filtered be-

* *Filtration of Public Water Supplies*, New York, 1895, p. 98.
† *Twenty seventh Annual Report Massachusetts State Board of Health*, p. 572 *et seq.*

comes $4.10. This being a single filter on the intermittent plan, it cannot be handled so advantageously as filters in series ; and the cost of operation per million gallons should be greater than in a large plant embracing a series of continuous filters, in which one or more filters could be taken out of service from time to time and cleaned at convenience.

The filter was operated for 1895 at an average rate of $\frac{1,095}{365} =$ 3,000,000 gallons per day. With an effective area of sand surface of 2.5 acres, and assuming the filter to have been in service two-thirds of the time, the average rate of filtration per acre was 1,800,000 gallons per day. Estimating the population of Lawrence for 1895 at 50,000, the average daily consumption of water amounted to 60 gallons per capita.

The following are the average bacterial results for the year : —

Bacteria in Merrimac River water,	5,000– 20,000 colonies per c. c.
Bacteria in effluent from filter,	38– 368 colonies per c. c.
Average bacterial reduction,	98.4 per cent.

This filter is reported to have cost $65,000, or $26,000 per acre of effective filtering surface.

In speaking of the merits of plain sand filtration, Mr. J. Herbert Shedd, C.E., who has given very earnest consideration to the matter of improvement of the Providence, R.I., water supply, says : — *

" The construction of sand filters for slow filtration is not an experiment. Their use and value have been demonstrated in great numbers of cases through long periods of years. The only reasons that I know for departing from this long-established practice is in the effort to get cheaper first cost, or because the necessary area for their establishment is not available. In the case of the city of Providence there are about 70 acres of suitable land near the pumping-station, bought for this purpose more than 20 years ago and still available. Since it has been found that a mechanical filter is likely to cost $281,000, plans have been made, levels taken, test pits dug, and estimates made for a sand filter for slow filtration on that land, with all necessary settling space, supply conduits and screens, leading mains, and other appurtenances, complete for connecting the plant with our present works. My estimate of the cost of

* *Engineering Record*, July 22, 1894.

supplying all materials and doing this work is about $208,000 ; but whether my estimates have any value or not, the commissioner of public works has in his possession a bid from responsible contractors who offer to do the whole work complete for $200,000.

"The cost of annual maintenance of the slow filtration plant will be, I think, very materially less than the cost of maintaining a mechanical plant of the same daily capacity."

PLAIN SAND FILTRATION.

The Report on the Providence experiments furnishes some interesting information upon plain sand filtration with a filter of

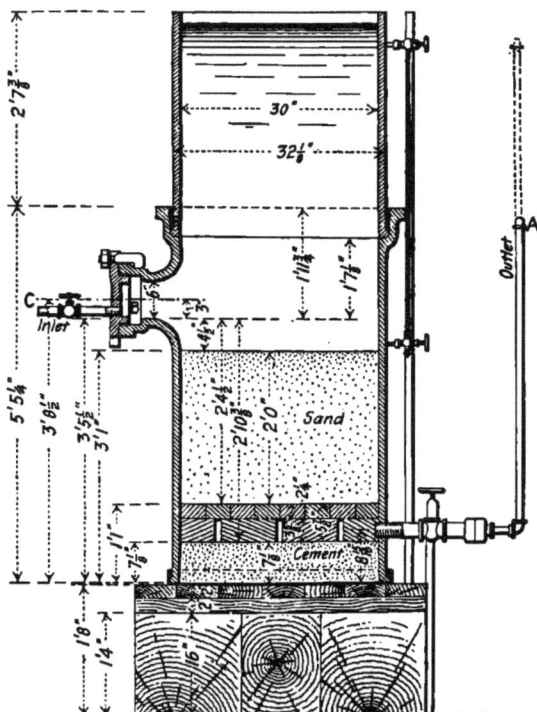

Fig. 10.   Experimental Filter, Providence, R. I.

the form shown in Fig. 10.   Two filters of this style were tested by Mr. Weston, from March 27 to Oct. 5, 1893, with occasional intermissions for cleaning filters and changing sand; and for tests of the influence of alum, on so-called natural filtration. These filters were worked at rates of 1,000,000 to 35,000,000 gallons per acre per day. (Fig. 10.)

Considering Filter No. 1, from May 15 (before which date the operation was discontinuous) to July 15 (after which date the conditions of operation were varied almost daily), the rates of filtration varied from 1,000,000 to 3,500,000 gallons per acre per day. Considering Filter No. 2, from April 15 (before which date the operation was quite irregular, doubtless due to the starting of novel experiments) to Sept. 13 (after which date the operation was discontinuous), the rates of filtration varied from 1,000,000 to 35,000,000 gallons per acre per day. In the review of the performance of Filter No. 2, the work is omitted from July 25 to July 29 (four days), when alum was used. These filters were restored to service after the sand-beds became clogged, sometimes by washing the sand with a reverse current of water, and sometimes by scraping the sand. The following table will show how this occurred by dates for the two filters: —

DATE.	FILTER No. 1.	PERIOD OF SERVICE, DAYS.	FILTER No. 2.	PERIOD OF SERVICE, DAYS.
1893.				
March 27,	Started,	. . .	Started,	. . .
April 21,	Sand renewed,	19	. . .	. . .
" 29,	Sand washed,	3	. . .	. . .
May 10,	Sand renewed,	4	. . .	. . .
" 11,	. . .	. . .	Sand repacked,	33
June 14,	Sand scraped,	26	. . .	. . .
July 14,	. . .	. . .	Sand washed,	51
" 16,*	Sand scraped,	26	. . .	. . .
" 24,	. . .	. . .	Sand washed,	8
" 27,	. . .	. . .	Sand washed,	3
August 23,*	. . .	. . .	Sand scraped,	21

When the filters were cleaned by washing, the current of water was reversed as in mechanical filters. At times the sand-beds were scraped in the usual way, taking off about one-half inch of

* After these dates the manner of operation was very irregular.

sand. The size of sand used in these filters is given in the Report as follows : —

DATE.	FILTER NO. 1.	FILTER NO. 2.
March 27,	Effective size 0.81 mm., uniformity coefficient, 2.2.	Effective size 0.81 mm., uniformity coefficient, 2.2.
April 21,	Effective size 0.18 mm., uniformity coefficient, 2.1.	
May 10,	Effective size 0.35 mm., uniformity coefficient, 2.0.	Repacked bed with same sand.
July 29,	Repacked bed with same size sand.	
Aug. 14,	Effective size 0.81 mm., uniformity coefficient, 2.2.	

Considering these filters after April 15, when they were started in service at regular and standard rates of filtration, Filter No. 1 was in operation for 63 days, of which 36 days gave bacterial efficiencies for the effluent of over 98 per cent, and 22 days gave bacterial efficiencies of over 99 per cent, with bacterial counts in the filtrate at times as low as 2, 4, 8, and 10 colonies per cubic centimeter. For the same interval of time, Filter No. 2 was operated for 69 days, of which 41 days gave bacterial efficiencies of more than 98 per cent, and 30 days gave bacterial efficiencies of more than 99 per cent, with bacterial counts in the filtrate as low as 6, 9, 10, and 12 colonies per cubic centimeter.

From July 17 to July 24, a period of seven days, Filter No. 2 was operated at an average rate of 29,043,000 gallons per acre per day, with an average bacterial efficiency of 98.5 per cent. During this period the highest bacterial efficiency was 99.9 per cent, the bacteria being reduced from 9,067 per cubic centimeter in the applied water to 10 per cubic centimeter in the filtered water, and the lowest bacterial efficiency was 92.9 per cent, when the bacteria was reduced from 565 per cubic centimeter in the applied water to 40 per cubic centimeter in the filtered water.

The average bacterial efficiency for the Morison Mechanical filter, using alum, from July 20, 1893, to Jan. 30, 1894,* is given as follows : —

* *Report on Results Obtained with Experimental Filters*, Providence, R.I., 1896, pp. 55–57.

For end growths,   97.21
For "ninety-hour growths,"   97.86

From Aug. 15 to Sept. 13 (1893), Filter No. 1 was operated with "alum and free flow" for a period of 23 days, while Filter No. 2 was operated as a plain sand filter for 22 days. During this interval of time both filters were packed with sand-grains of an "effective size" of 0.81 mm., and a "uniformity coefficient" of 2.2. The rates of filtration and bacterial efficiencies are tabled below : —

FILTER.	RATE OF FILTRATION. GALLONS PER ACRE PER DAY.	BACTERIA. PERCENTAGE REMOVED.
No. 1 (with alum),	30,100,000	82.11
No. 2 (without alum),	30,900,000	89.45

These figures indicate no advantage in the use of alum, notwithstanding the rate of filtration was less than one-fourth of the standard rate which Mr. Weston has proposed for filters of the mechanical class using alum as a coagulant. Filter No. 2 was always operated with an "effective size" of sand-grains of 0.81 mm., while Filter No. 1 was operated with sand-grains of an "effective size" of 0.81 mm., 0.18 mm., and 0.35 mm.

During the interval of time taken for comparison of filtration "with alum" and filtration "without alum," the "effective size" of sand-grains, condition of the applied water, and rates of filtration were the same. The "effective size" of sand-grains for the Morison mechanical filter was 0.59 mm., with a "uniformity coefficient" of 1.5.

The influence of sand finer in "effective size" than 0.81 mm. is shown by comparison of the operation of Filter No. 1, when it was packed with sand of an "effective size" of grain 0.35 mm., with Filter No. 2, which was packed with sand-grains of the larger size.

The average bacterial efficiencies of Filter No. 1, operating without alum, from May 25 to July 15, 1893, a period of 42 days, during which time the sand-bed was scraped once, were as follows : —

FILTER No. 1. Sand-Bed Scraped and Filter started in service May 15.

EFFECTIVE SIZE OF SAND, 0.35 MM.   UNIFORMITY COEFFICIENT, 2.0.

AVERAGES.

INTERVAL OF TIME.	RATE OF FILTRATION. GALLONS PER ACRE PER DAY.	PERCENTAGE OF BACTERIA REMOVED.
May 25–June 13,	2,300,000	98.3

During above test the numbers of bacteria per cubic centimeter in the effluent were often below 100, and at times as low as 8, 24, and 26.

Sand-Bed Scraped and Filter Started in Service June 15.

AVERAGES.

INTERVAL OF TIME.	RATE OF FILTRATION. GALLONS PER ACRE PER DAY.	PERCENTAGE OF BACTERIA REMOVED.
June 15–July 15	2,280,000	97.9

During this latter interval the numbers of bacteria per cubic centimeter in the filtrate were often less than 100, and at times as low as 2, 4, 9, 10, 11, 13, and 18.

The average bacterial efficiencies of Filter No. 2, operating without alum, from May 25 to July 13, 1893, a period of 40 days, during which time there was no scraping of the sand-bed, were as follows : —

FILTER No. 2. Sand Removed and Filter Started in service May 13.

EFFECTIVE SIZE OF SAND, 0.81 MM.   UNIFORMITY COEFFICIENT, 2.2.

AVERAGES.

INTERVAL OF TIME.	RATE OF FILTRATION. GALLONS PER ACRE PER DAY.	PERCENTAGE OF BACTERIA REMOVED.
May 25–June 13	2,316,400	98.1.

During this interval of time the bacteria in the effluent were as low as 14 to 16 per cubic centimeter.

Sand-Bed Unscraped Since Previous Use.

AVERAGES.

INTERVAL OF TIME.	RATE OF FILTRATION. GALLONS PER ACRE PER DAY.	PERCENTAGE OF BACTERIA REMOVED.
June 15–July 13	2,296,250	97.4

During this interval of time the numbers of bacteria in the effluent were as low as 9, 12, and 16 per cubic centimeter.

A comparison of these tables indicates no special advantage in the sand of smaller size of grain.

These results taken as a whole clearly show that plain sand filtration as conducted during the Providence, R.I., experiments is quite as efficient as mechanical filtration with "alum," and is not calculated to impart an astringency or acidity to the filtrate, which may be positively hurtful to some systems.

Mr. Weston's experiments with plain sand filters in the author's opinion are entitled to more consideration than they have been given in the official Report. Here are two sand filters, 30 inches diameter, operating naturally at rates 1,000,000 to 35,000,000 gallons per acre per day, with average bacterial efficiencies of 97, 98, 99, and occasionally 100 per cent (the higher results sometimes being obtained with the higher rates of filtration). The average efficiency for Filter No. 2, without alum, at rates of 25,000,000 to 35,000,000 gallons per acre per day for about the same length of time, is the same as the average bacterial efficiency of the Morison mechanical filter after the sand-bed was washed with a solution of caustic soda.

LOWELL, MASS., FILTER—BED.

The following description of this filter is taken from the *Manual of American Water-Works*, 1889–1890, p. 63. Population, 78,000.

Built in 1876, in gravel between the filter gallery and the river : 100 by 114 feet at bottom, which is 8 feet below the level of the Pawtucket dam. On the gravel is laid a dry stone drain, 15 inches square at the river end, 100 feet long, and 30 inches square at the end nearest the gallery, where it terminates in a 10-foot circular brick chamber, connected with the filter gallery by a 30-inch pipe. From the central drain 27 lateral stone drains are laid, each 8 by 12 inches. The filtering materials consist of :—

18 inches fine sand.
6   "   coarse screened sand.
10   "   coarse gravel (½-inch diameter).
36   "   ⅜-inch cobble stones.
70 inches total depth of filtering materials.

" In the spring of 1877 a freshet deposited 18 inches of sand and silt on the filter-bed ; and it was necessary to admit some water directly from the river until the deposit was removed in September, when for 83 days the filter-bed and gallery yielded the full (daily) supply to the city of 1,750,000 gallons. In 1878 the filter furnished the full daily supply of 1,879,810 gallons for 43 days. It was found that with a one-inch silt deposit the filter yielded but little water. From August, 1878, to June, 1879, the surface of the bed was not cleaned, and in this time 20 inches of silt had accumulated. After being cleaned, it supplied the gallery for only 9 days before another inch of silt entirely stopped the yield. Finding that the bed needed cleaning three times a month, that the cost would be $25 each time, and that it could only be done when the river was low and free from ice, further cleaning was given up, until 1888, when the new inlet was put in and the bed cleaned, it was practically useless, four-fifths of the water used being pumped directly from the river."

This filter consisted of a single bed with no provision for periodical resting and cleaning. From the description it would seem that the cleaning and restoring of the filter to its original condition were not thought of at the time of its construction. In fact, it was expected to work continuously, and never clog with intercepted suspended matter and the products of bacterial action. From the dimensions given, the filter had an "effective area" of 0.26 of an acre, and ran for 83 days, delivering water at the rate of 6,734,000 gallons per acre per day. At another time it was operated for 43 days at the rate of 7,230,000 gallons per acre per day, when it clogged and was taken out of service. For ten months the filter was run without cleaning, during which time 20 inches of silt accumulated on the bed.

The statement that it required cleaning three times each month is not remarkable, considering the rate of filtration, but that it cost $25 to clean one-quarter of an acre of sand filter *is* remarkable. The cost of cleaning the filters of the East London Water-Works is $25 per acre; but this is considered there a high price, and is accepted only to secure rapid work under contract, and have the filters out of service for the shortest periods of time. Why it should cost four times as much to clean the Lowell filter is not clear, unless, as it appears, there was no sedimentation of the

Merrimac River water before it was put on the bed. Assuming, however, that the filter might have been kept in successful operation at a cost of $900 per year, and the average yield of water was 1,800,000 gallons per day, or 657,000,000 gallons per year, the cost would have been less than $1.40 per million gallons; a very low price indeed.

It seems, however, that the filter was not combined with a settling-basin, could only be cleaned " when the river was low and free from ice," and no provision was made for treatment of the river water when this single filter was out of service.

Considering the time it was built, twenty years ago, and after modern filtration had been established for nearly thirty years in the London Water-Works, it is singular that so many mistakes occurred in the design of this Lowell filter.

HUDSON, N.Y., FILTERS.

The following description of these filters is taken from the *Manual of American Water-Works*, 1889–1890, p. 152.   Population, 10,000.

Filters. — Built 1874–1875. Two of them adjoining the reservoir.   One with an area of 9,071 square feet, and the other with an area of 23,017 square feet at top of filtering material.   Water is admitted to either basin through masonry wells, the walls of which are even with the top of the filtering materials.

The filtering materials from the top downward consist of : —

<pre>
 6 inches fine white sand.
18   "   coarse dark sand
 6   "   ¼-inch gravel.
 6   "   ½-inch gravel.
 6   "   1-inch broken stone.
 6   "   2-inch broken stone.
24   "   4–8-inch broken stone.
──
72 inches total depth of filtering materials.
</pre>

"The bottom of the basin has a 6-inch layer of concrete, sloping slightly towards center and outlet.   A dry masonry stone culvert leads along the bottom of basin to an effluent chamber, from which water passes to a storage reservoir, or can be drawn directly to the city. When dirty, the top layer of fine sand is removed with flat shovels to a depth of one inch, washed, and replaced. The larger filter was constructed in 1888."

The average daily consumption of water was stated as 1,483,389 gallons, which with an "effective filtering area" of 0.737 acre for the two filters, indicates an average rate of filtration of 2,013,000 gallons per acre per day. These filters have been in service since 1875.

POUGHKEEPSIE, N.Y., SETTLING—BASINS AND FILTERS.

The following description of these filters is taken from the *Manual of American Water-Works* for 1889–1890, p. 175. Population, 22,000.

Settling-Basins and Filters. — The former is 30 feet above the mean level of the lower pump-well, 25 by 60 feet, by 12 feet deep, and in three compartments. There are two filter-beds, each 73½ by 200 feet, by 12 feet deep, with 5 feet of filtering materials arranged as follows : —

> 24 inches sand.
> 6   "   ½-inch gravel.
> 6   "   2-inch broken stone.
> 24   "   4–8 inch broken stone.
> 60 inches total depth of filtering materials.

The materials rest on a concrete floor, in which are open culverts conveying the filtered water to an intermediate basin, 6 by 85 feet, by 16 feet deep. From this it passes to a reservoir, 28 by 88 feet, by 17 feet deep, and from here by 408 feet of 18-inch pipe to the pump-well.

" The filter-beds cost $54,000. The cost of removing ice, cleaning beds, and washing sand, in 1888, was $809.00 ; cost per million gallons, $1.32 ; cost of repairs was $86.00."

Taking the average daily consumption of water at 1,669,358 gallons per day, and the effective filtering area as 0.675 acre, the rate of filtration at the date mentioned was 2,473,100 gallons per acre per day. It has doubtless been much higher since 1888–1889. These filters have been in service since 1878.

FILTER GALLERIES.

These, as exemplified in the water-works of Lyons and Angers, France, are chambers in which the water is collected by infiltration from the surrounding pervious materials. As constructed, they consist of dry masonry walls and covers, placed at an elevation below low water in the adjacent river or other source of supply, and unlike filter beds, the materials through which the water percolates to these galleries cannot be conveniently cleaned or graded. Abroad it is believed that these filter galleries collect water from the river or other visible sources; but experience in this country indicates that such filter galleries, like wells sunk in the bank of a river, generally intercept water percolating through the drift. In fact, such wells sunk in the banks of the Ohio River, within the limestone formation of the channel and watershed, always furnish water quite as hard as that of wells further inland.

In some situations these galleries doubtless intercept or tap an "underflow" of streams, but such water is not precisely water filtered from these sources, but is the natural percolation of water through the drift parallel to the streams. The remarks in Chapters II. and X. upon natural filtration through the materials of the drift apply to these so-called natural filter galleries.

From Mr. Kirkwood's *Filtration of River Waters* * the following data are taken on the rate of percolation per acre of bottom area of some of these galleries :—

RATE OF PERCOLATION.

LOCATION.	U. S. GALLONS PER ACRE PER DAY.
Toulouse, France,	12,545,280
Lyons, "	6,403,320
Angers, "	13,068,000 (New gallery.)
Perth, Scotland,	7,927,920

The kind of water supplied by these galleries should be that of shallow wells sunk in the drift, and the chemical and bacterial contents may be inferred from the tests of water samples from such wells for any given locality. Aside from the fact that these

* D. Van Nostrand, N.Y., 1869.

galleries are liable to intercept surface water insufficiently filtered, and will eventually clog and fail to supply a profitable amount of water, the filtering materials are beyond the reach of daily super-vision and manipulation, and as a general proposition such sources are not to be recommended for domestic water supply.   There are localities where filter galleries will furnish an altogether acceptable water supply ; but very careful investigation of the water quality and environment of the source should be made before such water is adopted for drinking and dietetic purposes.

EUROPEAN FILTERS.

From the notes collected for the author during 1896, upon some European filters, the following data are taken with reference to the arrangement and nature of the filtering materials, and rates of filtration in U. S. gallons : –

ROTTERDAM, population, 276,338.
Water from the River Maas carried for 24 hours in settling-basins before it is put on the filters.
Area of filtering surface, 9 acres in 18 beds.
Standard area of filter, 0.50 acre.

ARRANGEMENT OF FILTERING MATERIALS.

Sand at top of bed (effective size, 0.34 mm.),*	30 inches.
Gravel (over underdrains),	12 "
Boulders,	12 "
Total depth of filtering materials,	54 inches.
Head of water on filters,	42 "
Average rate of filtration per acre per day,	1,818,200 gallons.
Average bacteria per c. c. in river water,†	6,000–10,000
Average bacteria per c. c. in filtrate,	90–99
Average bacterial reduction by filtration,	98.82 per cent.
Average present daily consumption of water, about	7,000,000 gallons.
Daily per capita consumption,	25 "

* The effective size of sand-grains in this and the following tables is given on authority of Mr. Hazen.
† Bacteriological tests made every day.

THE HAGUE, population, 187,545.
Water from wells sunk in the sand dunes.
Area of filtering surface, 3.66 acres in 6 beds.
Standard area of filter, 0.61 acre.

ARRANGEMENT OF FILTERING MATERIALS.

Fine dune sand at top of filter (effective size, 0.19 mm.),	30 inches.
Gravel,	12 "
Boulders,	12 "
Total depth of filtering materials,	54 inches.
Head of water on filters,	39 "

This water is of very excellent quality before it is put on the filter-beds.

Average rate of filtration per acre per day is 1,497,400 gallons, which is sometimes increased to 4,280,000 gallons per acre per day.

The thickness of sand-paring is about $\frac{3}{4}$ inch, the dirty sand being given to truck gardeners for use as a fertilizer.

Average present daily consumption of water, about	5,480,000 gallons.
Daily per capita consumption,	29 "

AMSTERDAM, population, 489,496.
Source of water supply: Haarlem sand dunes and River Vecht.
Area of filtering surface, 5.36 acres in 4 beds, 4.76 acres in 7 beds.

ARRANGEMENT OF FILTERING MATERIALS.

Fine dune sand at top of bed (effective size, 0.17 mm.),	30 inches.
Gravel,	12 "
Boulders (over underdrains),	12 "
Total depth of filtering materials,	54 inches.
Head of water on filters,	39 "

Two filters, each having an area of 2,860 square meters (0.706 acre), costing, it is stated, $20,000 or $14,200 per acre, have recently been built.

Rate of filtration per acre per day,	3,208,700 gallons.
Average daily consumption of water,	10,331,000 "
Daily per capita consumption,	21 "

PARIS SUBURBS, population, 600,000.

Supplied by Compagnie Générale des Eaux, from Choisy-le-Roi, Nogent-sur-Marne, and Neuilly-sur-Marne. This company uses the Anderson Revolving Iron Purifier and sand filters.

Area of filters at Choisy-le-Roi,	2.30 acres, 15 beds.
Area of filters at Neuilly-sur-Marne,	2.30 " 15 "
Area of filters at Nogent-sur-Marne,	0.75 " 4 "
Total,	5.35 acres, 34 beds.

ARRANGEMENT OF FILTERING MATERIALS.

Fine sand at top of filter,	24 inches.
Gravel,	6 "
Boulders,	6 "
Total depth of filtering materials,	36 inches.
Head of water on filters,	36 "
Rate of filtration per acre per day,	$\left\{ \begin{array}{c} 3,500,000 \\ 4,500,000 \end{array} \right\}$ gallons.

June, 1896, it was claimed that the several stations about Paris where this process was in operation were delivering 17,000,000 gallons of filtered water per diem, with a reduction of bacteria from 20,000 per cubic centimeter in the unfiltered water to 300–400 in the filtered water (by the Miquel method of cultivation), indicating an efficiency of 98.25 per cent.

With this iron process the top sand in the filters is worked from a maximum thickness of 24 inches to a minimum thickness of 12 inches. The filters are open ; and in winter, when an ice-cake of sufficient thickness is formed, the water level is lowered until the floating sheet of ice rests on the sand, when some of the matter which has accumulated at the surface of the sand and clogged the filter adheres to the under side of the ice, and upon filling the filter again from below and floating the ice, the surface of the sand is opened and the rate of filtration increased.

A statement is made in connection with the Anderson process at Paris, which, if true, is very significant ; i.e., that the filtered water may be carried in storage for as many as twenty days without an increase in the bacterial contents. It is supposed that the salts of iron have an inhibiting effect on the growth of the bacteria, algæ, etc., in the treated water.

ZURICH, population (1892) 93,000.

Source of water supply: Lake Zurich and springs.

Filtering area, 0.835 acre in 5 beds.

Three covered filters, 21,690 square feet, 7,230 square feet each.

Two open filters, 14,967 square feet, 7,483 square feet each.

ARRANGEMENT OF FILTERING MATERIALS.

Fine sand at top of bed (effective size, 0.30 mm.),	32 inches.
Coarse sand,	6 "
Small gravel,	4 "
Coarse gravel (over underdrains),	6 "
Total depth of filtering materials,	48 inches.
Head of water on filters,	39.6 "
Average rate of filtration per acre per day,	5,850,000 gallons.
Average consumption of filtered water per day,	4,884,000 "
Average consumption of spring water per day,	792,000 "
Total average consumption,	5,676,000 gallons.
Average consumption per capita per day,	61 "

LONDON.

According to Mr. Hawksley,* the total area of filters in use by the London companies (1892) was 110 acres, dealing with 119,000,000 U. S. gallons per day, from which it appears that the average rate of filtration was about 1,800,000 gallons per acre per day. The average area of the London filters is about one acre each.

* Appendices to *Minutes of Evidence*, taken by Royal Commission on Metropolitan Water Supply, 1893, p. 347.

CHAPTER XII.

MECHANICAL FILTERS.

THE mechanical filter is distinctly an American invention, and like many inventions is primarily designed to accomplish a large amount of work within a small compass and short time.

Certain physical operations have been wonderfully improved in both speed and quality by modern invention, but it cannot be said that this is true of water filtration. While the slowest rates of filtration do not invariably give the best results, at the same time certain moderate rates per unit of sand area cannot be increased without risk of impairing the quality of the filtrate. The mechanical filter is expected to operate at prodigious rates per unit of sand area, when compared with the very moderate rate of the European type of sand filter.

This can best be shown by comparison of the rates of the London filters for 1896 with the estimated best rate for the Morison mechanical filter in the Providence, R.I., tests : —

RATES OF FILTRATION PER ACRE PER DAY.

	U. S. GALLONS.
Average rate for all the London Filters, 1896,	2,120,000
Providence Experimental Mechanical Filter,	128,000,000

The sand used in the mechanical filter is of coarser grain than in the London filters, and this enormous difference of rate could not be maintained were it not for two conditions not found in the operation of the plain sand filter. (1) The frequent washings of the sand-bed, and (2) the use of alum as a coagulant to quickly form on the surface of the sand, the coagulum which takes the place, but cannot be regarded as the equivalent of the "Schmutzdecke," or natural film produced by subsidence of suspended matter and bacterial action at the surface of the plain sand filter.

The mechanical filter, so-called, is mechanical only so far as machinery operated by power is applied for the raking and agitation of the sand while being cleansed, and for the regular dosing of the applied water with the alum solution. The process of filtration, excepting as the flocculent alum precipitate may affect it, is altogether natural.

Mechanical filters may be of two types, — those which operate by a gravity head or draft on the sand-bed, and those which operate

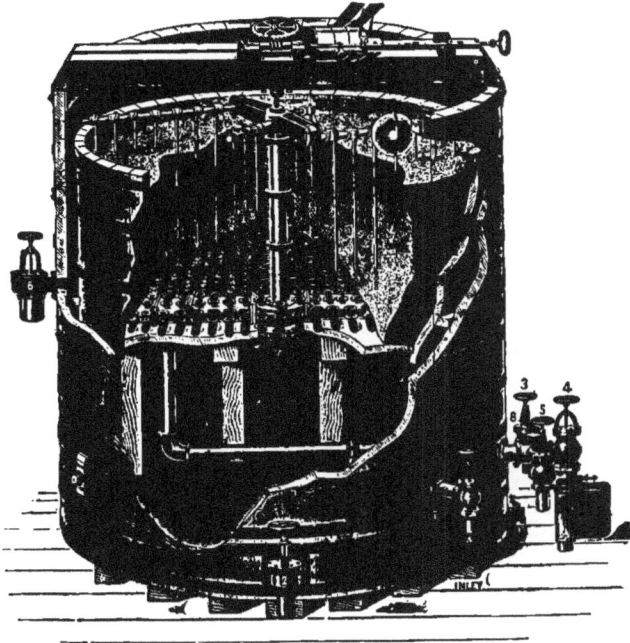

Fig. 11. Jewell Gravity Filter.

under pressure; sometimes the full pressure of the water-works system. In either case the machine consists of a tank of wood or metal, vertical or horizontal, in which the bed of sand is carried on a system of screens or strainers, and arranged with a rake or agitator, which is slowly revolved around in the tank through the bed of sand. When the sand is being stirred by the revolving rake a reverse current of water is passed through the filter-bed, to wash away such suspended matter as may have been intercepted from the applied water during the previous interval of use of the filter.

The Gravity Mechanical Filter shown in Fig. 11 is manufactured by the O. H. Jewell Filter Company of Chicago, and consists of a settling-tank and sand-bed combined in one tank, the lower part containing the settling-tank and the upper part the filter. The head is produced by a vacuum in the effluent pipes under the sand-bed. In this type of filter the revolving rakes are at rest on the sand-bed while the filter is in service, and are put in rotation after the sand-bed has been "loosened up" for washing by a reverse current of water. Provision is made for washing the sand either with filtered or unfiltered water.

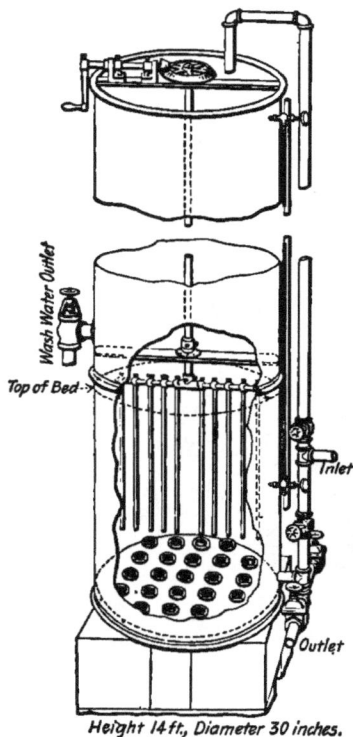

Height 14 ft., Diameter 30 inches.

Fig. 12. Morison Experimental Filter, Providence, R.I.

The most elaborate Report now available on the performance of this type of filter is that made by Mr. Edmund B. Weston, C.E., on what is termed the "Morison Experimental Filter," from which, through the kindness of Mr. J. Herbert Shedd, city engineer of Providence, R.I., the author is permitted to abstract for the purpose of this work.

The drawing, Fig. 12, is reproduced from the Report mentioned, in which the filter is described as follows by Mr. Weston: —

"Upon the screens shown at the bottom of the filter, the filtering medium or filter-bed of crushed quartz is located, the total depth being two (2) feet and ten (10) inches. The effective size of the grains of quartz which compose the upper two (2) feet is 0.59 mm., and the uniformity co-efficient 1.5.

The lower ten (10) inches of quartz is of a much coarser quality. The screens allow the water to pass through them during the different operations of working the filter. downward while filtering, and upward during the process of washing the filter-bed. They prevent the quartz or any foreign substances from entering the collecting-pipes or passing off with the filtered water.

" The manner in which the filter was operated during the experiments is as follows : At the end of a run, or immediately before starting the filter, the filter-bed was thoroughly washed by forcing up through the screens and filter-bed a reverse flow of water under pressure, the mechanical rake or agitator, shown in the cut, being operated at the same time, which added materially to the efficient cleansing of the filter-bed. The water was forced up through the bed, and the agitator kept in motion, until the water flowing from the overflow drain-pipe was as clear as it was before it was used for washing the filter-bed. The necessary valves were then operated, and the water and the sulphate of alumina turned onto the filter.

" The rates of the filtration of water mentioned in this report all represent an average rate per acre per 24 hours unless otherwise specified. The standard rate of filtration decided upon at the commencement of the experiments was 128,000,000 gallons per acre per 24 hours. When the term sulphate of alumina is used, it is intended as an abbreviation of basic sulphate of alumina.

" In making the experiments with this filter the following details were carefully investigated, as well as many other points relative to the efficient working of the filter, viz. : —

" 1. The chemicals best adapted for the purification of the Pawtuxet River water.

" 2. The best method of applying the chemicals, and the quantity to add to the applied water for each gallon of water filtered.

" 3. If any portion of the chemicals that were added to the applied water were present in the filtered water.

" 4. The rate in gallons per acre per 24 hours which could be efficiently filtered.

" 5. The bacteriological and chemical purification of the water.

" 6. The percentage which the color of the water would be reduced by filtration.

" 7. The washing of the filter-bed.

" 8. The time which would be required for washing the filter-bed.

" 9. The quantity of water which would be required to wash the filter-bed.

" 10. The quantity of water which it would be necessary to run to waste after washing the filter-bed.

" 11. The length of time which the filter would run after starting, before it would be necessary to shut down and wash the filter-bed on account of the water gradually rising to its prescribed limit in the filter, owing to the filter-bed becoming gradually clogged up.

"12. The effective stability of the quartz and supplementary precipitate bed; viz., whether it could be depended upon to do its work thoroughly during the whole of the time that the filter was in operation, or whether at times it would be liable to crack or break, or have its efficiency reduced in any manner.

"13. The loss of head due to the water flowing through the filter-beds and screens.

"During the preliminary experiments, the chemicals used were basic sulphate of alumina, chloride of alumina, carbonate of soda, bicarbonate of soda, caustic soda, and chloride of iron. The soda salts were used in connection with sulphate of alumina. It was found, however, that basic sulphate of alumina added to the applied water produced the best results. Basic sulphate of alumina, therefore, is the only chemical that has been used since the preliminary experiments.

"The theory of mechanical filtration, when basic sulphate of alumina has been added to the applied water, may be described as follows: The alumina causes an artificial precipitation. A portion of the alumina is decomposed, forming sulphates of other bases and a flocculent precipitate of aluminic hydrate. A portion of it also combines directly with the organic matter present in the water, coagulating the same, and thus helping to increase the precipitation. A sufficient quantity of the precipitate having been deposited upon the top of the sand or quartz-bed of the filter, and plugged into the interstices of the upper layer of sand or quartz-grains, the filter is ready for service.

"At the commencement of the experiments with the Morison mechanical filter, it was discovered that satisfactory results could not be obtained by simply dropping the sulphate of alumina into the applied water at the rate of $\frac{1}{2}$ grain per gallon, as it would take from one to three hours after the filter was started for a sufficient quantity of the precipitate to form in order to do good work. After experimenting in different ways, it was found that if a "free flow" of about a pint of coagulant, containing about nine hundred and eleven (911) grains of sulphate of alumina for an average rate of filtration of about 128,000,000 gallons per acre per 24 hours, was allowed to run into the filter, immediately after the water was let on, in a space of time of not more than six (6) minutes, a quantity of coagulant corresponding to one-half ($\frac{1}{2}$) grain of sulphate of alumina per gallon of filtered water being dropped in at the same time from a different receptacle than that containing the "free flow," a sufficient amount of precipitate would be formed to do good work in one-half hour or less after the water commenced to flow from the filter.

"At the commencement of a run of the filter, the applied water was at first gradually let into the filter, it being regulated at the same time. After the normal quantity commenced to flow into the filter a constant flow was maintained, and the depth of water in the filter gradually increased proportionately during the run as the supplementary precipitate bed was formed, and the filter-bed became plugged with precipitate. The rise of water practically accommodated itself to the circumstances, and caused a constant flow of water through the filter, which I considered extremely essential in order to obtain good results.

" One of the most serious problems that it was necessary to solve when the experiments were commenced, was to ascertain if the basic sulphate of alumina that was added to the applied water was entirely decomposed before the water was discharged from the filter."

A sample of the sulphate of alumina used had the following composition : —

	PER CENT.	ONE-HALF ($\frac{1}{2}$) GRAIN CONTAINS IN GRAINS.
Insoluble residue,	0.52	0.0026
Alumina (Al_2O_3),	15.78	0.0789
Sulphur Trioxide (SO_3),	36.79	0.1840
Water (by difference),	46.91	0.2345
	100.00	0.5000

After a series of experiments upon this filter, extending from April 5, 1893, to Jan. 30, 1894, Mr. Weston reached the following conclusions : —

The chemical best adapted for the purification of the Pawtuxet River water was basic sulphate of alumina, the quality used containing 15.8 to 17.5 per cent of alumina.

The best method of applying the chemicals, and the quantity required per gallon of water, have been described as $\frac{1}{2}$ grain per gallon plus "free flow" for not more than six minutes, equivalent to $\frac{6}{10}$ grain of sulphate of alumina per gallon of water for an average run of 16 hours, 43 minutes.

Upon the appearance of any portion of the chemicals added to the water in the filtrate, he says : —

" The results that I have mentioned, that were obtained by applying the logwood and acetic acid test for alum, in conjunction with filter paper, have demonstrated, I think, that none of the basic sulphate of alumina was present during the experiments in the filtered water, in its original state, after the water had been flowing from the filter twenty-one (21) minutes. The only indication of alumina found in the filtered water was a minute quantity of finely suspended hydrate, resulting from the addition of the alumina, that came through the filter-bed with the water that was being filtered. . . .

" An analysis by Professor Thomas M. Drown . . . shows that 0.0292 of a grain of alumina ($Al_2 O_3$) per gallon was found in a sample of Pawtuxet River water, that had been taken directly from the river, and afterwards filtered through a double thickness of Swedish paper, and that 0.0584 of a grain of alumina ($Al_2 O_3$) per gallon was found in a sample of the same water after sulphate of alumina had been added to it, at the rate of one-half ($\frac{1}{2}$) grain per gallon; and the very slight flocculent precipitate produced, filtered off through a double thickness of filter paper, shows an increase of alumina ($Al_2 O_3$) of 0.0292 of a grain."

The rate at which the water was "filtered successfully" ranged from 90,000,000 gallons to 193,000,000 gallons per acre per 24 hours, "the average rate of filtration being about 128,000,000" gallons per acre.

The average bacterial efficiency of the filter for two short intervals of time, selected from the ten months of experiment, viz., Oct. 17 to Nov. 11, 1893, a period of 25 days, and from Jan. 24 to Jan. 30, 1894, a period of 7 days, was a reduction of 98.6 per cent of the bacterial contents of the applied water. For various reasons Mr. Weston rejects the work of the filter for 87 per cent of the time of test, and bases the bacterial efficiency upon these two short intervals of time. Upon the subject of bacterial efficiency, Mr. Weston says : —

" I do not consider that the efficiency of a filter should be entirely based upon the average results obtained, although this is generally the standard upon which the efficiency is based, but that the worst results obtained should be duly considered. In order to present my ideas upon this subject more clearly I will assume a rather improbable case. For example, if 100 individual results were used in working up an average, 90 of these results might each show an efficiency of 100 per cent, and 10 of them might each show an efficiency of only 80 per cent, or in other words, 10 per cent of the total results would be 18 per cent below the average result, which in my opinion would be sufficient grounds to condemn a filter. Yet the average of the whole number would be 98.0 per cent, which is a very good result."

The author concurs with Mr. Weston, with the additional suggestion that the efficiency of a filter for hyglenic purposes should be measured altogether by its worst results, and not by the best or even the average results.

The filtration of a public water supply should assume that under the most unfavorable conditions of the applied water, the filtrate shall comply with a given standard of hygiene, and any estimate of the influence of such water upon the health of the people who drink it should be based upon these worst conditions. In short, the filtration of a public water supply should assume a certain uniformity in the quality of the filtrate, without regard to the manual operation of the filters, or to the condition of applied water. The filter itself should be so constructed, and the regulations under which it is operated such, that the quality of the filtrate shall satisfy some acceptable standard at all times. Phenomena and physical aberrations may be tolerated in scientific investigations, but the practical purification of a polluted public water supply should involve no phenomena and no vagaries to the prejudice of the public health.

The reduction of color by filtration, using alum with the " Morison filter," ranged from 66.3 per cent for the night observations to 77.9 per cent as an average for the day observations.

The average time required to wash the bed of sand in the filter was about 11 minutes ; and the amount of water required to wash the sand-bed, and the amount which was run to waste after the filter was washed and started in service, was about 7.8 per cent of the quantity filtered. Of this quantity 4.9 per cent was required to wash the filter-bed, and 2.9 per cent was run to waste after the filter was started again.

The average length of "run" of the filter between cleansings was 16 hours and 43 minutes, and the average loss of head for a delivery of 128,000,000 gallons per acre per diem of 24 hours was 2.44 feet. Mr. Weston estimates the cost of operating a Morison mechanical filter plant of 15,000,000 U. S. gallons daily capacity, as $5.69 per one million gallons of water filtered.

From a single experiment by Dr. T. M. Drown, in connection with the Providence filter tests, it appears that the addition of one-half ($\frac{1}{2}$) grain per gallon of the sulphate of alumina to the Pawtuxet River water, increased the alumina from 0.0292 grain per gallon to 0.0584 grain per gallon, and increased the sulphuric acid in the water from 0.3129 to 0.5214 grain per gallon.

Although Mr. Weston has made a very long and exhaustive study of the mechanical filter, with "alum" as a coagulant, in his summary he rejects the majority of his data, and draws his conclusions from : —

Two days' operation of the filter in July.
Seven days' operation of the filter in October.
Eight days' operation of the filter in November.
Two days' operation of the filter in December.
Twenty-four days' operation of the filter in January.

Or out of ten months' continuous experiment, he takes 43 days, as showing the possibilities of this method of water filtration ; of which time, six days embrace a treatment of the sand-bed hitherto untried with any type of filter. The average amount of alum used during these 43 days was about $\frac{7}{10}$ grain per gallon of water.

So far as the chemical and bacterial reductions in the applied water are concerned, it may be accepted that the mechanical filter, used with "alum" as a coagulant, will accomplish about the same results as will natural filtration ; but with the latter no injurious property can be imparted to the water, while with "alum" properties more objectionable than the pollution sought to be removed may be found in the filtrate.

The following costs of construction and operation of mechanical and plain sand filters are taken from estimates made by Mr. Weston for the city of Providence, R.I. The cost of filters is based on an available daily capacity of 15,000,000 gallons.

MECHANICAL FILTERS.

NUMBER AND KIND.	COST OF FILTERS PER MILLION GALLONS OF DAILY CAPACITY.	COST OF FILTRATION PER MILLION GALLONS OF WATER TREATED.
60 Steel Filters,	$16,344.80	$7.67
60 Cypress "	15,296.80	7.86
51 Steel "	14,160.30	7.25
51 Cypress "	13 262.30	7.41

PLAIN SAND FILTERS.

KIND OF FILTERS.	COST OF FILTERS PER MILLION GALLONS OF DAILY CAPACITY.	COST OF FILTRATION PER MILLION GALLONS OF WATER TREATED.
Filters with vaulted masonry coverings,	$35,000.00	$8.86
Filters with timber coverings,	21,906.53	8.14
Open filters,	19,414.66	6.87

In the figures for cost of operation of the mechanical filters, the cost, including alum, is taken in all cases at $4.52 per million gallons of water treated ; and the cost of operation of the plain sand filters, as deduced by Mr. Weston from the Reports of the Massachusetts State Board of Health at Lawrence, is taken at $4.39 per million gallons of water treated.

The cost per million gallons of water filtered is taken in the table as the whole cost, including interest at four per cent on cost of filters, buildings, and all appurtenances, and charges for deterioration of plant, cost of chemicals (for mechanical filters), and all labor required to operate the works.

Other uses of the mechanical filter, in several cities in New Jersey, are given in an interesting paper by Mr. M. N. Baker, C.E., contributed to the New Jersey Sanitary Association, 1895, from which the following quotations are made : —

"Without attempting to trace the various stages through which the mechanical filter has passed, it may be said that it aims to purify large volumes of water with a small body of filtering material, relying upon frequent washings to keep the material clean."

"Mechanical filters are now used on over one hundred American water supplies, against perhaps ten filter-bed plants worthy the name. Many factors have contributed to the greater use of mechanical than slow sand filters in this country. Chief of these is the commercial aspect of mechanical filtration and a former entire misconception of the principles of, and the results which may be accomplished with, filter-beds. Mechanical filters have been vigorously pushed by sales agents wherever bad water has been reported. Filter-beds stand or fall on their own merits, as they are not patented, and no one is financially interested in securing their adoption. The misconceptions regarding filter-beds have come to light with the recognition of the germ theory of disease, and improved methods and interpretation of the bacterial examinations of water. For years water contained disease and other germs, and filter-beds removed many of them without any one knowing it.

"Most of the plants built by the mechanical filter companies have been designed to remove suspended matter and color where these were so marked as to render the water almost intolerable. These ends many of the mechanical filters have accomplished most admirably. Meanwhile, most communities have remained satisfied with water that looks well, without regard to the dangerous impurities it may contain, or have secured new supplies from more favorable sources. With the modern advances in sanitary science, attention has recently been turned to the importance of removing sewage impurities from polluted waters, if the latter must be used; and of late filter-beds and mechanical filters have been constructed with this end in view.

"I believe it probable that good bacteriological results are possible with mechanical filtration. I am certain that they can be obtained with sand filter-beds, and that suspended matter, vegetable stains, and iron can be removed by means of mechanical filters.

"Filter-beds will also remove color, suspended matter, and iron, if supplemented by aëration, as well as sewage impurities."

The following data from the Somerville and Raritan Water-Works are given by Mr. Baker:—

Source of supply, Raritan River.

Population supplied (1890), 6,417.

Capacity of filter, 1,500,000 gallons per day.

Average daily filtration for 1894, about 800,000 gallons.

Cost of filters, exclusive of buildings, $15,600. Of the operation of these filters, Mr. Baker says : —

"As this plant was put in to remove matters in suspension, its efficiency should be judged by its removal of total solids. These were reduced from 26.72 to 15.98 parts per 100,000, a reduction of 10.74 parts in 26.72, or about 42 per cent. The color is reported as having been changed from dark brown to faint. The reduction of organic matter, as indicated by the albuminoid ammonia, was nearly 70 per cent."

The analyses from which these figures are taken contain measurable quantities of nitrites and nitrates for the river water, while none are given for the filtered water. Successful filtration generally indicates an increase of nitrites and nitrates. Referring to the ammonias, the albuminoid ammonia is reduced from .049 to .015, and the "free" ammonia is increased from .013 to .052 part per 100,000.

The permanent hardness of the water by addition of sulphates was increased from 3.75 parts to 6.75 parts per 100,000, while the temporary hardness (carbonates) was reduced from 3.50 parts to 0.50 part per 100,000, the gain in sulphates being exactly balanced by the loss in carbonates. Alum is used as the coagulant.

Long Branch, according to Mr. Baker, has a mechanical filter plant of 3,000,000 gallons daily capacity, treating water from Whale Pond Brook. These are pressure filters, working under a head of 40 pounds. The loss of head in passing the water through the filter is stated at five-tenths pound. Five per cent of the total water purified is required for washing the sand in the filters. The filters, including buildings, cost $31,000.

From the analyses given in Mr. Baker's paper the following data are taken : —

PARTS PER 100,000 OF WATER.	BEFORE FILTRATION.	AFTER FILTRATION.
Free ammonia,	0.132	0.0035
Albuminoid ammonia,	0.0445	0.0095
Nitrites,	0.0025	0.0015
Nitrates,	0.087	0.087
Permanent hardness,	. . .	1.00
Temporary "	2.25	1.24
Total solids,	9.52	7.14
Organic and volatile matters,	4.24	1.74
Bacteria per c. c.,	268.00	3.0

Potash alum is used in this filter.

THE JEWELL GRAVITY FILTERS AT LORAIN, OHIO.

Through the kindness of the Jewell Filter Company of Chicago, the author is enabled to include the results of its process of water purification at Lorain, Ohio, for the months of March and April, 1897. From the notes furnished, which are quite complete, the following *résumé* is drawn : —

MARCH, 1897.

Bacteria in untreated water,	3,725
" " filtered water, .	88
Percentage of reduction,	97.61
Grains of alum used per gallon of water,	1.87
Average water treated daily,	2,712,400 gallons.

APRIL, 1897.

Bacteria in untreated water,	1,835
" " filtered water,	31
Percentage of reduction,	98.29
Grains of alum used per gallon of water,	1.99
Average water treated daily,	2,774,500 gallons.

In this case the alum per gallon of water treated is about 2 grains, which, at $1\frac{6}{10}$ cent per pound, represents a cost of $4.80 per million gallons of water for the chemical alone, an amount equal to the average cost of plain sand filtration, according to the reports from works where such filters are in daily use. The actual consumption of alum per gallon of water is over three times the amount which Mr. Weston, in the report on mechanical filters for the city of Providence, regarded as necessary for proper filtration.

Adding to the cost for alum the estimate by Mr. Weston of the cost for labor, wash-water, water run to waste, etc., viz., $2.80, the total cost of mechanical filtration, based on the Lorain experience, will be $7.60 per one million gallons of water treated.

According to Mr. James H. Blessing, of the New York Filter Company, in a statement to the city of Albany, N.Y.,[*] the cost for mechanical filtration at that place, including labor, alum, etc., will be from $2.44 to $2.94 per million gallons. This estimate is very difficult to reconcile with the estimated cost at Providence, and the probable actual cost at Lorain ; in fact, Mr. Blessing makes the cost for Albany from one-half to two-thirds the cost for alum alone at Lorain, and considerably less than one-half of the total cost as figured by Mr. Weston for the proposed mechanical filter plant for Providence, R.I.

MECHANICAL FILTERS, ALBANY, N.Y.

Mr. Hazen,[†] in his report on filtration for Albany, estimates the cost of mechanical filtration as follows : —

---

[*] An Address to the Common Council, Feb. 27, 1897.
[†] *Report to Board of Water Commissioners*, Albany, Feb. 13, 1897, p. 27.

COST OF FILTRATION PER MILLION GALLONS.

LOCATION OF FILTERS.	LUMBER DISTRICT.	BLEECKER RESERVOIR.
Labor and power for operation of filters,	$1.50	$1.50
Alum, 143 lbs. at 1.6ᶜ,	2.29	2.29
Wash-water,	. . .	0.50
Total,	3.79	4.29
Mr. Blessing's estimates,	2.44	2.94

The estimated cost of mechanical filters for Albany is given as follows : —

COST OF MECHANICAL FILTERS PER MILLION GALLONS OF DAILY CAPACITY.

LOCATION.	HAZEN.	BLESSING.
Lumber district,	$12.938.24	$ 6,004.42
Bleecker Reservoir,	12,118.22	10,431.37

The cost of filtration quoted for Albany does not include (as in the report) the cost of lifting the water to the filters, which will vary in different locations, and with gravity sources may not be required at all. The cost of filters includes the *pro rata* allowance for contingencies. Mr. Hazen estimates on gravity filters for both locations. Mr. Blessing estimates on gravity filters for the lumber district, and on pressure filters for the Bleecker reservoir.

The prices for filters per million gallons of daily capacity do not include land, nor such structures as are required at Albany to make the filtered water available in service.

MECHANICAL FILTRATION FOR PHILADELPHIA.

From a proposition of the Morison-Jewell Filtration Company to the city of Philadelphia * the following data is by permission extracted : —

Daily capacity of filters,	30,000,000 gals.
Rate of filtration per acre of sand area per day,	128,000,000 "
Time allowed for subsidence of water in settling-tanks,	*One hour.*
Total cost of filters, foundations, and buildings,	$300,000.00
Cost per 1,000,000 gallons of capacity,	$10,000.00

* June 8, 1897.

The manufacturers' estimated cost for operation of these filters, with an allowance of ¾ grain of sulphate of alumina per gallon of water, is given as $3.61 per one million gallons of water filtered, which would be increased to $6.43 per million gallons if the consumption of alum should be as high as 2 grains per gallon.

MECHANICAL FILTERS, ELMIRA, N.Y.

The city of Elmira, N.Y., is supplied with water from Morison-Jewell mechanical filters, using sulphate of alumina as a coagulant. These filters have a daily capacity of 6,000,000 gallons, and are operated at the rate of 100,000,000 gallons per acre per day of 24 hours. The water passes through the settling-tanks by continuous flow at a rate which is equivalent to the detention of the raw river water in the tanks for about 30 minutes before it passes to the filters. Dr. Ravenel,[*] of the University of Pennsylvania, has made the following bacteriological analyses of the water before and after filtration.

The first of the following tables gives the bacterial results for mechanical filtration without a coagulant, while the second shows the bacterial efficiency with basic sulphate of alumina used at the rate of 1.4 grain per gallon of water : —

BACTERIAL CONTENTS OF WATER, WITHOUT COAGULANT.

DATE.	RAW WATER.	AFTER PASSING SETTLING-TANK.	FILTERED WATER.
June 10, 1897.	885 per c. c.	746 per c. c.	36 per c. c.
11 "	513 " "	556 " "	Samples lost.
12 "	625 " "	527 " "	40 per c. c.
13 "	351 " "	208 " "	132 " "
14 "	434 " "	366 " "	34 " "
15 "	425 " "	216 " "	13 " "
16 "	566 " "	407 " "	15 " "
17 "	432 " "	358 " "	21 " "

BACTERIAL CONTENTS OF WATER, USING BASIC SULPHATE OF ALUMINA 1⅖ GRAIN PER GALLON OF WATER.

DATE.	RAW WATER.	AFTER PASSING SETTLING-TANK.	FILTERED WATER.
June 10, 1897.	885 per c. c.	576 per c. c.	26 per c. c.
11 "	513 " "	413 " "	40 " "
12 "	625 " "	457 " "	12 " "

* Communicated by the Morison-Jewell Filtration Company, New York, July, 1897.

Date.	Raw Water.	After Passing Settling-Tank.	Filtered Water.
June 13, 1897.	351 per c. c.	129 per c. c.	10 per c. c.
14 "	434 " "	258 " "	0 " "
15 "	425 " "	333 " "	6 " "
16 "	566 " "	315 " "	13 " "
17 "	432 " "	117 " "	12 " "

In these tests the water was taken from the Chemung River, and carried for short intervals of time in settling-tanks. For the first test without, and for the second test with a coagulant.

The average numbers of bacteria, and bacterial efficiencies of sedimentation and filtration, without a coagulant, were as follows : —

Average bacteria in river water,	529	per c. c.
Average bacteria in subsided water,	423	" "
Average bacteria in filtered water,	26.5	" "
Reduction of bacteria by subsidence,	20	per cent.
Reduction of bacteria by subsidence and filtration,	95	" "

(In striking the average of bacteria per c. c. for the filtered water without a coagulant, the determination for June 13 is omitted ; as the figures given clearly indicate an abnormal result, the cause of which is not explained in the excerpt of the report in possession of the author.)

In the second test a coagulant was used, with the following average numbers of bacteria per c. c. of water and bacterial efficiencies, by subsidence and filtration : —

Average bacteria in river water,	529	per c. c.
Average bacteria in subsided water,	325	" "
Average bacteria in filtered water,	15	" "
Reduction of bacteria by subsidence,	38.6	per cent.
Reduction of bacteria by subsidence and filtration,	97.16	" "

The addition of sulphate of alumina to the Chemung water increased the efficiency of subsidence and filtration 2.16 per cent, but in this instance the percentage reductions are of minor importance to the low numbers of bacteria found in the filtrates.

THE USE OF ALUM FOR FILTRATION.

If the decomposition of alum in mechanical filters depends upon the amount of bases, as lime, soda, etc., in the water, then no free or unappropriated sulphuric acid can at any time be present, because all such will be found in combination with the alumina (alum), or with the lime, etc., as sulphates ; and in this case an excess of alum applied to the water would result in a hydrated sulphate of alumina, some of which may appear in the filtrate.   Alum can be dissolved in distilled water wholly free from organic matter or earthy salts ; but no decomposition of the alum will in such case occur, because of the lack of a base to appropriate or unite with the sulphuric acid.   Astringency would be imparted to the water ; and a physiological question then arises, upon the effect on the absorbent vessels of the digestive tract, of the continuous use of water containing an astringent.

So far as information from medical sources has come to the author upon this question, it indicates an objection to the continuous use of a drinking-water purified by alum ; the disorders traceable to it being impaired digestion, irritation of the mucous membrane of the stomach, and when gastric troubles already exist, a dangerous aggravation of these may follow the continuous use of water containing perceptible astringent properties.   For the bath and laundry, and for some industrial purposes, water purified by an addition of alum is well known to be objectionable.

When mechanical filters are used for the treatment with alum of polluted soft waters, as are the waters of many of the rivers of the central and western portions of the United States, lime as milk of lime is sometimes added to the water before the alum is introduced, to furnish a base for the sulphuric acid in the sulphate of alumina to unite with.   This practice, the author is informed, is in use in several water-works supplied with Jewell filters, with an improvement over the use of alum alone, in the quality of the filtrate, and a reduced cost for chemicals.   In the case of one city using Mississippi River water, it is reported that, by the addition of lime to the water, the work of the filters is more regular, and the consumption of sulphate of alumina kept within 2 grains per million gallons of water treated.

The superintendent of a Western water-works, in writing to the author, says : —

"When the river is soft, which is the case after heavy rains, we use lime-water in the pump-well, thus supplying carbonate of lime for the alumina to act upon. This has proven an economical measure, as less alumina is required when the carbonates are present in large quantities, and compared with sulphate of alumina, lime is inexpensive."

The published circular of one of the prominent manufacturers of mechanical filters contains the statement : "As a general rule, when operating filters at full capacity . . . the amount of alum . . . required varies from $\frac{1}{16}$ to 2 grains per gallon," and "within certain limits the alum required is inversely proportional to the rate of filtration." The smaller amount of alum mentioned ($\frac{1}{16}$ grain per gallon) is very much less than the amount reported to the author from any public water-works which employs mechanical filtration. Indeed, the larger amount (2 grains per gallon) seems to more nearly represent the consumption of alum in practice.

The author has been informed by manufacturers and users of mechanical filters, that one of the difficulties with the use of alum in the waters of our Western rivers is the variable quantity required for good results from day to day. That while $\frac{1}{4}$ grain or less per gallon of water would be sufficient one day, 6 grains would be necessary to obtain satisfactory results another day. This represents not only a large cost for alum, but raises a question of the reliability of a process of water purification subject to such a wide range of behavior in actual service; and this large variation in the quantity of coagulant required, it is stated, is not always accompanied by known corresponding changes in the quality of the unfiltered water.

The table on page 202 shows the influence of rate of filtration and variable quantities of alum per gallon of applied water on the bacterial efficiency of the Lorain filters.*

Before dismissing this subject, the author desires to quote a pertinent paragraph in conclusion of a report to the Philadelphia

* *Ohio Sanitary Bulletin*, Columbus, Ohio, October, 1897, p. 117.

LORAIN, OHIO, MECHANICAL FILTERS.

(From Examinations by Mr. F. S. Hollis.)

RATE OF FILTRATION. GALLONS PER ACRE PER DAY.	ALUM. GRAINS PER GALLON.	BACTERIA PER C.C. OF WATER.		PERCENTAGES.	
		LAKE WATER.	FILTRATE.	BACTERIAL REDUCTION.	BACTERIA REMAINING IN FILTRATE.
66,480,984 ·	2.58	1,441	16	98.9	1.1
68,999,040	2.50	385	6	98.4	1.6
69,626,304	2.27	367	9	97.5	2.5
80,280,792	1.07	154	14	90.9	9.1
71,508,096	0.94	189	26	86.3	13.7

Water Department, by Drs. N. Wiley Thomas and John Marshall, on the subject of "alum" filtration for the city water supply : —

"It appears practically impossible to rapidly filter the city's supply without the use of a coagulant; and while any method of filtration must of necessity be largely experimental, yet in view of the unsatisfactory results of our examination of the water obtained from the Roeske filter, and in consideration of the approximation of the Long Branch filter to the spirit of the specifications — the water after treatment being sensibly improved — (although it does not literally fulfill the conditions in the specifications stated, yet it might possibly do so at Belmont), we beg leave to suggest the erection and operation of a plant of the character proposed by the New York Filter Company at the Belmont Water-Works, under the considerations proposed, provided that every possible precaution be taken to prevent an excessive use of alum, if this substance be employed as a coagulant; and, if the sulphate of alumina be selected, that corresponding care be exercised that it shall be free from dangerous impurities, and shall be introduced only in sufficient amount to produce the necessary coagulation; and finally that limestone be made a part of the filter-bed, to insure the presence of an adequate amount of lime compounds not already converted into sulphate, to take up the products of the decomposition of the alum, as well as to facilitate the breaking up of that compound."

An examination of the *Manual of American Water-Works* for 1897 reveals the use of various kinds of filters in the water-works of one hundred and sixty-one cities and villages. About two-thirds of this number are represented by the different forms of mechanical filters, of which the largest works are collected in the table on page 203. The daily aggregate capacity of all the mechanical filters in water-works of the United States is about 190,000,000 gallons.

City.	Daily Capacity in Gallons.	City.	Daily Capacity in Gallons.
Wilkes-Barre, Pa.,	10,000,000	Cedar Rapids, Iowa,	4,000,000
Chattanooga, Tenn.,	9,000,000	Elgin, Ill.,	4,000,000
Davenport, Iowa,	7,500,000	Newport, R. I.,	4,000,000
Atlanta, Ga.,	7,000,000	Burlington, Iowa,	3,500,000
Elmira, N. Y.,	6,000,000	Biddeford and Saco, Me.,	3,000,000
Oakland, Cal.,	6,000,000	Columbia, S. C.,	3,000,000
Quincy, Ill.,	5,000,000	Decatur, Ill.,	3,000,000
Bangor, Me.,	5,000,000	Greenwich, Conn.,	3,000,000
Little Rock, Ark.,	5,000,000	Keokuk, Iowa,	3,000,000
Knoxville, Tenn.,	5,000,000	Lorain, Ohio,	3,000,000
Niagara Falls, N. Y.,	4,500,000	Long Branch, N. J.,	3,000,000
Terre Haute, Ind.,	4,500,000		

The only large city which has attempted to purify its water supply by alum and mechanical filtration is New Orleans.* Louisville, Ky., has been conducting experiments for the past two years upon mechanical filtration with alum, the results of which are not yet available by the public. The typhoid fever statistics of the smaller cities using mechanical filters have not been compiled, but the author's investigations along this line indicate a lower efficiency for rapid sand filtration with alum, than by plain slow sand filtration as employed in the purification of polluted waters abroad.

" While much is claimed for the bacterial efficiency of mechanical filters, the fact remains that the claims are not so firmly verified by scientific research as are those of slow sand filtration." †

REMOVAL OF IRON FROM GROUND WATERS.

From Mr. Baker's description of the mechanical filters used in connection with the water-works of Asbury Park, N.J.,‡ the following information has been drawn : —

The filters were introduced to reduce the amount of iron in the ground water which constitutes the supply for these works. The capacity is 2,000,000 gallons per acre per day, and each pair of filters consists of two steel tanks, 6 feet diameter and 28 feet long,

* *Nineteenth Annual Report*, New Orleans Water-Works Company, 1897, p. 5.
† *Manual of American Water-Works*, New York, 1897, p. N.
‡ Proceedings New Jersey Sanitary Association, 1895, p. 92.

of ⅛-inch plates, with double riveted longitudinal seams.   The first
tank of each pair of filters contains quartz or sand, and the second
tank contains animal charcoal.   The depth of filtering material is
about four feet.   During winter the filters are washed once every
24 hours, and during summer once every 12 hours.   No coagulant
is used.   Before reaching the filters the water is aërated by the
Pohlé air lifts which are used to raise the water from the wells to
the receiving-tanks.   The water is obtained from 7 wells, 4½-inch
casings, each 600 feet deep, and 2 wells, 6-inch casings, one 1,021
feet and the other 1,132 feet deep.   The cost of the filters, including foundations, is stated as $20,000.

From experiments by Dr. T. M. Drown the following net results
were obtained : —

The iron in solution in the water of the two deeper wells was
1.125 and 1.1378 parts per 100,000 respectively.   For the 600
feet deep wells, from several determinations, the iron amounted to
0.1791 part per 100,000.

Aëration and filtration of the water gave the following reductions in the amount of iron : —

Filtering through sand alone,					87.9 per cent.	
"	"	"	"		92.7	"
"	"	"	"		96.9	"
"	"	"	"		95.5	"
"	"	"	"		97.7	"
"	"	"	and charcoal,		95.0	"
"	"	"	"	"	98.0	"
"	"	"	"	"	98.2	"

Concerning the necessity of filtration through charcoal, Dr.
Drown says : —

"If we take the last two days only, when the pumps were working at their
maximum rate, the removal of iron by the sand filter was 98.3 per cent, and by
both filters 98.51 per cent, or only 0.21 per cent additional removal by the
charcoal filter."

The filters at Asbury Park have been in operation since January, 1895 ; they are of the pressure type, the water being pumped
under a pressure of 54.5 pounds to the consumers, with a loss of
3 to 5 pounds in passing the filters.

The reduction of iron in ground waters by aëration, and filtration through sand, has been practiced for some years in Germany.

Dr. Dunbar, the director of the Hamburg Institute of Hygiene, has made quite an extensive investigation of the various processes employed,* from which the following facts are taken : —

The earlier method, pointed out independently by Anklam and by Oesten, consists of aëration of such water in long canals, or by dropping the water in finely divided streams from an altitude of 2 meters (6.5 feet). With some waters this has given good results, with others it has failed almost entirely. Thus in one instance the oxide of iron ($Fe_2 O_3$) was 1.10 mg. per liter in the raw water, and 0 in the treated water, showing a complete reduction or removal of the iron. In another instance the reduction of the iron oxide was only from 24 mg. to 20 mg. per liter, showing a reduction or removal of only 16 to 17 per cent of the iron in the untreated water.

The Piefke method consists of the percolation of the water through a chamber filled with coke. The efficiency of this method is said to be increased as the coke becomes covered with the iron and other substances precipitated from the water. Upon a large scale this method has reduced the iron in ground water from 40 mg. per liter to merely a trace.

The Kronke method of iron reduction in water consists of the treatment of the water first by chemicals, usually a salt of iron, and then by lime. By this process all the iron can be eliminated from water. The chemicals consist of 1 gram of ferric chloride and 5 to 10 grams of lime to 100 liter of water. The apparatus required consists of a mixing-tank, a measuring-vessel, and a filter to intercept the precipitated iron. The use of this process has given reductions of the iron in the untreated water as shown in the first table on the following page.

The cost of the iron salts and lime required by this method, according to Dr. Dunbar, varies from $\frac{1}{10}$ to $\frac{1}{4}$ cent per cubic meter (264.2 gallons) of water.

The process for reduction of iron in water by flow through a

---

* " On the Nature and Treatment of Ground Waters Containing Iron, etc.," *Zeitschrift für Hygiene*, vol xxii., 1896, p. 68 *et seq.*

OXIDE OF IRON IN WATER.

Untreated Water. mg. per Liter.	Treated Water. mg. per Liter.	Percentage of Reduction.
8.00	0.10	98.75
9.20	0.00	100.00
10.00	0.00	100.00
1.95	0.10	94.87
24.00	0.15	99.37

bed of animal charcoal, in which the deferrization is due either to oxidation in the pores of the filter, or to the influence of the calcareous constituents of the filter material, shows in some instances a complete removal of the iron.   Such filters diminish in efficiency from day to day, but can be restored to their original capacity by immersion of the animal charcoal in dilute hydrochloric acid.   The influence of time on such a filter is shown in the following table : * —

REDUCTION OF OXIDE OF IRON IN WATER BY FLOW THROUGH
A BED OF ANIMAL CHARCOAL.

Days of Service.	Original Fe_2O_3 mg. per Liter.	After Flow Through Filter (Fe_2O_3). mg. per Liter.	Percentage of Reduction.
1	. .	0.25	98.96
2	. .	0.25	98.96
3	. .	0.40	98.34
4	24.0	0.55	97.71
5	24.5	0.65	97.35
6	. .	0.80	96.74
7	. .	0.75	96.94
8	. .	1.50	93.88
9	. .	2.50	89.80
10	. .	1.50	93.88
11	. .	1.40	94.29

The Massachusetts State Board of Health has very carefully investigated the subject of iron in ground waters, and the following paragraph has been taken from its Twenty-seventh Annual Report : —

* "On the Nature and Treatment of Ground Waters Containing Iron, etc.," *Zeitschrift für Hygiene,* vol. xxii., 1896, p. 135.

"Many experiments have been made at different times with a view to a removal of the iron by oxidation and subsequent filtration of the water through sand to remove the precipitated iron oxide. The results obtained by this means have been very variable. But in general it may be said, that when the iron is present in the water in small amount, say, not over 0.3 of a part per 100,000, the iron will separate out of the water almost completely on exposure to the air for 24 to 36 hours, in the form of a rusty precipitate, which can be removed entirely by filtration through sand at a rapid rate. Forced aëration by filtering through sand with a current of air was found in almost all cases to hasten the oxidation and separation of the iron oxide."

The performance of the iron reduction plant at Reading, Mass., from a series of analyses extending from July 27, 1896, to Oct. 6, 1896, indicates reductions ranging from 83.16 to 100 per cent of the amount originally in the water. In this instance the plant consists of a Warren mechanical filter, used with lime, forced aëration, and sulphate of alumina, for the precipitation and coagulation of the iron. In one instance the iron originally in the water is stated as 0.356 part per 100,000, and in the treated water as 0.020 part per 100,000, showing a reduction of 94 per cent.* Analyses by Professor Henry Carmichael, Boston, September, 1896, gave the iron oxide in the original water as 0.1070 part per 100,000, and in the filtered water as 0.0107 part per 100,000, showing a reduction by the Warren process of 90 per cent.

* "Removal of Iron from Ground Water," M. N. Baker, *Engineering News*, Nov. 26, 1896.

CHAPTER XIII.

HAMBURG SETTLING-BASINS AND FILTERS.

THE following description of the water purification works at Hamburg is based upon a very elaborate paper by Mr. Meyer, the chief engineer.* These works were under construction at the time of the cholera epidemic, September, 1892, and stimulated by this awful calamity (which was largely due to the condition of the water supply of the city), the work on the filters during the intervening months was carried on day and night by the aid of electric lights, and finished in May of the following year.

These works are the most modern in all proportions and appointments, and illustrate on a grand scale the combined effect of sedimentation and filtration on the water from the River Elbe ; a source of supply which will bear comparison with some of the sewage-polluted rivers of this country.

The water is first pumped from the Norder Elbe into four settling-basins, each 393.6 feet wide by 1,148 feet long, and 11.15 feet deep. The effective depth of these basins is stated as 6.56 feet, and the available water capacity of all as about 84,500,000 U. S. gallons. The usual time allowed for sedimentation is 19 to 30 hours, according to information furnished the author by Mr. Rud Schröder, inspector of the Hamburg Water-Works.

These settling-basins are excavated in the earth, with inside slopes three horizontal to one vertical. The bottom and slopes are puddled, and covered with a pavement of brick or tile. Of the total depth of water, 4.59 feet is below the invert of the effluent pipe, and represents the space allowed for accumulation of mud, silt, etc., in the bottom of the basin. The material precipitated by subsidence from the river water can from time to

* *Das Wasserwerk der Frein und Hansestadt Hamburg,* by F. Andreas Meyer, Hamburg, 1894.

time be flushed out of the basins through a 36-inch cast-iron waste-pipe, which is controlled by a stop valve in the embankment.

"The main conduit of masonry, from the settling-basins on Billwarder Island to the filters on the Kalte Hofe, is 9,020 feet long, 8.5 feet diameter, until it reaches the group of filters, around which it is reduced to 5.25 feet diameter for a length of 885.6 feet. From this main conduit short branch pipes 3.936 feet diameter lead to the influent chambers of each of the filters."

"The influent chamber to each filter contains two compartments. In the first is placed a double-seat (balanced) valve connected by means of a lever or walking-beam to a float in the second compartment, by means of which, when the water on the filter reaches the desired elevation, the valve is closed automatically. The water flows upon the filter through two openings in the side of the chamber, the bottoms of which are at the same elevation as the surface of the sand in the filters (see Fig. 13).

"All the filters except one are rectangular in plan, this one being shaped to the topography of the island. All the filters are open, and constructed with inside slopes, two horizontal to one vertical. Sloped embankments were used, partly because the marshy soil would not support walls of masonry, and partly because the ac-

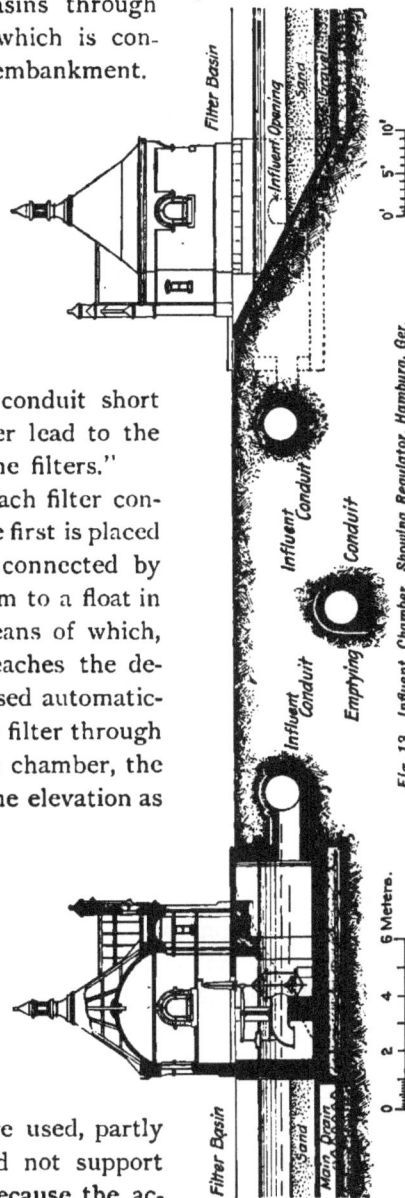

Fig. 13. Influent Chamber, Showing Regulator, Hamburg, Ger.

tion of the expanding ice on the paved slopes would not so readily injure them."

According to the Hamburg officials, open filters have an advantage over closed filters in being more easily cleaned, operated, and inspected. Exposure to the air can work no injury to the water on the filter; upon the contrary, it is held that the decomposition of organic matter is aided by contact with the air. The water in the settling-basins and filters, which becomes warmer than the river water during the summer, is again cooled in the long conduits and covered reservoir.*

"The location of Hamburg, near the German Ocean, precludes the probability of ice forming on the filters for long periods. It should be mentioned, however, that during the winter the water in the River Elbe is generally quite clear, and the intervals between scrapings of the sand are therefore considerably lengthened.

"The Hamburg filters have very large dimensions compared with other works, namely, 7,650 square meters (1.89 acre) each. The objection to large filters heretofore has been that the cleaning of them is not so easily accomplished as are those of small area. If this objection was real, there is no doubt that smaller beds would be made of those now used in the Hamburg waterworks. The experience had with these filters seems to show that the cleaning can be easily accomplished; and there is no reason why the beds should be made smaller than is necessary from an economic standpoint, in order not to have an excess of filtering area in reserve, or out of service during the time of scraping and renewal of the sand. For this reason the size of the single filters in any system of filtration should not exceed a given per cent of the total filtering area. In these works, containing eighteen filters, it does not appear that the unit area has been made too large. By reducing the areas of filters, the walls of which are sloped, a great deal of otherwise useful surface would be lost in the increased length of embankments, the number of influent and effluent chambers would be increased, and the land required for

* The author is informed that the water in the covered storage reservoirs at Rothenburgsort is usually cooler by 2 degrees Fahr. in summer than the water as it is pumped from the river to the settling-basins.

a given effective filtering area would also be increased. Finally, the cost of construction and operation of the works would be increased on the one hand, while, on the other, the convenience of operation would be diminished. It therefore seemed to be more advantageous for Hamburg to have large filter-beds ; and the experience of four years has demonstrated that neither in the operation of the filters, nor in the bacteriological results from the filtrate, can any objection be found.

"The imperviousness of the filters and embankments in the more or less sandy soil of the Kalte Hofe was obtained in the following manner : —

"Upon a layer of good marsh soil, 14 inches thick, was placed a layer of plastic clay puddle 4 inches thick. The clay was prepared either by ordinary clay-cutters, or by grinding in pug mills, such as are used in the manufacture of tile and brick. The bottom was paved with bricks laid flatwise in cement mortar, while the inner slopes were paved with a layer of bricks on edge. The upper edge of the slope paving was finished with a strip of concrete. The outer slopes of the embankments were sodded. The embankments between the filters were finished with a gravel path, in the middle of which the narrow gauge railway tracks for the sand cars were laid.

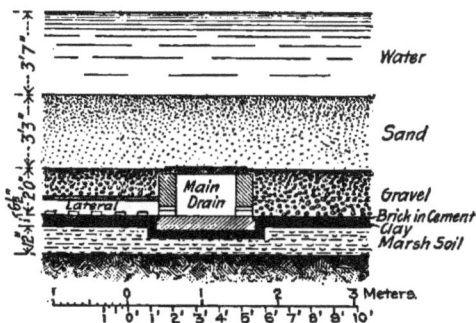

Fig. 14. Section of Main Drain and Filtering Materials, Hamburg, Ger.

"After the water has percolated through the sand and gravel to the bottom of the filters, it is received in collecting-drains, constructed as shown by Fig. 14. The main collecting-drain, which extends from the effluent chamber of the filter, is built upon a separate foundation in the filter-bed. It is 22 inches high, 32 inches wide in the clear, with brick side walls, and cover stones of granite. Into this the side drains, 7.5 inches high and 6 inches wide, are connected.

"The branch collecting-drains of brick, laid dry, are entirely surrounded by gravel. The top of the granite slabs on the main drain projects into the sand about 4 inches. The water which collects in the gravel layer either flows directly into the main collector, through openings in the brick side walls, or enters the branch collectors through similar openings, and then flows to the main collector. From the main collector the clear water enters the effluent well shown in Fig. 15.

"The arrangement of the filtering materials is shown by Fig. 14. The water stands in the filter at about 3.6 feet above the

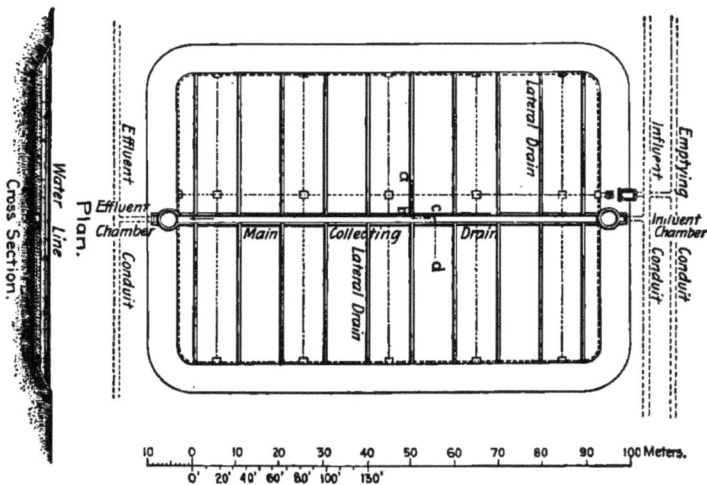

Fig. 15. Plan of Filters, Hamburg, Ger.

sand, and must penetrate a thickness of 3.28 feet (one meter) of fine sand, when the filter is first put in operation, which, upon successive parings, may be diminished to a thickness of 16 inches. The dirty sand is scraped off in successive thicknesses of three-eighths to one-half inch, and conveyed to the sand washer to be cleaned, and then takes its place again in the filter. The layer of sand rests upon a layer of gravel 24 inches thick, the sizes of which are so arranged that the upper finer material cannot penetrate the lower coarser material, and the latter cannot enter the collecting-drains.

ARRANGEMENT OF FILTERING MATERIALS.

Fine sand	{ Effective size,	0.30–0.34 mm. }	40 inches.
	{ Uniformity coefficient, 2.0 –2.3 }	
Gravel, different sizes,			24 "
Total depth of filtering materials,			64 inches.
Head of water on filter,			42 "

"To clean the filtering materials after these were brought from the various natural deposits, five sand-washing machines were erected at different points on the work.

"The gravel which was taken from the pits had to be freed from the mud and sand attached to it, and also assorted into the various sizes corresponding to the layers in the filters. This double object is accomplished by means of slightly inclined cylindrical iron drums, having numerous projections on the interior. The gravel being placed at the upper end, the drum is revolved, while numerous jets of water are played upon the material. At the lower end are placed a number of shaking sieves of various degrees of fineness, one above the other, by which the gravel is separated according to the commercial sizes, and then falls into wagons placed under the sieves.

"The sand is taken from pits and banks. Cylindrical iron drums were also used for the purpose of cleaning the sand, arranged in such a way that of the raw material, when thrown upon a shaking sieve, the finer particles were washed through this sieve, leaving the coarser material upon it. It was then introduced into the lower end of the slightly inclined, slowly revolving drum (see Fig. 29).

"By means of a number of spiral vanes upon the inside of the drum, with small intervening spaces, the mixture of sand and water was conveyed to the upper end of the drum, where it was discharged into a hopper. As the sand left the drum it was again played upon by a strong stream of water, which was directed partly into the interior of the drum, and partly on the sand which was flowing out.

"By this arrangement the sand gradually came in contact with cleaner water as it rose to the upper end of the drum, while the foul water found an exit from the lower end of the drum. The washed sand was then shoveled into dump cars and conveyed to the filters.

The small gravel obtained upon separation and grading of the sand was washed, and used as the top layer of gravel in the filters.

During a day and night turn of the washing apparatus, the filtering material prepared for use was about 2,614 cubic yards, for which were required : —

> 8 drums worked on stone and coarse gravel.
> 4 drums worked on smaller gravel.
> 26 drums worked on sand.

The total quantity required (for eighteen filters) amounted, in round numbers, to 104,640 cubic yards of gravel and stone, and 248,520 cubic yards of sand. For the cleaning of the stone, gravel and sand, filtered water was used exclusively, except for the materials which were placed in the first filter, for which, of course, filtered water was not then available.

"The regulation of the quantity of water flowing from the filters is accomplished in the following manner. The effluent well contains several compartments, through which the water must pass successively. From the main collecting-drain, the water enters the first compartment, and rises to an elevation corresponding to the elevation of the raw water on the filter. The water passes from the first into the second compartment over an adjustable weir, by means of which the quantity flowing from the filters will always be the same. The dimensions of the weir are such that the lower edge can be placed at a point 2.30 feet below the water level of the filter. When the weir is at its highest position the flow cf water is checked entirely, and the filter is taken out of service (see Fig. 16).

"One attendant can regulate the position of the weirs, and serve ten filters if necessary. To the weir is fastened a scale, and a float placed about three feet to the rear of the weir operates a pointer which indicates on the scale the difference in height of the water levels. The float is placed to the rear of the chamber to avoid the influence of the currents of water flowing over the regulating weir.

"When the difference of height is constant, i.e., when the pointer covers a certain mark on the scale corresponding to the quantity of water which the filter was intended to yield, the flow over the weir will be uniform for equal intervals of time. Thus, if the rate of percolation through the sand be 2.56 inches per hour, we can deduce the height from the formula, $Q = a.\ b.\ h.\ \sqrt{2gh}$, in which $b = 1.0$ m. : $g = 9.81$ m., the coefficient, a, being obtained from observation of the fall of the unfiltered water when the supply valve was closed. The term a was deduced as 0.503, and the quantity of water per second (Q) was observed to be 0.136 c. m., and (using 7,650 sq. m. as the useful area of a filter), we obtain $h = 0.155$ m.

"It was intended to measure the quantity of filtrate by the difference in height between the water levels of the two well chambers separated by the weir, and to register this difference in height by an automatic apparatus, but attempts in this direction have not given satisfactory results.

"From the second of the well chambers the water passes through an iron pipe into a third compartment, and from this into a branch canal 2.624 feet wide, and then to its respective branch clear-water conduit.

"In determining the size of the filter works, a velocity of filtration of 2.5 inches per hour, or 5 feet per day vertical, has been used as a basis (this is a measure of the quantity of water

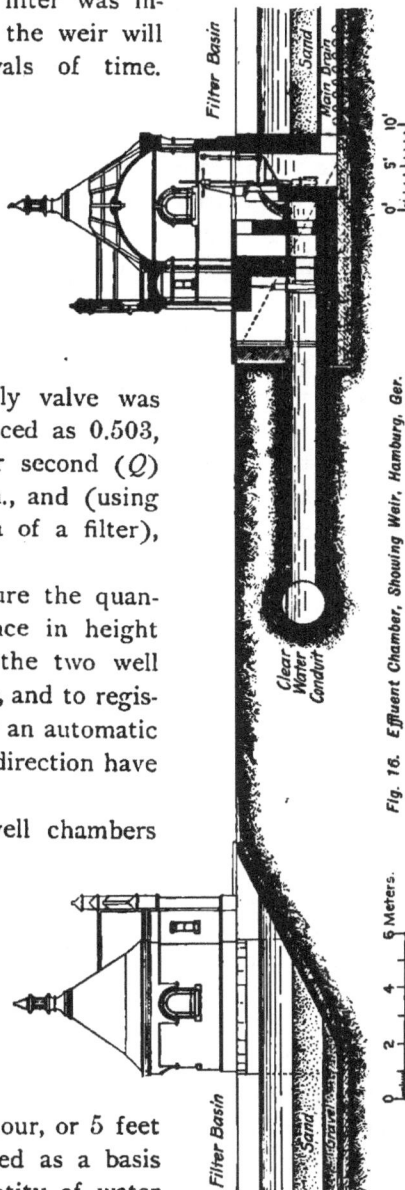

Fig. 16. Effluent Chamber, Showing Weir, Hamburg, Ger.

leaving the filter when the influent valve is closed) ; and in operation the attempt is made to not exceed this rate of percolation,
and to avoid rapid changes in the rate of filtration. But variations
in consumption (as between holidays and week-days, or between
a warmer and a colder day) can be compensated by a temporary
increase in the rate of filtration, as it will scarcely be possible to
have (at Hamburg) clear-water reservoirs of such size as will provide for large hourly variations in the demands for water.

It has not been proven by the experience with the Hamburg
filters to the present time that the filtrate is affected by such
variations in the rate.* In fact, the daily records of the operation
of the various filters indicate that, under certain circumstances,
there is no increase in the numbers of bacteria in the water when
the rate is changing.

The two following diagrams for Filters Nos. 12 and 16, which
have been compiled from the daily records of the Hamburg Hygienic Institute, indicate the influence of changes in the rate of
filtration, on the bacterial contents of the filtered water.

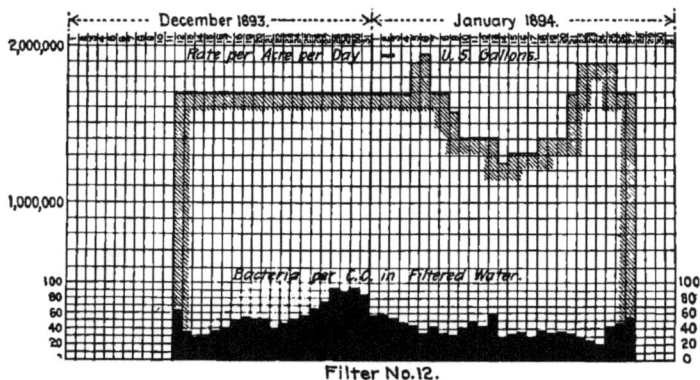

Fig. 17. Diagram Showing Operation of Filter No. 12, Hamburg, Ger.

Filter No. 12 was started in service Dec. 12, 1893, and stopped
for scraping of the sand Jan. 27, 1894, having run without interruption for 47 days. Filter No. 16 was started Dec. 6, 1893, and
stopped Jan. 25, 1894, having run without interruption for 51 days.

* April, 1897.

These two diagrams are an interesting study of the operation of plain sand filters on a large scale. Referring to that for Filter No. 12, it will be noted that the rate of filtration was 1,689,096 gallons per acre per day, for the first 24 days. On the 25th day, the rate was 1,900,224 gallons per acre, for the 26th day, 1,951,972 gallons, and on the next day it was again 1,689,096 gallons per acre; after which, to the 47th day, the rate varied from 1,329,379 gallons to 1,900,224 gallons per acre per day.

During this interval of time the bacteria per cubic centimeter ranged from 23 colonies on the 44th day, to 93 colonies on the 17th and 19th days; never reaching the limit assigned by the

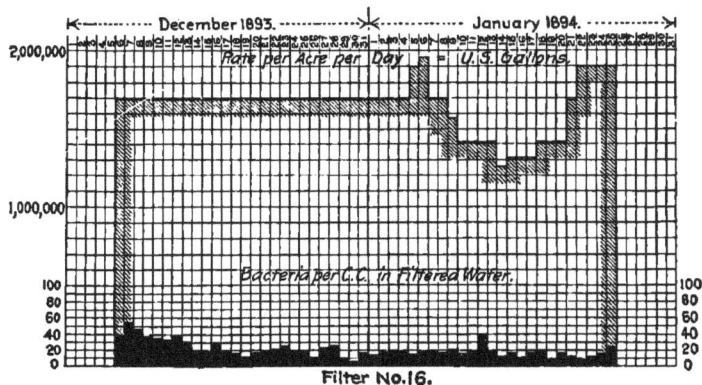

Fig. 18. Diagram Showing Operation of Filter No. 16, Hamburg, Ger.

German Imperial Institute of Hygiene (100 colonies per cubic centimeter of the filtrate), and averaging, for the whole time the filter was in service, 47 colonies per cubic centimeter of the filtered water.

Filter No. 16 was operated for a period of 30 days at the rate of 1,689,096 gallons per acre per day, then for one day at the rate of 1,900,224 gallons per acre per day, then for one day at the rate of 1,951,972 gallons, and for the next two days at the standard rate of 1,689,096 gallons per acre per day; after which, for the remainder of the period of 51 days, the rate varied from 1,329,379 gallons to 1,900,224 gallons per acre per day.

For the 51 days of service of the filter, the bacteria per cubic

centimeter of filtrate varied from 55 colonies on the 2d day of
service to 6 colonies on the 25th day, the average for the whole
time being 21 bacteria per cubic centimeter of filtrate.

The general bacterial efficiency of the Hamburg filters is
shown by the following table : —

SOURCE OF SAMPLE.	BACTERIA PER C. C. OF WATER.
Unfiltered water from the Elbe,	800–3000
From the filters,	20– 30
Average bacterial reduction, per cent,	98.64

Whenever a filter has reached a point in its periodical "run"
where it requires a head of water on the sand in excess of the
maximum allowed, viz., 42–44 inches, in order to obtain the
standard rate of delivery, it is taken out of service, the sand
scraped, and after observing the usual precautions in refilling, is
started again.

At Hamburg the drainage pipes of the filters are 20 inches
diameter, and controlled by an ordinary stop valve. All the drainage pipes discharge into a common masonry conduit or sewer about
4 feet diameter, which traverses the Kalte Hofe, and connects with
a pump well on the bank of the River Elbe.

(Mr. Meyer is silent upon the manner of discharging the
contents of this pump-well. Water drawn from the bottom of a
filter after it is taken out of service will be filtered water, and if
not changed in quality in passing through the drainage conduit,
could with safety be pumped into the clear-water conduit which
conveys the water from the filters to the clear-water basin at
Rothenburgsort. The first run of a filter after it is started in
operation is probably also discharged into this same drainage conduit or sewer, and collected finally in the same pump-well, from
which it should be pumped into the river. The double use of
this drainage conduit is open to criticism. In one aspect of the
case it indicates the waste of filtered water which might, with a
proper arrangement of pipes or conduits, be saved and used ; and
in another, the possible after pollution of water which had left
the filter in condition for domestic use.)

To refill and start a filter, water from the clear-water conduit is allowed to flow backward through sluice gates in the effluent well to the central collecting-drain, from this to the lateral brick drains, and finally upward through the gravel and sand until it stands at a depth of eight inches above the surface of the sand. Further filling is then accomplished by opening the valve in the influent chamber, after which the automatic float and valve in this chamber, in connection with the adjustable weir in the effluent chamber, regulates the head on the sand and the discharge of the filter, within the limits fixed in practice.

Each filter is connected with a clear-water conduit of brick masonry 8.5 feet diameter, 2,460 feet long, which lies parallel to the dike of the Elbe. This conduit at one point is connected with the old conduit through which the water was taken from the river for the old settling-basins prior to May, 1893. The connection was made by means of a side-shaft, and so arranged that, during the construction of the filters, each filter could be allowed to discharge its filtrate into the old conduit ; and after a sufficient number of filters were put in service to supply the whole quantity of water consumed by the city, the connection between the old intake from the river and the new filtered-water conduit was temporarily closed. During September of 1893, a leak was discovered in the temporary bulkhead, and the connection between the old and new conduits was closed with a permanent bulkhead of concrete.

From the clear-water conduit on the Kalte Hofe, the water is carried by an inverted siphon of welded steel pipe 6.56 feet diameter, across the Billwarder Bay, to a basin or clear-water reservoir on the Rothenburgsort, from which the filtered water is pumped to the city.

The clear-water basin is covered with a masonry vaulting resting on pillars, the arches of which are coated with a layer of asphalt, to exclude the water which may percolate through the earth and sand which is placed above the arches, and the whole covering is finally finished with a layer of sod. Drain tile is placed over the arches, to carry off the seep water which may find its way through the covering.

The capacity of the clear-water basin (1897) is stated to be

6,182,280 U. S. gallons, while the average daily consumption of water for 1896 is given as 31,524,080 gallons, indicating that this clear-water reservoir was filled and emptied about five times each day. The maximum daily consumption for 1896 was 38,407,811 gallons, at which time the clear-water basin contained less than four hours' average consumption. The author is informed that, during the summer, the temperature of the water falls about 2° Fahr., between the river and the clear-water reservoir, while in the winter the temperature rises between these two points about the same amount.

The average length of "run" of a filter between scrapings, at Hamburg, is about forty days. But, as the author is informed, under favorable conditions of the water from the river, during the winter of 1896–1897, one filter successfully delivered, between scrapings of the sand, a column of water 105 m. (344.5 feet) high, which is equivalent to 112,215,438 U. S. gallons per acre, or at the standard rate of percolation for these filters (1,689,096 gallons per acre per day), represents an uninterrupted service for 66 days.

The average daily per capita consumption of water by Hamburg for 1896 was 50 U. S. gallons.

THE SCHRÖDER SAND–WASHER.

The sand-washers now in use at the Hamburg Water-Works are the invention of Mr. Rud Schröder, inspector of the filters; and each set consists of seven conical boxes or hoppers of iron or steel, in the lower ends of which are fitted Korting ejectors. Filtered water under a head of thirty-six feet is supplied to the ejectors from a manifold, while the sand is fed into the first hopper by manual labor. The mixture of sand and water is carried up through a vertical pipe by the action of the ejector, and discharged into the next hopper of the series. The current of water through the ejector performs two offices; one, the transportation of the sand from hopper to hopper, and the other, the separation and washing of the dirty sand. The dirty wash-water overflows the upper edges of the hopper, and is carried off by suitable troughs. Seven hoppers of the form shown in the drawing (Figs. 19 and 20) are found sufficient to effectually wash the sand scraped from the filters, and restore it to a condition fit to go into the filters again.

From the vertical pipe in each hopper a trough conveys the mixture of sand and water to the next hopper of the series. By Fig. 22, it will be seen that these ejector washers are arranged in sets of two, each set consisting of a sand-chute, a small receiving-

Sand-Washing Plant, Hamburg, Ger.

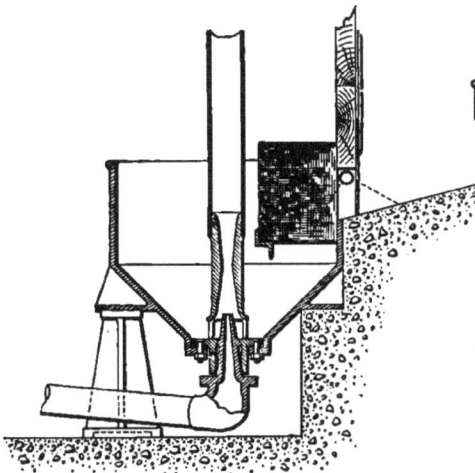

Fig. 19 (Hopper No. 1).   Fig. 20 (Hopper No. 2).

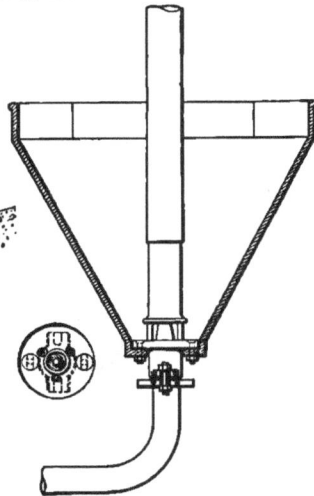

hopper at the bottom of the sand-chute, and six larger elevated hoppers. From the last hopper the washed sand is discharged onto a platform, from which it is shoveled into the tram-cars. The surplus water from the sand is conveyed away by troughs to the rear of the platform.

These hoppers are about 2 feet 6 inches square, excepting the first of the series, which is 2 feet square. The first hopper which receives the sand is about 1 foot 8 inches deep, while the remaining hoppers are about 2 feet 2 inches deep. The converging chute into which the "fouled" sand is dumped is 4 feet 2 inches

Fig. 21.
Longitudinal Section.

Plan.

Fig. 22.

Fig. 23.
Transverse Section A-B.

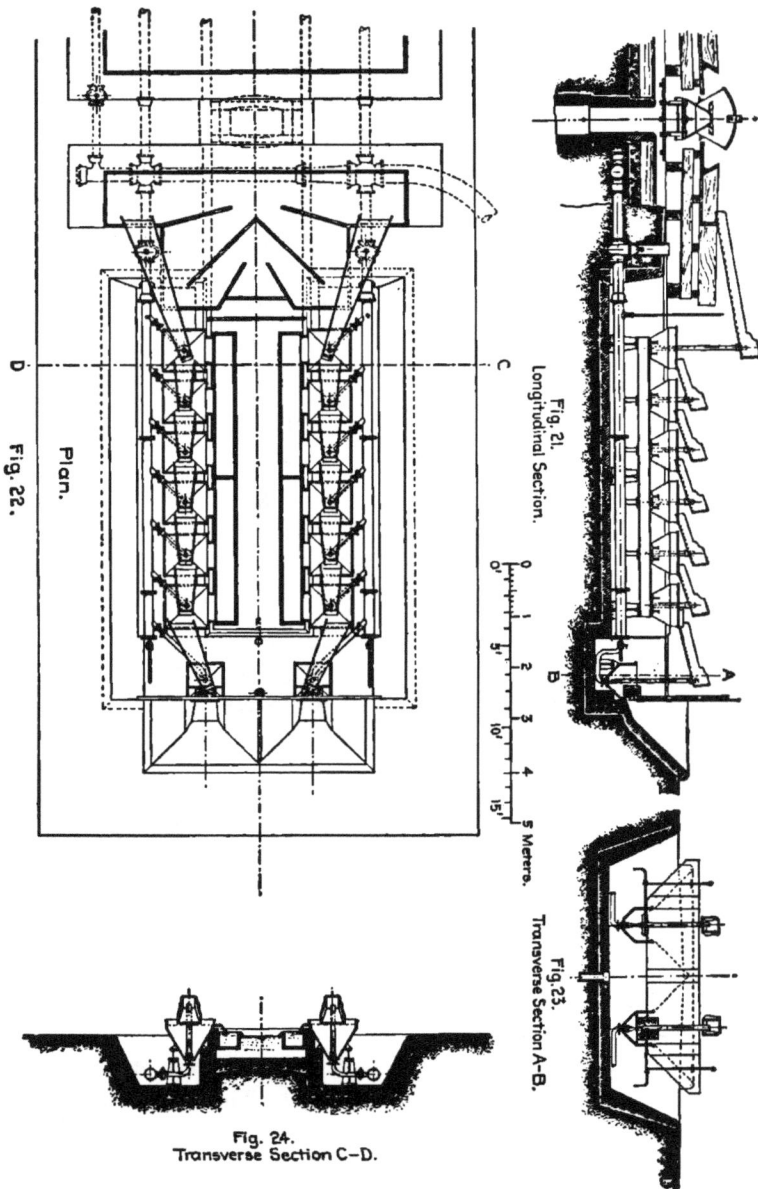

Fig. 24.
Transverse Section C-D.

Sand-Washing Plant, Hamburg, Ger.

by 6 feet 6 inches at the top, and 4 feet deep. This is provided with a gate and screen at the bottom, through which the flow of sand to the first of the washing-hoppers is regulated. The water-pipe from the manifold to the ejector is $1\frac{1}{4}$ inches diameter, and the elevator pipe above the ejector is 3 inches diameter. A chilled iron throat is screwed into the lower end of the elevator pipe to resist the grinding action of the mixture of sand and water.

From Mr. Schröder's description of this apparatus,* as used with the Hamburg filters, one complete set of washers and all appurtenances cost about $2,400. Four sets of washers are sufficient for the service of 18 filters of 1.89 acres each, or 34 acres of filtering area. The expenditure of water per cubic yard of sand washed averages 4,043 U. S. gallons, applied under a head of 36 feet. As stated before, filtered water only is used for sand-washing. This style of washer is regarded at Hamburg as being more economical in labor than the drum washers employed at Berlin and in the London Water-Works, although requiring about twice the quantity of water for washing the sand and operating the ejectors.

The capacity of one set of the Hamburg sand-washers is stated by Mr. Schröder to be 4 c. m., or 5.23 cubic yards, of sand cleaned per hour. The author is informed that these ejector sand-washers have been in constant service since 1894, cleaning annually about 25,000 c. m. (32,675 cubic yards) of "fouled" sand from the filters, and have during this time given entire satisfaction.

The following notes are from the operation of these Water-Works for 1896 : —

Total consumption of water for all purposes, 11,506,300,000 U. S. gallons.
Consumed in washing sand from filters, 91,800,000 U. S. gallons.
Percentage of filtered water required by the Schröder sand-washers, 0.80.

(In Chap. XVII. it will be noted that the English type of sand-washers, in use at Berlin, and formerly used at Hamburg, require about $\frac{4}{10}$ of one per cent of the filtered water for washing the "fouled" sand scraped from the filters.)

---

* *Zeitschrift des Vereines Deutscher Ingenieure*, vol. xxxix., Hamburg, 1894.

THE MAGER SAND—SCRAPING DEVICE.

The winters of Hamburg have been sufficiently rigorous since the filters were started in service to produce some inconvenience in the scraping of the sand-beds after the ice forms on the water, which has occurred as early as November, and continued until late in February. The following diagram, from the records of the Hamburg Water-Works, illustrates the time of formation, duration and thickness of the ice-cover over the filters, during the winter of 1896–1897.

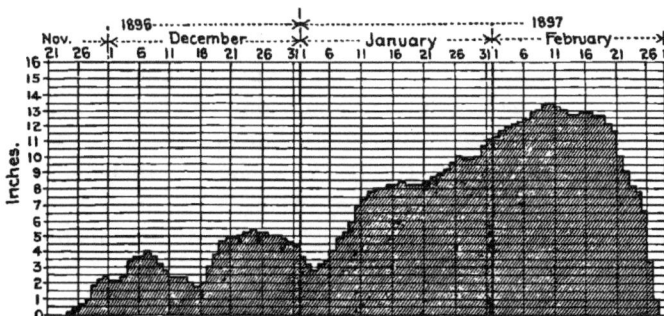

Fig. 25. Diagram Showing Ice on Filters, Winter of 1896-1897, Hamburg, Ger.

From this diagram it will be seen that the ice began to form on the filters Nov. 23, 1896, and continued until Feb. 27, 1897, attaining a thickness of about 13 inches. During this time several of the filters in service were cleaned by the Mager apparatus, to be described.

Before the invention of the Mager sand-scraping apparatus the filter-beds were cleaned by hand-dredging from the after end of a scow, which was slowly moved across the water from side to side of a filter, by means of a wire rope stretched from bank to bank, which engaged with a whim or capstan mounted on the scow. In order to conduct the work in this manner, it was necessary to first cut away or break and remove the ice from that portion of the water where the traverse of the scow and scrapers was to be made. The scrapers were mounted on long poles, and provided with bags or other receptacles for the sand scraped from the surface of the bed. As rapidly as these receptacles were loaded, the scow was stopped, the scrapers and accumulation of "fouled" sand lifted on board and dumped. The scrapers were then put in position again, and the motion of the scow resumed across the filter.

The traverse of the scow and hand-scrapers was from side to side of the filter, reversing the position of the scrapers with each traverse, and shifting the position of the wire rope a distance equal to the width of the swath or path scraped during the preceding traverse.

The hand scrapers were always worked from the after end of the scow, and upon accumulating on board a load of "fouled" sand, this was wheeled to the bank, and carried to the sand-washers.

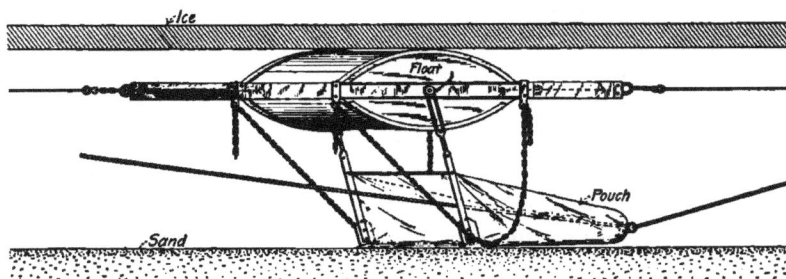

Fig. 26. *Device for Scraping Ice-Covered Sand-Filters, Hamburg, Ger.*

By successive traverses from slope to slope the whole area of the sand-bed was scraped, and the filter restored to service.

The use of this apparatus required the breaking of the ice over the whole water area, and involved an expense of labor and time which brought about the invention of the apparatus shown in Fig. 26.

The Mager device consists of a large float which impinges against the under side of the ice cake, and a metal scraper hung from the float by a pair of oscillating arms. Two chains, connected to the scraper and the float, limit the oscillation of the arms, and with reference to the float, regulate the depth of the swath cut in the surface of the sand. To the scraper is attached a bag which receives the "fouled" sand as it is cut from the surface of the bed. The float and scraper is introduced at one end of the filter under the ice, and by means of two capstans, placed one upon each of the two longer embankments of the filter, and two wire ropes attached to the float, the float and scraper is dragged from side to side of the filter without removing or breaking the ice-cover.

When the scraper has made a full traverse across the filter, by pulling upon one of the two lines connected with the sand-bag, it is turned inside out like a stocking, and the contents emptied on the inner slope of the embankment. Upon traversing the filter in the opposite direction, the scraper is reversed, and upon reaching the further slope the sand is discharged by pulling upon the other line and reversing the bag. In this manner the float and scraper is drawn from side to side of the filter until the whole bed of sand is scraped, the "fouled" sand being left upon the slopes or at the edge of the sand-bed.

As each traverse is made, the capstans on the embankments are moved along the filter a distance equal to the width of the swath cut in the sand by the previous traverse of the scraper.

This apparatus requires only the cutting away of a narrow strip of ice at each end of the filter, and at the side slopes, for the introduction and removal of the float and scraper, for the operation of the wire cables which drag the float under the ice from side to side of the filter, and for handling the lines which reverse the sand-bag and discharge its contents.

A comparison of the time required to scrape the sand-bed with the scow and hand scrapers, with the time required by the Mager float and scraper, indicates a reduced cost of labor for the latter ; and a comparison of the after periods which the filter will run, and the volumes of water delivered before a new scraping is required, indicates a gain in the efficiency of the filter ; i.e., the periods of subsequent operation are longer, and the quantities of water delivered by the filter are greater, than with the apparatus previously in use.

From tables in a paper by Mr. E. Mager, descriptive of this apparatus,* the following data are derived : —

* *Process of Cleaning the Open Filters of the Hamburg Water-Works During the Winter.* By Ed. Mager, Engineer, Hamburg, 1897, pp. 4, 6.

BY THE OLD METHOD OF SAND-SCRAPING.

Average time required to clean one filter,	4.3	days.
Least " " " " " "	3	"
Greatest " " " " " "	7	"

Generally 4 days were sufficient to scrape the sand from a bed of 1.89 acres area.

Average length of time the filters were in service after scraping,	15	"
Least time the filters were in service after scraping,	4.0	"
Greatest time the filters were in service after scraping,	29.0	"
Generally the filters were in service after scraping,	17.4	"
Average yield of (one) filter after scraping,	28,493,336	U. S. gallons.
Least yield,	7,040,402	" "
Greatest yield,	48,725,085	" "
Generally the average yield after scraping the sand was,	33,588,010	" "

Upon a second scraping of one filter by the former process, 6 days were required to remove the "fouled" sand, after which the filter was in service for only 5 days, and the yield was 7,645,155 gallons.

With the Mager apparatus for scraping the sand-bed under the ice, the average time required for the cleaning of three filters was 2.3 days each. The average period of operation of the filters was 17 days, and the yields of filtered water were as follows : —

Average yield,	38,774,256	U. S. gallons.
Least "	24,767,165	" "
Greatest "	57,910,790	" "

Upon a second cleaning, one of the filters required 5 days for scraping the sand, with an after operation of 12 days, and a yield of 19,235,873 gallons.

Generally, after cleaning the sand-bed with the Mager apparatus, the yield of filtered water is from one-third to one-half as much as when the same bed is laid dry and scraped with shovels in the usual way.

At present the average time required for the scraping of a sand-bed of 1.89 acres with the Mager apparatus is about 40 hours.

Referring to the diagram (Fig. 25), during the interval of time when the surface of the water on the filters was frozen, filters were cleaned with the Mager apparatus as follows : —

NUMBER OF FILTER.	DATE OF SCRAPING.	DURATION OF AFTER SERVICE. DAYS.	NUMBER OF FILTER.	DATE OF SCRAPING.	DURATION OF AFTER SERVICE. DAYS.
7	December 10,		16	January 1,	
7	January 11,	31	16	January 22,	21
7	January 14,		6	January 9,	
7	February 15,	32	6	February 21,	43
8	December 26,		4	January 16,	
8	January 15,	20	4	February 7,	22
8	January 19,		12	January 22,	
8	February 9,	21	12	February 24,	33

Another method which was resorted to during the past winter for scraping the sand-bed is described by Mr. Schröder. The ice was cut away from one-half the bed, and the water level lowered until the ice-cake rested on the sand. Workmen were then put upon the dry portion of the bed, and removed the "fouled" sand by hand-scraping. The filter was then filled with water, the ice-cake floated over to the opposite side, and the water again lowered until the remaining half of the filter was laid bare. This half was then scraped by hand in the same manner, after which the filter was filled and put in regular service. An operation like this of course requires that the temperature of the air shall be above the freezing-point during the interval of time when the water is off the filter.

About the first week of November, 1897, the daily newspapers of the United States contained an account of an epidemic, or unwarranted increase, of typhoid fever in Hamburg during the fall of that year. Desirous of ascertaining if this was caused by the failure of the filters to properly purify the raw Elbe water, or if the increase in typhoid was traceable to other causes, the author requested an explanation of the Hamburg officials ; and from the letter in reply the following quotations are extracted : —

"The investigations by the Medical Board have shown that the increase in typhoid fever during the fall of 1897 was due either to the use of raw milk or unfiltered Elbe water, and there was no evidence to show any connection between this rise in the typhoid rates and the filtered public water supply.

"The use of the raw water for drinking-purposes is partly due to the following facts : —

"For a time after our epidemic of cholera in 1892 (when naturally the people had a dread of the unfiltered Elbe water), no cases of typhoid occurred. With the lapse of time, this fear of the raw river water has somewhat subsided ; and notwithstanding the warning signs set up at frequent intervals along the harbor against using (for drinking or dietetic purposes) the unfiltered river water, some people associated with the river interests are reckless enough to use this water.

" Excepting such cases as were due to raw (unsterilized) milk, it may therefore be of interest to you to know that all other cases of typhoid fever have been stated by our Medical Board as being derived from the use of raw river water in the harbor, and not from the use of our filtered water, which remains up to date of excellent quality."

CHAPTER XIV.

THE FILTERS OF THE BERLIN WATER-WORKS.

THE original filters of the Berlin Water-Works at the Stralau station, built in 1855–1856, were uncovered, and as described by Mr. Kirkwood,* consisted of six beds, with an area of about 4.86 acres, or 0.81 acre to each filter. The filtering materials consisted of small boulders, gravel, and sand. No lateral drains were used to convey the filtered water to the central drain, the boulders at the bottom of the bed performing this office.

The arrangement of the filtering materials was as follows : —

Fine sand at top of bed (effective size, 0.35 mm.),	18	inches.
Coarse sand,	12	"
Coarser sand,	6	"
Gravel under the sand, and boulders at bottom of filter,	22	"
Total depth of filtering materials,	58	inches.
Depth of water on filters,	54–60	"

According to Mr. Kirkwood, ice from 15 to 20 inches in thickness had formed over the filters during "long and severe winters ;" and as a protection to the filter walls, the ice-cake was broken around the edges "by workmen appointed to that duty." This difficulty with the ice, and the impossibility at that time of properly cleaning the sand-beds in winter, led to the adoption of covered filters in the Lake Müggel Works, to be described. As originally constructed, the filters at the Stralau station were open ; but since 1893 these filters have been covered.

The new water-works of Berlin are located on the north shore of Lake Müggel,† a branch and enlargement of the River Spree,

---

* *Filtration of River Waters*, by J. P. Kirkwood, 1869, p. 112.

† *The Filtration of the Müggel Lake Water Supply, Berlin*, by Henry Gill, Institution of Civil Engineers, London, 1895, p. 14.

about 12 miles from the center of the city. Lake Müggel, so-called, is 2.90 miles long and 1.43 miles wide, with a depth over the greater part of the area of 26¼ feet.

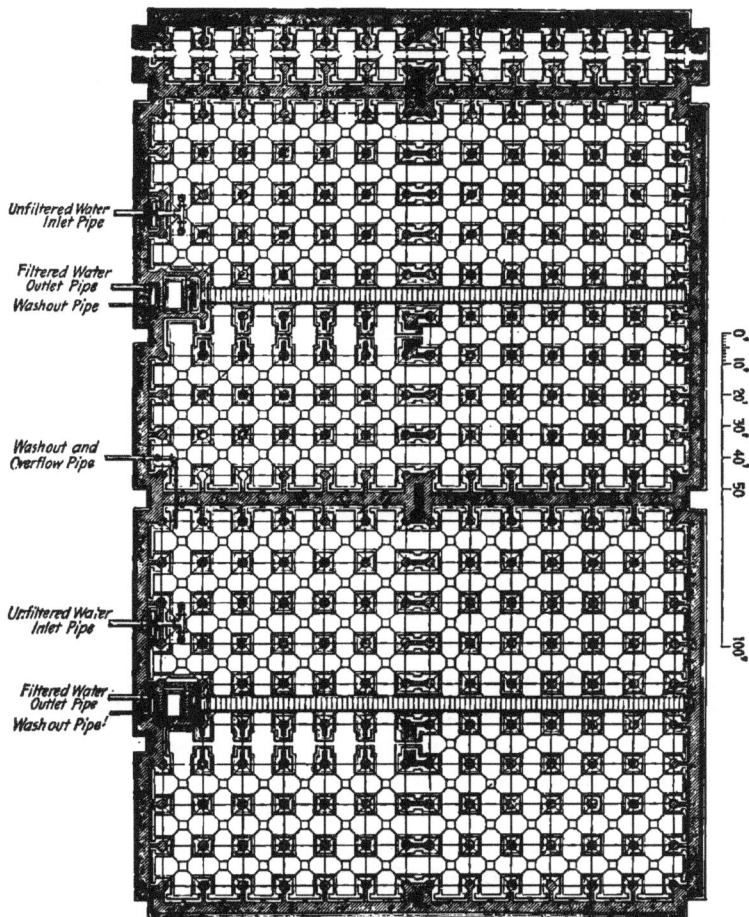

Fig. 27. Plan of Filters at Lake Müggel, Berlin, Ger.

The works are designed to supply 47,280,000 gallons of water per day, and contain 44 filters, each of an area of 0.576 acres, or a total sand surface of 25.344 acres, divided into four groups of 11 filters each. It is assumed in these works that 3 filters of each group will at all times be out of service for cleaning and renewal of the sand, or be held in reserve; hence $\frac{8}{11}$ of the total filtering capacity only will be available. The estimated rate of filtration is 2.448 gallons per square foot of sand surface per hour, or 2,559,237 gallons per acre per day. The available filter area is assumed to be 18.432 acres, and the daily capacity as 47,171,856 gallons per day.

The filtering materials are arranged as follows : —

Fine sand at top of bed (effective size, 0.35 mm.),	24 inches.
Gravel,	12 "
Boulders,	12 "
Total depth of filtering materials,	48 inches.
Head of water on filters, maximum,	31.5 "
Head of water on filters, minimum,	3.6 "

(Mr. Gill estimates the voids or water space in the compacted sand as $\frac{1}{3}$ of the whole mass.)

The rate of discharge from a filter is a nearly constant quantity; and to effect this with an increasing head on the sand-bed, the water flows from the effluent chamber to the clear-well through a submerged orifice, the head over which is maintained at a uniform height by the adjustment of a sluice gate, placed in the division wall of the effluent chamber, between the sluice chamber and the weir chamber. The adjustment of the gate from day to day serves to maintain the difference of level between the water on the filter and the water in the sluice chamber, to obtain the desired rate of percolation through the sand, and the proper head on the submerged orifice in the weir chamber. (See Fig. 28.)

By this device (the invention of Mr. Gill) any variation in the demand for water can neither increase nor diminish the rate of flow through the filters, and will only lower or raise the level of water in the clear-well.

The Müggel filters are covered with groined arches, the supporting piers of which are placed 14.37 feet center to center in each direction. At the center of each arch over four piers, an opening is placed, which admits of a thorough lighting up of the bed of sand for the purpose of cleaning.

According to the experience at Zurich, the cost of operating is lower for the closed filters than for the open filters,* while the reverse seems to be true at Berlin; for the closed filters are said to entail a cost of $10.00 † per million U. S. gallons, the highest cost for any European filtration works from which reports have been obtained by the author. Aside from the special difficulties due to the formation of ice on the open filters in climates like that of Berlin, the cost of scraping, removing, and renewing the sand should

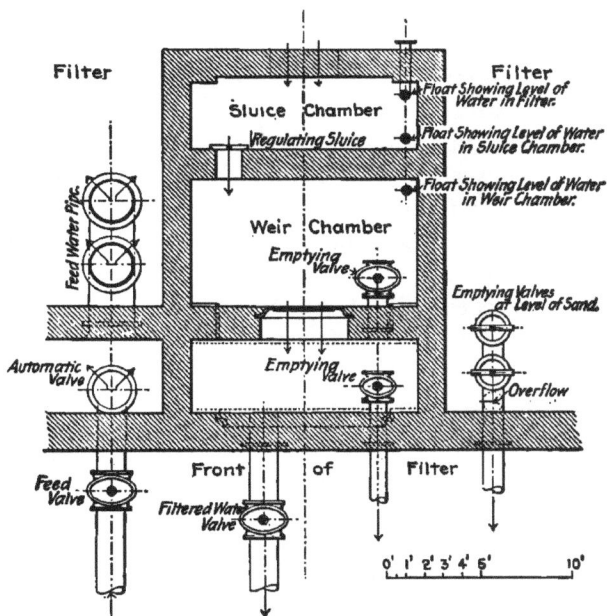

Fig. 28. Plan of Regulating Chamber.
(*Gill on the Filtration of the Müggel Lake Water-Supply.*)

be the least with open filter-beds, and why the closed filters at Zurich (after omitting the charge for breaking the ice) should cost less for operating than the open filters, requires some explanation.

At Berlin the clear-water reservoir is also covered with a masonry vaulting; and the whole work, as described by Mr. Gill, is of the most substantial kind.

---

* *Water Supply of Zurich*, Preller, p. 37.
† Said to include interest and sinking-fund charges.

The new water-works at Lake Müggel were planned to supply a population of 1,700,000 with an allowance of 27.5 U. S. gallons per capita, which would indicate an approximate present pumpage and filtration of 46,750,000 U. S. gallons of water per diem.

From an elaborate description by the late Mr. Henry Gill of the method for operation of the filters at Lake Müggel, the following *résumé* is taken.

The filter is started in service by filling from below with filtered water. The water is allowed to percolate slowly upward through the bed of sand in order to displace the air and fill all the voids between the sand-grains. In filling a filter the influent and effluent gates are closed, and the water drawn back through an independent valve and pipe from the clear-well. As soon as the water has risen 4 inches above the bed of sand, the influent gate is opened, and further filling is cautiously conducted with unfiltered water. After a head of 1.6 feet above the sand has been attained, the unfiltered water is quickly run on the filter until the full operating head is reached. Mr. Gill recommends that a filter be filled at a rate of not more than 4.7 inches per hour, to avoid disturbance of the sand.

After a filter has been filled, it should be rested with the water over the sand-bed for 24 hours, in order that the pores of the sand-bed may be partially closed by sedimentation; and in cases when this length of rest is inadmissible, and the filter must be put in service earlier to maintain the supply of filtered water, it should be brought very gradually up to its normal work.*

Sudden variations in head or pressure on the sand-bed should be avoided, to prevent injury to the film of silt and the products of bacterial action at the surface of the sand. After the normal rate of filtration has been attained, the deposit on the surface of the sand increases from day to day, and the effective head necessary to obtain the normal discharge of water from the filter will also have to be increased by adjustment of the sluice gate in the

---

* In the *Journal of the Sanitary Institute*, October, 1895, p. 387, Professor Percy Frankland says:—

"It is of importance to hasten the formation of the surface slime; and to this end the water should be run onto the filter, and left there undisturbed for twelve hours before filtration is actually commenced."

effluent chamber. With these filters, according to Mr. Gill's rules, when the difference of water level on the sand-bed and in the sluice chamber reaches 1.64 feet, the filter must be taken out of service.

Upon taking a filter out of service the influent and effluent valves are closed, and the water level lowered to the layer of gravel, or to the floor of the filter, no water being left in the bed of sand. It is desirable, each time a filter is taken out of service, to thoroughly aërate the sand-bed. The upper surface of the sand is pared with shovels, the cut in the surface not exceeding 0.4 inch. Care should be observed to avoid taking off a thicker layer of the "fouled" sand. The scraped sand is gathered in heaps in the center of each vault, and carried in barrows to the sand-house for washing and storage.

Mr. Gill thinks that a closed filter, after cleaning, should be exposed to the atmosphere for several days (excepting in winter, when the temperatures are below the freezing-point), and thoroughly ventilated before it is started again.

"Fouled" sand from a filter is washed and stored until required to renew the thickness of bed in the filter. In all cases the original thickness is reduced to 16 inches. After the last paring has been taken from the surface, the bed is filled with washed sand until the original thickness is obtained.

After sand has been scraped from a filter and taken to the washing-machine, it should be so thoroughly washed that a sample stirred in a beaker of distilled water will produce no turbidity.

The sand-washers used at Berlin (Fig. 29) are of the revolving-drum type, the kind originally in use at Hamburg, and which were discarded there for the ejector washers described in Chapter XIII.

In the operation of these washers, the rate at which the material is worked through the drum will depend upon the speed of rotation, while the quantity of water supplied to the drum is regulated by a tap or valve. By varying the speed of rotation and the flow of water, a thorough washing of the material, no matter how foul it may be, can be accomplished by the time the sand reaches the discharge end of the drum.

A circular weir at the inlet end can be raised or lowered, and thus increase or diminish the volume of water retained at all times in the drum.   It is advisable (especially in summer) to wash the

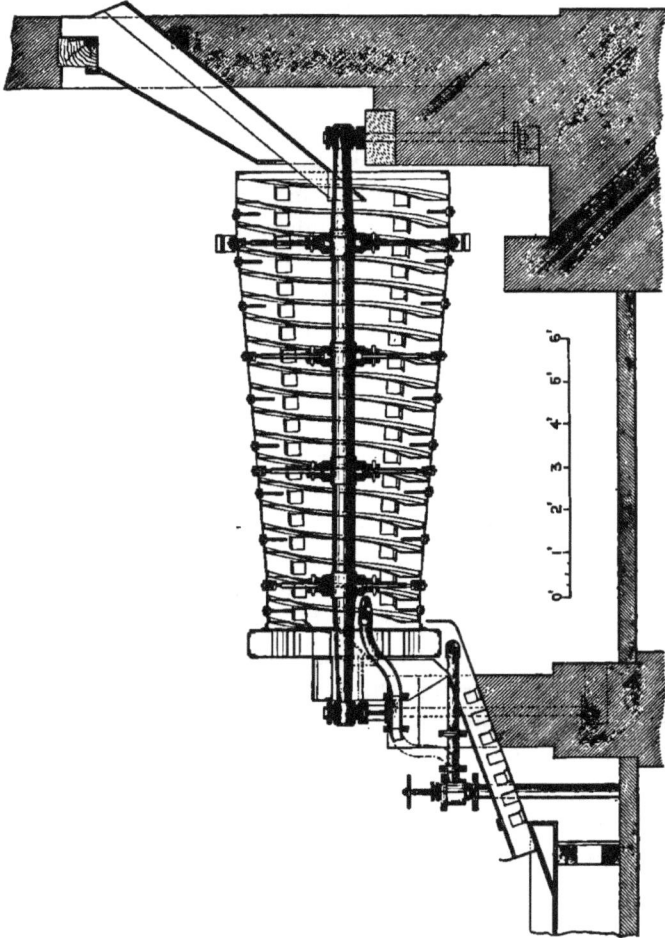

Fig. 29. Sand-Washing Machine, Berlin, Ger.

scraped sand as soon as it comes from the filters, and store it ready for future use.

The earliest recorded comparison (see Chapter XI.) of sterilized sand, and sand washed but not sterilized, was made at the Stralau station of the Berlin Water-Works, with the result that the best filtrate invariably was obtained from a bed of washed, unsterilized sand.*

The water from Lake Müggel is very variable in bacterial contents, having sometimes as many as 6,000 colonies per cubic centimeter, and at other times so few as 200 colonies per cubic centimeter. In the operation of the filters it is the aim to keep the bacterial contents of the filtrate within the German standard, i.e., 100 colonies per cubic centimeter of water; and seldom do the numbers of bacteria exceed 90 per cubic centimeter in the filtered water, while counts as low as 40 per cubic centimeter are often made. Not considering the time when the bacterial contents of the lake water is very low, the general reduction of bacteria by the filters is nearly 99 per cent.

* *Lake Müggel Water Supply,* Gill, p. 9, 10.

CHAPTER XV.

THE FISCHER FILTER AND ANDERSON PURIFIER.

THE FISCHER PLAQUE FILTER.

THIS is an invention of Mr. Fischer, Director of the water-works of Worms, Germany, where it has been in operation for four years past, and consists of hollow plates or bricks about one meter (40 inches) square and 20 cm. (8 inches) thick, with 5 cm. (2 inches) of space in the middle of the plate, which gives an effective thickness of filtering-plate of 3 inches. These plates, or plaques, are made of a mixture of clean sharp sand and finely pulverized glass, obtained from the waste of glass-works, broken bottles, etc. This mixture, when fused, may be given any form desired, and upon cooling forms a porous mass through which water may be filtered under pressures depending primarily upon the density of the material. The head under which this form of filter works at Worms is given in the Consular Report* as 3 to 4 feet.

From a drawing which accompanies the Report, it appears that the hollow brick, or plaque as it is called, is made up of two solid plates, 40 inches square and 3 inches thick, bolted together on a frame of metal (?), with which the plates make water-tight joints, and leaving a water space or cell between the plates 2 inches in width. These hollow plates or bricks are set on edge in two tiers, as shown by the drawing, in a suitable water-tight tank or reservoir, with a water space of 3 or 4 inches between adjacent pairs of plates. The reservoir is then filled with water until a head is obtained sufficient to secure the desired rate of filtration through the plates.

The water passes through the 3-inch thickness of plate from the tank to the cell inside, from which, by suitable pipes, it is

* Advance Sheets of U. S. Consular Reports, February, 1897.

drawn off to the clear-water reservoir. The suspended matter in the water is intercepted at or near the outer surface of the plates ; and when the pores become so plugged as to reduce the capacity of the filter to a rate of delivery at which it becomes unprofitable to operate it, the water is drawn from the tank, and by reversing the current the filtered water is caused to pass from the central cells outward through the pores of the plates, and the accumulated suspended matter intercepted at the surface is washed away, and flushed from the plates and the tank by a hand hose.

The principle of filtration is the same as that employed in the Berkefeld and Pasteur type of fil-

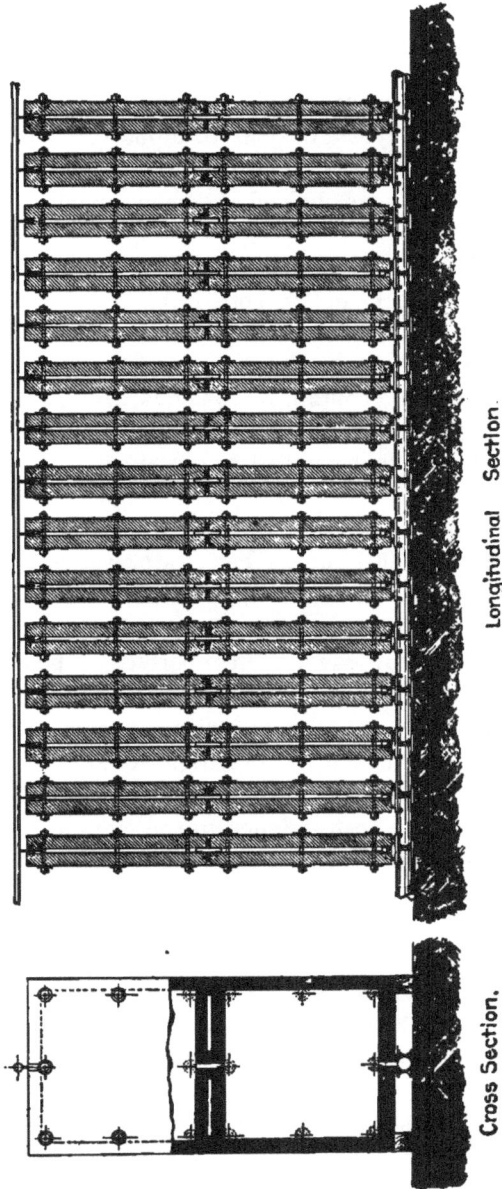

Fig. 30. Fischer Method of Filtration, Worms, Ger.

Longitudinal Section.

Cross Section.

ters, and the method of reversing the current to wash the filter the same as is employed in the mechanical filter.

The original sand filter at Worms contained 13,000 square feet of filtering surface, and filtered at the rate of 792,510 U. S. gallons per day, equivalent to 2,655,700 gallons per acre per day; while a battery of 500 of these Fischer plates or hollow bricks is said to have yielded the same amount of filtered water as the sand filter.

Estimating the effective area of one face of a plaque at one square meter, and of both faces at two square meters, or 21.528 square feet, then 500 such plaques (of which 30 are shown in Fig. 30, each pair of plates being bolted together making a hollow brick) would contain 10,764 square feet, and the rate of percolation through the 3 inches of porous material would be 73.6 gallons per square foot per day, equivalent to a vertical rate of 9.8 feet per day.

(It is stated in the Report that the estimated cost of a sand filter of 13,000 square feet of area was $30,000, which would make the cost per acre more than $100,000. This figure seems to be in error; for nothing approaching it in cost has heretofore, within the author's knowledge, been reported. Open filters in series, including clear-well and accessories upon an elaborate plan, can be constructed in this country within a cost of $40,000 per acre, and estimating concrete coverings at $11,000 per acre, the cost of covered filters may be as low as $51,000 per acre, which is about one-half the cost assigned in the Report for the sand filters in use at Worms prior to the introduction of the Fischer filter.)

The Fischer filter cost $9,600, or about $12,000 for 1,000,000 gallons of daily capacity.

The Report states, " From a long series of analyses and careful observations made by the sanitary authorities at Worms, it appears that the efficiency of the two systems of filtration, which are there worked side by side, are practically identical, so far as regards their effect upon the chemical purity of the water; but the percentage of bacteria left by the Fischer process is somewhat greater than is left by the sand filter, when clean and in good working condition."

The porosity of these Fischer plaques is doubtless greater than the porcelain tubes of the Pasteur-Chamberland filter, through which bacteria are known to grow within a few days after sterilization ; and since sterilization of these sand and glass plaques is not practicable, — only washing with a reversed current of filtered water, — there is danger of the same deterioration of quality of filtrate which has often been observed by the continuous use (unsterilized) of the Pasteur tubes.

THE ANDERSON REVOLVING IRON PURIFIER.

The following description of this device and its mode of operation is taken from a recent publication by the Anderson Purifier Company entitled *Water Purification :* —

"This process consists in passing the water while on its way to the settling-beds through a wrought-iron cylinder (Fig. 30 *a*), supported horizontally on hollow trunnions forming the inlet and outlet to the cylinder. This is kept in continual slow rotation, and contains a charge of metallic iron in small pieces. The iron is continually lifted and showered down through the water by means of scoops fixed within the cylinder. The speed of rotation of the machine is about 6 feet per minute at the periphery. The water is passed through at the rate of from a third to a fifth of the capacity of the cylinders per minute, thus keeping the water in contact with the iron for from three to five minutes, according to the quality of the water. The cylinders are made in various sizes; for example, a machine 18 feet long and 5 feet in diameter is capable of treating nearly a million gallons per day, and is charged with about 2 tons of any sort of scrap iron, one of the most convenient forms being punchings from boiler plates.

" This churning with scrap iron causes the water to take up a small quantity of iron, from a tenth to a fifth of a grain per gallon, which, in precipitation, effects the purification of the water.

" On leaving the cylinder these particles of iron are in the form of ferrous hydrate ; but as the water is immediately exposed to the influence of the air, this becomes quickly changed to ferric hydrate, which is precipitated in particles more or less coarse according to the nature of the water under treatment. On leaving the cylinder the water is passed into a settling-bed, or simple troughs, in which the iron is completely oxidized by exposure to the air, and in which the precipitate immediately settles.

" The action of the ferric hydrate on all impurities in the water is one of coagulation, the formation of a precipitate in the water tending to throw out of solution the dissolved organic substances. This explanation of the action of the iron process upon the organic impurities of a water applies equally well to its action upon microbes. Experience shows that the microbes become entangled in the precipitate, and either subside with it to the bottom of the settling-tank, or remain upon the surface of the filter."

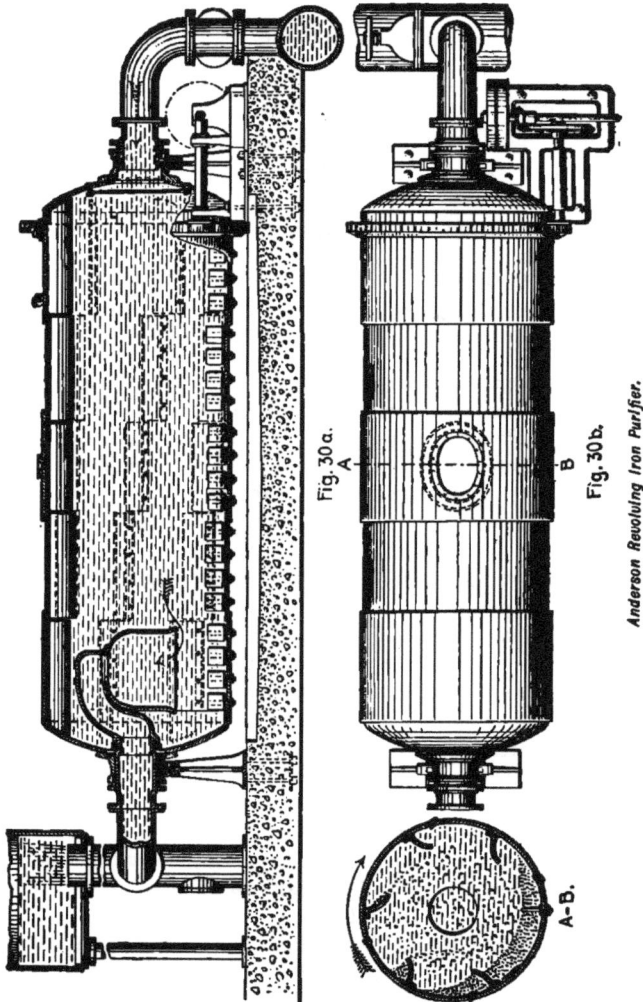

Fig. 30 a.

Fig. 30 b.

Anderson Revolving Iron Purifier.

A-B.

After extensive experiments had been made with this process upon the sewage-polluted water of the River Seine at Boulogne-sur-Seine, with very gratifying results according to the report of Dr. Miquel, it was adopted by the Compagnie Générale des Eaux, for the supply of the suburbs of Paris. The process has been made a part of the works at Choisy-le-Roi, Nogent-sur-Marne, and Neuilly-sur-Marne, and is proportioned for the treatment (at all the stations) of 18,500,000 U. S. gallons per diem.

From Dr. Miquel's bacterial tests of the performance of this process at Boulogne-sur-Seine, the following averages for a period of six months, February to July inclusive, 1893, are taken : —

	COLONIES PER C. C. OF WATER.
Unfiltered water from River Seine,	396,000
Filtered water,	1,702
Percentage of reduction,	99.57

The water of the River Vanne, at the same time, contained 1,110 colonies per cubic centimeter. This is a very pure water from protected mountain sources, 107 miles distant, and in Paris is regarded as the standard for dietetic water.

The method pursued by Dr. Miquel and other French workers in bacteriology is calculated to show the bacteria per cubic centimeter of a water sample about ten times as high as the method employed in Germany, England, and America ; and for comparison with our statements of the bacterial counts from various waters his figures should be divided by this number, which will give about the following results : —

	BACTERIA PER C. C.
Seine water (unfiltered),	39,600
Seine water (filtered),	170
Vanne water,	111

The special merit of the Anderson process is found in its ability to increase the rate of precipitation of the suspended matter, including bacteria, without the use of chemicals as a coagulant, the same result being accomplished by the "ferrous hydrate," formed by the contact of the iron particles with the water, which upon aëration is precipitated as a "ferric hydrate."

According to the circular from which the above information was drawn, the expense of operating the small plant, including the filters, at Boulogne-sur-Seine, was about $1.50 per million U. S. gallons. The process is not in use in any English water-works, although tried at one time under unfavorable conditions at the water-works of Worcester.* Of this test Dr. Dupre says: —

"1. The revolving purifier process, judged merely from a chemical point of view, has been a considerable success as regards at least 7 out of the 11 fortnightly samples examined; and if the process could be conducted in such a manner that all the filtered water equaled these, there would be nothing left to desire; while from a bacteriological point of view it has been eminently successful in practically every case.

"2. From a sanitary point of view most of the samples of filtered water are open to no objection.

"3. The process, as hitherto worked at Worcester, does not effect any very noticeable reduction in the color of the water whenever there is much peaty matter present.

"4. From a sanitary point of view the presence of peat is not, however, a serious evil.

"5. Similar results might no doubt have been obtained by means of sand filtration only. To obtain them in this way it would, however, be necessary to increase the present filtering area by at least 50 per cent, since the rate of filtration should then not exceed 4 inches per hour; whereas the present rate of supply cannot be kept up under a rate of at least 6 inches per hour, and even then no provision would be made to supply the place of filters thrown out of work for cleaning."

The author's experiments with a small Anderson purifier (on the Ohio River water) have given as averages of several tests from 86.13 to 97.28 per cent reductions of the bacteria in the raw water; but, as stated in Chapter III., this purifier, and especially the filter used in connection with it, were not calculated to favor the process, and should not be weighed against the more elaborate experiments of Dr. Miquel, 1893, on the process as used at Boulogne-sur-Seine.

The claims by the manufacturers for the Anderson process of treatment before the water enters the subsiding reservoirs are: —

"1. Filtration, after the water has been purified by means of the revolving purifier process, is carried on at about twice the customary speed, thus effecting a saving of about half the area of filter surface required.

* Report of Dr. A. Dupre, London, November, 1892.

"2. The saving thus effected much more than counterbalances the cost of the revolving cylinders.

"3. The purification is much more thorough and much less liable to accidental disturbance, and removes a greater percentage of microbes.

"4. The working cost is low, as the iron employed is very cheap, and with efficient settlement the cost of filter cleaning is very small."

The cost of a revolving purifier plant, including all usual connections, is stated at $5,000 per million gallons of daily capacity. A series of cylinders, and the usual connections and appurtenances (not including the filters), required to treat 20,000,000 gallons of water daily, would thus cost $100,000.

According to Mr. E. Devonshire of the Anderson Purifier Company, the cost of plain sand filters abroad is $15,000 to $20,000 per million gallons of daily capacity, while with the reduced filter area required by the Anderson process, these figures are reduced to $9,000 and $12,000 per million gallons of daily capacity; and he estimates the average cost of a combined purifying and filtering plant at $15,500 per million gallons of capacity per day. It is stated by the company that the cost of treatment by this process, including the care of the sand filters, "will not exceed $2.00 per million gallons."

CHAPTER XVI.

FILTERS PROPOSED FOR CINCINNATI.

THE water supply of Cincinnati has for years been in a deplorable condition, and different measures for relief have been proposed at various times during the past thirty years.   As early as 1865 Mr. James P. Kirkwood proposed settling reservoirs and plain sand filters for the treatment of the Ohio River water before it was supplied to the consumers. This method of water purification, with such modifications as the intervening time has suggested, was recommended by the Commission of Engineers appointed to report plans and estimate of cost for extension and betterment of the city water-works.*   The plans embrace subsidence in large reservoirs for four days previous to the delivery of the water to the filters.

The premises and conclusions upon the matter of water purification, as set forth in the Report of the Engineer Commission, abridged and corrected for the present purpose, were as follows : —

" Experiments indicate that subsidence for four days will remove from the Ohio River water a very large percentage of the suspended matter, and relieve the filters of that part of the work which is chiefly concerned in the clarification of the water.   The effect of this will be to cause the filters to pass a larger quantity of water per unit of area between successive parings or cleanings of the sand."

" Much of the work now required of the filters abroad will be accomplished in the subsiding reservoirs ; and by a fair division of the work between the subsiding reservoirs and the filters, relying upon the former largely for clarification and improvement of the color, and upon the latter wholly for the reduction of the bacteria

---

* This commission reported March 20, 1896.

(and finer suspended matter), better results can be had in the quality of effluent and economy of operation than by filtration alone."

" The subsiding reservoirs have been designed for ready cleansing from the silt and other suspended matter in the water which will be deposited upon the bottom and slopes, and are so arranged in unit capacity that at all times at least 250,000,000 gallons, and usually 300,000,000 gallons, cf sedimentation capacity will be in service."

"The filters were designed for a total capacity of 66,000,000 gallons per day, and a least effective capacity of 60,000,000 gallons per day. The net aggregate area of water and sand surface is 22 acres, allotting two acres to each of the eleven filters. The estimated rate of delivery is 3,000,000 gallons per acre per day."

" To obtain the highest quality of effluent with the maximum allowable rate of filtration, regulators will be used on both the inflow and outflow pipes, limiting the head on the sand-bed and the loss of head between the water on the filter and the level of water in the effluent chambers to such measures as may be found to give the most satisfactory results in practice."

The subsiding reservoirs are six in number, and each has a capacity of 50,000,000 gallons when filled to a depth of 30 feet. The bottom dimensions are 705 feet by 210 feet, with dimensions at the full water-line of 855 feet by 360 feet. The top width of embankment has been fixed at 20 feet, with inside slopes 2½ horizontal to one vertical, and outside slopes 2 horizontal to one vertical. The bottom and inside slopes are to be covered with 2 feet of puddle, over which will be a pavement of concrete 6 inches thick. The top of the embankment will be paved with concrete and small broken stone rolled in place, to form a foot-walk and driveway around and between the reservoirs.

The dimensions of sand-bed and water surface of each filter are 220 feet wide by 400 feet long. The depth of the filter, from the top of coping to the concrete floor, is 11 feet. The filters have been planned with masonry walls, vertical on the inside and battered by offsets on the outside. Under the bottom of the filter a layer of puddle 12 inches thick has been shown, and over this

puddle is placed a concrete floor 6 inches thick. The walls are
started on a course of puddle 12 inches thick, with a broad footing,

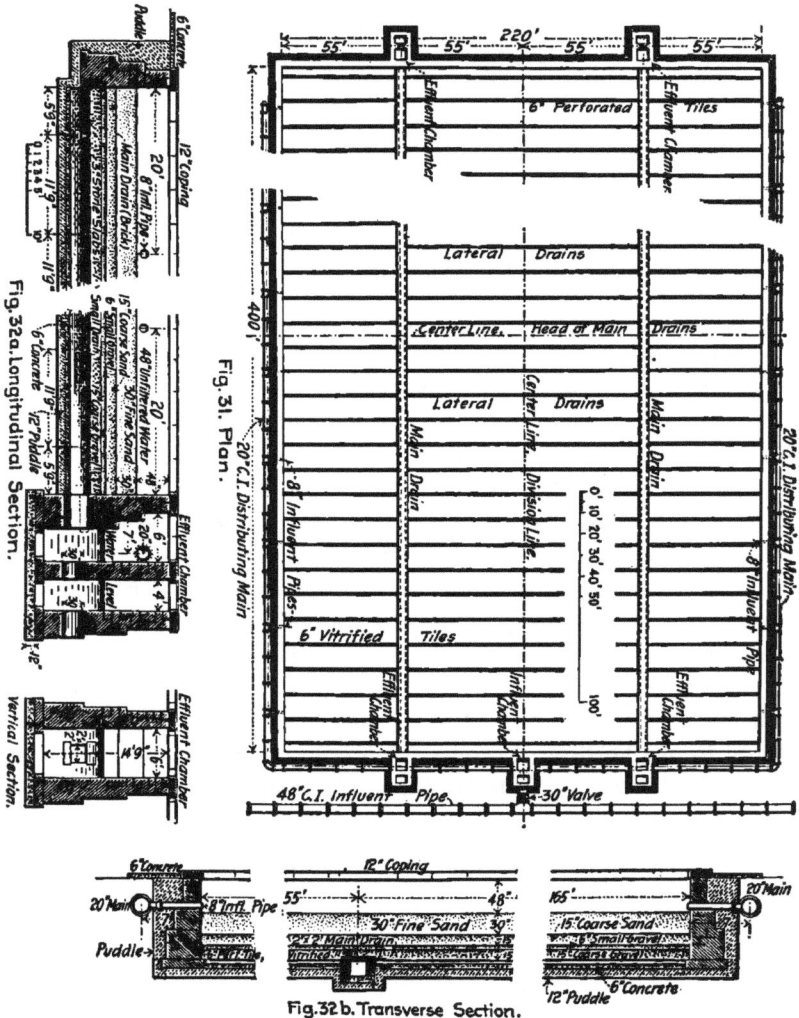

Figs. 31 and 32. Proposed Filter Bed for the City of Cincinnati, O., 1896.

and around the walls puddle of varying widths will be packed up
to the level of the ground.

Each filter has two acres of sand and water surface,* and is provided with two main drains laid to a grade of 6 inches in 200 feet, each main drain being graded from the center of the length of the filter chamber to the effluent chambers at the ends of the filter, to collect the water from one-fourth the area of the filter, and discharge this right and left to the effluent chambers." The dimensions of each section are, therefore, 110 feet by 200 feet.

One filter of 2 acres sand area is divided into four parts or sections of $\frac{1}{2}$ acre each, from which the filtered water is collected, and delivered to the four effluent chambers ; and any variation in the quality of filtrate supplied by each $\frac{1}{2}$ acre of the filter can be detected by proper tests of the water at the effluent chambers. The sections, Figs. 32 *a* and 32 *b*, show the method of construction proposed. The excavation will be carried to such bottom elevation as will provide for the filling between and for the embankments around the filters, with due allowance for shrinkage in volume of material by rolling and the action of the elements.

The concrete floor and masonry side and end walls constitute the basin or reservoir for the reception of the main and lateral drains and the filtering materials. Each section of the floor is a shallow trough, with a general grade toward its respective effluent chamber. The regulator on the influent side of the filter consists of a 30-inch balanced valve, and a metal float which closes the influent valve when a head of 4 feet over the sand layer is reached. Upon the effluent side the yield of the filter is conducted to the clear-well through a 24-inch pipe, controlled by a balanced valve and float, which limits the delivery of each $\frac{1}{2}$ acre of the filter to 1,500,000 gallons per day.

" The main drains are built of brick, with portholes in the three upper courses to receive the water from the small lateral drains, and are covered with close jointed stone slabs 3 inches thick. The walls of the main drains are 12 inches thick, and rest on a concrete foundation 6 inches thick."

The main drains are 2 feet wide and 2 feet high in the clear, two of which are provided for each acre of filtering surface.

" The lateral drains are of vitrified salt-glazed tile, with butt

* Compare Hamburg Filters, Chap. XIII.

joint of arched section with flat bottoms, and perforated on the top and sides. The inside dimensions are 6 inches wide and 8 inches high. These are laid on the concrete floor to a grade of 3 inches in 52.5 feet. The lateral drains are spaced 11.8 feet center to center.

"The filtering materials are arranged as follows : —

Fine graded sand (at top of filter),	30 inches.
Coarse sand,	15 "
Small gravel,	6 "
Coarse "	15 "
Total depth of filtering materials,	66 inches.
Depth of water over sand,	48 "

"Each filter is provided with one influent and four effluent chambers ; and each chamber is provided with an automatic regulating-valve to control the depth of water over the sand-bed, and regulate the rate of flow from the filters to the clear-well. Each filter is supplied through a 30-inch branch pipe, connected with a 48-inch supply main. Each branch pipe is provided with a stop-valve to shut off the flow to the filter when it is out of service and being cleaned. Provision also is made for the draining of the water to such level below the surface of the sand-bed as may be desired, or to empty the filter of water altogether.

From the influent chamber two lines of 20-inch cast-iron pipe pass right and left across the ends and down the longer sides of the filter, from which short pieces of 8-inch cast-iron pipe deliver the unfiltered water on the filter-bed. These branch pipes are placed 40 feet center to center.

The author believes that the influent pipes should enter the filter a few inches (not more than one foot) above the sand, to avoid the necessity of a complete refilling of a filter with filtered water, and the disturbance of the sand surface by the fall of water from the influent pipes while filling a filter to the standard level.

"The clear-well is planned as a masonry structure, with walls vertical on the inside and battered by offsets on the outside, and is started on a layer of puddle 18 inches thick, over which is placed a layer of concrete 6 inches thick. Outside the walls puddle of varying widths will be rammed up to a level with the ground. The clear-well inside has a length of 1,180 feet and a width of 148 feet, giving a net area of 4 acres, which, with a depth of 15 feet, contains 20,000,000 gallons, or one-fourth of the daily capacity of the high-service pumping-engines.

" Much thought has been bestowed upon the problem of open and closed filters for Cincinnati, and due consideration has been given to the practice of filter construction abroad. In latitudes where the winters are rigorous it is essential that the filters be covered to secure good results.

" In temperate climates, like that of London, all the filters are open. In the extreme climates of St. Petersburg, Warsaw, and Koenigsberg the filters are covered to avoid the danger due to a complete freezing over of the water on the sand-bed, and more especially to prevent freezing of the sand when the filter is taken out of service.

" The filters of Berlin (a city in a climate nearly like that of Cincinnati), are covered, while the latest filter works of Germany, those of Hamburg, are of the open type.

" The normal temperature of the winter months should govern in this matter ; and a comparison of the temperatures of the three winter months for the past eleven years for Cincinnati, with the mean January temperatures of Berlin and Hamburg, are given in the following table : —

MEAN NORMAL WINTER TEMPERATURES.

City.	December.	January.	February.
Cincinnati,	36.75	30.66	34.27
Berlin,	. .	31	. .
Hamburg,	. .	31	. .

" From this it appears that the mean January temperature of Cincinnati is about the same as that of the German cities noted ; but of the eleven years embraced in the average for Cincinnati, seven had mean January temperatures below the freezing-point.

" In the light of the long and valuable experience of the other German cities in the matter of filter construction and operation, it is difficult to conceive how Hamburg could have made a mistake in a matter apparently so easy of solution as the covering or non-covering of its filters. Altona, adjoining Hamburg, and subject to the same winter climate, had used open filters for thirty-two years before Hamburg built its filters ; and although some complaint had arisen in Altona against open filters, it does not seem that this was strong enough to cause the use of covered filters in Hamburg.

The commission decided to recommend filters without coverings, with a provision in the report for the vaulting of the filters, should experience demonstrate the necessity of these. Information from Hamburg, received since the Report was submitted, indicates that the covering of filters in climates similar to Cincinnati is not essential to satisfactory results, either in the quality of filtrate or in the management of the filters during the winter.

The project of water purification for Cincinnati contemplates eleven open filters, each of two acres of sand and water surface ; and estimating in the usual manner for engineering structures, the cost of the filters, including all necessary pipes, valves, regulators, etc., is $65,146.50 for one filter. The cost of clear-well of masonry construction was $162,696.90, and the total cost for the filtering-works was estimated as follows : —

ORIGINAL PLAN FOR CINCINNATI FILTERS.

11 filters, 2 acres of filtering area each, at $65,146.50,	$716,611.50
Clear-well, 20,000,000 gallons capacity,	162,696.90
	$879,308.40
Add 10 per cent for sand-washing and conveying machinery, contingencies, etc.,	87,930.84
45.06 acres of land, at $150.00,	6,759.00
Total for 11 filters, clear-well, and all appurtenances,	$973,998.24
Cost per acre of filtering area,	44,272.65
Cost per 1,000,000 gallons of estimated capacity,	14,757.55

Subsequent to the report of the commission the author investigated the cost of these filters, if constructed after the Hamburg plan, with sloped walls of earth instead of masonry, the sand surface to remain the same as before ; viz., two acres, influent and effluent chambers of masonry, and all distributing and collecting pipes and channels of the same construction as before, from which the following *résumé* is drawn : —

AMENDED PLAN FOR CINCINNATI FILTERS

11 filters, 2 acres of filtering area each, at $53,960,	$593,560.00
Clear-water reservoir, 20,000,000 gallons capacity, at $3,000 per million,	60,000.00
	$653,560.00
Add 10 per cent for sand-washing and conveying machinery, contingencies, etc.,	65,356.00
52.5 acres of land, at $150.00,	7,875.00
Total for 11 filters, clear-water reservoir, and all appurtenances,	$726,791.00
Cost per acre of filtering area,	33,036.00
Cost per 1,000,000 gallons of estimated capacity,	11,012.00

In this estimate the clear-water reservoir is also considered as a plain earthen reservoir with sloped walls, paved with concrete six inches thick, same as filter basins.

The estimates of cost for a system of plain sand filtration for Cincinnati were made from plans prepared with unusual care in view of the novelty of the proposition to filter 60,000,000 gallons of river water per diem, and it is not known that any feature of successful filtration was omitted in the plans or overlooked in the estimate. The prices for materials and construction adopted in the detailed estimates are really higher than the prices prevailing at this time (1897), and the author is confident that entirely satisfactory and durable works can be constructed within the estimates given.

With reference to the great cost of the filter works at Berlin, Mr. Gill's plans have been studied very carefully ; and aside from the fact that he has included in the cost of the purification works the cost of certain features of the Lake Müggel works, which in the author's opinion are not strictly chargeable to the filters, but should be charged to the pumping-works, the whole work was conducted upon a very costly scale, scarcely justified even in permanent works of public water supply.

(During a long experience with public works the author has seen much money wasted in certain details of construction which have been due to inexperience or perverted judgment upon the part of the constructors. Thus reservoirs, thoroughly constructed, complete in every essential, and as durable as such structures may be, have been completed by some engineers at a cost of $2,500 per million gallons of available capacity, while in other situations equally as favorable for this class of works, the engineer has succeeded in using up over $4,000 per million gallons of reservoir capacity, with no material gain in the quality of the finished structure. Point lace on the legs of a pair of overalls, or the sleeves of a machinist's jacket, would add nothing to the utility of these garments, while costing many times as much as the garments themselves. In like manner the author has seen works overloaded with trimmings which attract the eye, while obviously lacking in some of the essentials for convenient service and durability. In the construction of filters and appurtenances the same extravagance which is often displayed in other engineering structures may enter into these with no benefit whatever to the works themselves.)

The manner in which the filters and appurtenances for the Hamburg Water-Works were forced to an early completion by working night and day, in order to avoid the possible return of cholera in 1893, manifestly increased the cost of labor, and possibly of materials, over the cost of what might have been obtained with slower and more deliberate construction ; and yet these works are very complete in every essential of modern filter construction, and cost a trifle over one-half, per acre of effective area, than that of the filters in the Berlin Water-Works. The Berlin filters are covered ; but allowing $13,000 per acre for concrete vaulted covers, then the Hamburg filters would have cost but two-thirds as much as the Berlin filters.

(The people are always ready to condemn the prodigality of a private spendthrift, and how much more justly may we condemn the public spendthrifts who, through ignorance and arrogance, presume to squander the contents of the public purse.)

CHAPTER XVII.

COST OF FILTERS AND FILTRATION

So many variable conditions enter into the cost of constructing a system of water filters, that any figures given in a work of this kind must be accepted rather as suggestions than estimates which can be used with safety in any locality. The topography and nature of the ground upon which filters are to be constructed, the local prices of labor and materials, the nearness and quality of available filtering materials, the character throughout the year of the water to be filtered, the necessity of previous sedimentation with certain waters, the quality of filtrate to be obtained, and many other obvious conditions, must be taken into consideration in determining and designing a system of filters on a large scale for public water supply. The same ingenuity and judgment in the use of available locations and materials of construction are to be taken advantage of in the building of works of filtration, as in other engineering structures. Successful filtration seems to be more dependent upon management than on the construction of the works, and plain construction, such as we find in the purification works of Hamburg, with the skill and vigilance there displayed in the management of the filters, will meet all practical requirements.

PHILADELPHIA, PA.

Mr. Hazen, in a Report to the Woman's Health Protective Association,* estimates the cost of filters there (omitting value of land) as given in the first table on page 256.

These prices include settling-basins, low-lift pumps, filters and clear-wells, and the pipes, valves, and regulators required to connect the filters in service. In all instances noted above, the maxi-

---

* *A Practical Plan for Sand Filtration in Philadelphia*, 1896.

STATION.	DAILY AVERAGE CAPACITY, GALLONS.	GROSS COST.	COST PER AVERAGE MILLION GALLONS.
Belmont,	14,000,000	$ 317,000	$22,643.00
Queen Lane,	26,000,000	587,000	22,577.00
Cambria,	60,000,000	1,578,000	26,300.00
Frankford,	20,000,000	389,000	19,450.00

mum capacity of the filters is 50 per cent above the average, and a statement of cost upon the total or maximum daily capacity of filters will be as follows : —

STATION.	COST PER MAXIMUM MILLION GALLONS.	STATION.	COST PER MAXIMUM MILLION GALLONS.
Belmont,	$15,095.30	Cambria,	$17,533.30
Queen Lane,	15,051.30	Frankford,	12,966.60

From Mr. Shedd's estimates on filters for Providence, R.I., the following costs are obtained : —

TYPE OF FILTER.	DAILY CAPACITY, GALLONS.	GROSS COST.	COST PER MILLION GALLONS OF CAPACITY.
Mechanical,	15,000,000	$281,000	$18,733.30
Plain sand,	"	208,000	13,866.60
Proposal on plain sand,	"	200,000	13,333.30

According to Mr. Hazen,* covered filters on the European model will cost $70,000 per acre, or allowing for a rate of filtration of 2,500,000 gallons per acre per day, the cost per million gallons of daily capacity will be $28,000 ; but upon comparison with careful estimates by the author, on open and covered filters, for the city of Cincinnati, this price is excessive.

Open filters, not including clear-well, sand-washing and conveying machinery, and land, if built on favorable ground, should cost, in the vicinity of Cincinnati, as follows : —

With vertical masonry walls, per acre of filtering area, $32,573.30
With earthen embankments, and slopes paved with
    concrete, per acre of filtering area, $26,980.00

* *Filtration of Public Water Supplies*, p. 120.

Estimates furnished the author by an expert in concrete construction indicate that concrete coverings for above filters will cost about $11,000 and $13,000 respectively per acre of effective sand surface ; making the cost of covered filters as follows : —

COVERED FILTERS.

With vertical masonry walls and concrete coverings, per acre of filtering area,	$43,573.00
With earthen embankments, slopes paved with concrete and coverings of concrete, per acre of filtering area,	$39,980.00

In his Report to the city of Albany, Mr. Hazen modifies his estimate of cost somewhat.* Here he gives the cost of eight filters (0.70 acre each) at $251,000, to which may be added $10,000 for piping about filters, etc., making the cost of covered filters $46,607 per acre, a price which agrees more nearly with the results of the author's estimates of cost of construction.

The clear-well, or reservoir, to equalize the delivery from a system of filters, should have a capacity equal to ⅓ or ¼ the maximum daily yield of filters ; and this, if constructed as a plain reservoir with paved inner slopes, will cost from $2,500 to $3,500 per million gallons of capacity.

Assuming 10 filters, open pattern, with earthen walls and paved inner slopes, of the dimensions given in the description of the Cincinnati filters (Chapter XVI.), the total cost of filters and clear-well, exclusive of land, should not exceed : —

10 filters, 2 acres each,	$539,600.00
Add 10 per cent for sand washing and conveying machinery, and contingencies,	53,960.00
Clear-water basin, of a capacity of 20,000,000 gallons, at $3,000 per million,	60,000.00
Total, exclusive of land,	$653,560.00
Cost per million gallons of daily capacity (allowing one filter to be always out of service, and 2,500,000 gallons average daily rate of filtration per acre),	$14,523.55

* *Report on Filtration of Water Supply*, Albany, 1897, p. 27.

In the estimates for plain sand filters for the proposed extension and betterment of the Cincinnati Water-Works, the clearwell was designed as a masonry structure of 4 acres area and 17 feet deep, and estimated to cost $163,000, or at the rate of $7,409 per acre of filtering area.

Estimating on open filters and clear-well of masonry construction, which may be desirable or necessary in some locations : —

10 filters, 2 acres each,	$651,466.00
Add 10 per cent for sand washing and conveying machinery, and contingencies,	65,146.60
Clear-well,	148,180.00
Total, exclusive of land,	$864,792.60
Cost per million gallons of daily capacity (allowing one filter always to be out of service, and 2,500,000 gallons average daily rate of filtration per acre),	$19,217.60

COST OF FILTERS, INCLUDING CLEAR-WELLS AND ALL APPURTENANCES.

Berlin, covered (Lake Müggel),*	$68,000 per acre.
Berlin, uncovered (Stralau),	48,570 "　　"
Hamburg, uncovered,	38,857 "　　"

The Berlin covered filters, as will be observed upon reference to the description of these in Chapter XIV., are of a very costly construction; and some of the appurtenances included in the cost are usually found in existing water-works to which filtration may in the future be applied. The Hamburg filters are of the most recent and modern construction, and approach more nearly the estimated cost for open filters in series in this country.

From Mr. Preller's paper on the Zurich Water-Works,† the cost of covered filters was $70,857 per acre, and for the open filters $46,464 per acre, prices which are higher than those of other works in Germany. These prices are stated to include only the filter basins and filtering materials, and possibly the pipes, valves, and conduits necessarily included in the construction of the filter basins and influent and effluent chambers.

---

* Mr. Gill states the cost of the covered filters at Lake Müggel as £15,000 per acre, equal to $72,750.00. Mr. Anklam, superintendent of these works, furnishes the prices given above.

† Proceedings *Institution of Civil Engineers*, London, 1892.

The cost of the Lawrence, Mass., filter was $26,000 per acre ; and this price it is understood covers all the work in construction of the filter and its connection with the previously existing filter gallery, which then became the clear-well of the filter.

The city of Ashland, Wis.,* recently constructed three small plain sand filters, each of ⅛ acre area, at a gross cost of $40,178.00. It was estimated that the extra cost of these filters due to local difficulties was $5,367.00, and the net cost under ordinary conditions was assumed at $34,811.00 for one-half acre. These filters are covered with masonry instead of concrete vaulting, which also materially increased their cost. Two of these filters have sand of an "effective size" 0.27 mm. and "uniformity coefficient" 1.9 ; and one has sand of an "effective size" 0.40 mm. and a "uniformity coefficient" 1.6. The sand in all beds is 4 feet thick.

RATES OF FILTRATION FOR PLAIN SAND FILTERS.

The rates of filtration per acre per day, as practiced in different cities, are given as follows : —

At the time of Mr. Kirkwood's visit to Europe the daily average rate of percolation was 3,920,400 gallons per acre, equal to 12 feet vertical per day. Mr. James Simpson, engineer of the Chelsea and Lambeth Water-Works (the pioneer in sand filtration), adopted a standard rate of 86.4 gallons per square foot (3,763,584 gallons per acre per day), corresponding to a vertical rate of percolation of 11.55 feet per day. The present average rate for the London filters is about 1,800,000 gallons per acre per day, corresponding to a vertical rate of percolation of 5.52 feet.

The filters of the New River Works sometimes reach a rate as high as 3,136,320 gallons per acre per day,† while the rate at which it becomes no longer profitable to operate a filter is placed by Mr. Hervey of the West Middlesex Works at 1,303,000 gallons per acre per day ; and when the rate of percolation reaches 2 inches per hour the filter is taken out of service, the sand-bed scraped, and the filter started for another period of useful work.

---

* *Engineering News,* Nov. 25, 1897, p. 338.
† According to Mr. E. L. Morris, engineer of these works.

The Hamburg rate is 1,700,000 gallons per acre per day, corresponding to a vertical rate of 5.22 feet. Mr. Gill proposed for the Müggel Lake filters for Berlin a vertical rate of 8 feet per day, equal to 2,606,630 gallons per acre per day. The rate at Zurich is 5,850,000 gallons per acre, equal to a vertical rate of 17.95 feet per day.

The rate proposed for a sand filter to be used in connection with the Marston Lake Water Supply for the city of Denver, was 195,500,000 gallons per acre per day, corresponding to a vertical rate of percolation of 600 feet.* (There is a suggestion in the paper which describes these filters that they were to be operated with a coagulant, but a late report on them indicates that this was abandoned, if ever used.) A filter devised for Tacoma, Washington, is said to work at rates of 22,000,000 to 44,000,000 gallons per acre per day, corresponding to vertical rates of 67.5 and 135.0 feet per day.† Plain sand filtration cannot be continuously conducted at such rates as these with any improvement in the quality of the water ; and they are here mentioned in order that the contrast between these rates and the rates which long experience abroad has sanctioned may be impressed upon water-works officials, with the hope that such works of water purification as may be attempted in this country, instead of showing an utter disregard of fundamental principles, will, if it is possible, be constructed and operated upon plans which will yield even better results than the works found in the cities of Europe.

Mr. Hazen, in estimating upon the cost of filters and filtration, employs a rate of 2,500,000 gallons per acre per day, corresponding to a vertical rate of percolation of 7.68 feet.

From the reports of the Massachusetts State Board of Health, satisfactory results, both chemically and bacterially, in the filtrate, were had with rates of filtration as high as 7,500,000 gallons per acre, corresponding to a vertical rate of 23 feet per day.

The Ashland (Wis.) plain sand filters, for the year ending February 28, 1897, were worked at an average rate of 2,180,064 gallons per acre per day, equivalent to a vertical rate of 6.69 feet.

---

* *Transactions American Society of Civil Engineers*, vol. xxxi., pp. 158–60.
† *Transactions American Society of Civil Engineers*, vol. xxxv., p. 44 *et seq.*

DURATION OF SERVICE OF FILTERS.

The period or interval of time between cleanings or renewal of the sand surface of a filter has a direct bearing on the cost of filtration. Obviously the clearer the water and the lower the rate of percolation the longer will be the interval of service. With a given condition of the water as it comes to the filter the capacity can be stated in millions of gallons filtered between cleanings, and the capacity divided by the average rate of percolation per day will give the number of days of filter service.

Thus, a filter which, between parings of the sand-bed, will deliver 60,000,000 gallons per acre, at an average rate of percolation of 2,000,000 gallons per acre per day, will have a period of operation of 30 days. A filter which will deliver 100,000,000 gallons per acre, between parings of the sand-bed, at an average rate of percolation through the sand of 2,500,000 gallons per acre per day, will have a period of operation of 40 days.

The period of operation for the London filters ranges from · 30 to 40 days, depending upon the condition of the water as it is drawn from the River Thames or River Lea, and the time allowed for subsidence in the storage reservoirs before the water is put on the filters. From the evidence taken by the Royal Commission on Metropolitan Water Supply the period of operation was given.as short as 21 days in one instance, and as long as 70 days in another. One witness stated that some of the filters of his works had been in service over forty years, without any attention being given to them other than the scraping, washing, and replacing of the cleaned sand in the beds from time to time.

The Hamburg filters, omitting the short periods which have been mentioned as occurring during the winter, have worked for periods of 47, 51, and 66 days. However, the usual period of service at Hamburg is about 40 days. At Zurich the covered filters are reported to have an average period of service of 50 days, while the open filters require cleaning every 40 days of use. In these works the sand-bed is scraped successively until the remaining thickness is reduced to 12 inches.

At Berlin the filters are scraped after about every 40 days of service; and once in four years the whole bed of sand is taken out, washed, and replaced in the filter.

During the experiments conducted by Mr. Weston, with small plain sand filters at Providence, at rates of percolation less than 80,000,000 gallons per acre per day, the periods of operation ranged from 30 to 50 days, while at the higher rates of percolation the period of operation was about 20 days.

The general practice by the London water companies, in restoring a filter to service from time to time, is to scrape off about ¾ inch of the clogged sand until a minimum thickness (varying with the different companies) of the sand-bed is reached, whereupon the whole bed of sand is readjusted in position. The sand remaining after the last scraping is then taken out of the filter, and replaced by the sand previously scraped from the bed and washed, above which the other sand in the filter is spread, scraped off, and washed in due time. By this method the whole bed of sand at long intervals is scraped off, taken to the washer, and returned to the filter. Thus during one complete cycle of "filling" and "scraping" of the sand-bed, the whole body of sand will be rotated, the lower sand coming to the top of the filter, and the previous top sand going to the bottom, thus avoiding the probability of converting the lower portion of the sand-bed into a favorable soil for the cultivation of bacteria.

As stated in a previous chapter, the filters of some, if not all, the London water-works are generally scraped and the sand delivered on the banks of the filter by contract, the price paid being, as stated by Mr. W. B. Bryan, engineer of the East London Water Company, £5, or about $25.00 per acre.

The period of operation of the sand filter at Lawrence, Mass. (1895), was about 27 days, and at each scraping of the sand-bed ¾ inch was taken off and washed. The sand is washed by machinery. During 1895, 1,500 cubic yards of "fouled" sand were scraped from the filter and washed, at a cost of 68 cents per cubic yard, or $1.02 per million gallons of water filtered. About 1½ cubic yards of sand were scraped per million gallons of water drawn from the filter. At Hamburg about two cubic yards of sand are scraped off the filters and washed per million gallons of water filtered. There the cost per cubic yard of scraping and washing sand is considerably less than the cost of washing alone at Lawrence. This is partly to be accounted for by the much larger quantity of sand scraped and washed at Hamburg, and by the lower cost of common labor.

In the report of the Ashland (Wis.) filters mentioned on page 259, it is stated that the cleaning of the sand of one bed (⅛ acre) for the year ending February 28, 1897, consumed ½ day, and cost $8.50, making the cost of removing and cleaning the sand per acre $51.00. The total cost for cleaning and renewing the sand for one year was $899.37, during which time the filters delivered 397,860,000 gallons of water, with a cost of $2.26 per million gallons filtered. While the cost per acre for cleaning and renewing the "fouled" sand is very high even for small filters like these, the cost per million gallons of water filtered is correspondingly low, and suggests the probability of a poor quality of filtrate.

LOSS OF WATER IN CLEANING FILTERS.

The cost of washing sand at Berlin is stated at 2,020 gallons of water per cubic yard; while at Hamburg, with the ejector washers, the consumption of water is said to be 4,040 gallons per cubic yard of sand. At Zurich the cost of washing sand by machinery is given at 17½ cents per cubic yard, but no mention is made of the quantity of water required, while the cost of washing and placing the sand in the filters is reported as 46 cents per cubic yard. This is for the new sand, and the price doubtless is larger than for washing and replacing the "fouled" sand scraped from the filters.

In Chapter XII., the statement is made upon the authority of Mr. E. B. Weston that the filtered water required to wash the sand-bed of the Morison mechanical filter during the Providence tests, and the water run to waste after the filter was started, represented about eight per cent of the water filtered, leaving thus 92 per cent available for consumption.

The data upon the proportion of filtered water from mechanical filters actually available for consumption is rather meager, and some of that which we have not very exact. Quoting from Mr. Baker's paper on the use of mechanical filters by certain cities of New Jersey,* the mechanical filters at Long Branch require about 5 per cent, while the filters at Asbury Park require about 10 per cent, of the total pumpage for washing the sand-beds. At Key-port, "Filtered water is used in washing. When the filters had been in operation only some two months, it was stated that 15 per cent of the water pumped was required for washing, but that the contractor had promised to reduce this."

In a circular published by one of the manufacturers of me-chanical filters, it is stated in one instance that 3.97 per cent of the total pumpage was used for washing the sand-bed.

With the mechanical filters at Lorain, Ohio, it is stated that 5.22 per cent of the filtered water is used in washing the sand.†

At Hamburg the water for sand-washing (1896) represented less than one per cent of the total delivery by the filters, while at Berlin less than one-half per cent of the filtered water is lost in washing the sand scraped from the sand-beds.

COST OF FILTRATION.

The cost of operating sand filters abroad, according to the statement of the officials, are so various and widely different as to suggest that some of these include items of expense not necessa-rily connected with filtration *per se*, but which are embraced in the ordinary expenses of water-works operation, while some are given so ridiculously low as to raise a suspicion of error in the opposite direction.

The cost per million gallons of water treated (not including interest and sinking-fund charges, and omitting the charge for re-moval of ice) for the Lawrence, Mass., filters for 1895 was $4.10 ; and estimating interest charges on $65,000 at 5 per cent, and sink-ing-fund payments invested at 4 per cent for 40 years, the total cost per million gallons for that year was $7.69. Taking account

---

* M. N. Baker, *Proceedings New Jersey Sanitary Association*, 1895, p. 84 *et seq.*
† *Ohio Sanitary Bulletin*, October, 1897, p. 115.

of the cost of clearing the filter of ice, and including interest and sinking-fund charges, the total cost per million gallons of water filtered was $10.34.

On page 121 of Mr. Hazen's book on *The Filtration of Public Water Supplies*, the cost per million gallons for treatment of 8,000,000 gallons per day, including interest and sinking-fund charges at six per cent (no time of redemption given), is estimated at $12.50. Omitting interest and sinking-fund charges, the cost is figured at $5.30. In his report to the Woman's Health Protective Association of Philadelphia, he puts the cost, with previous sedimentation, at $3.50 per million gallons; while at Albany, with preliminary sedimentation, he estimates the cost at $2.50 per million gallons, and without preliminary sedimentation, at $3.50 per million gallons. (These prices do not include interest and sinking-fund charges.)

The cost of filtration, not including interest and sinking-fund charges, at Zurich, is stated as 61 cents for the covered filters, and 94 cents for the open filters, per 1,000,000 U. S. gallons. The average cost for both open and closed filters, including interest and sinking-fund charges, is deduced from Mr. Preller's notes as $6.71 per million U. S. gallons filtered.

A very careful estimate of all items of expense entering into the operation of the filters proposed for Cincinnati, with due allowance for loss of sand in handling and washing, superintendence, daily laboratory work, and depreciation of such portions of the apparatus as is subject to wear, based upon 60,000,000 gallons of water treated daily, gave $3.50 per million gallons, exclusive of interest and sinking-fund charges; although $4.00 per million gallons was used in estimating the probable cost of filtration in the report on these works.

The cost of filtration in any instance (omitting interest and sinking-fund charges) will depend very largely upon the management of the filters. In London the cost per million U. S. gallons ranges from $1.15 to $2.00, and probably averages less than $1.50 per million U. S. gallons.

In the review of the sand filters at Poughkeepsie, N.Y.,[*] the

* *Manual of American Water Works*, 1889–90, p. 175.

cost per million gallons of water filtered is given as $1.32, a price which indicates that these filters were not then worked with a view to the high quality of filtrate obtained in works abroad.

Investigations during the present year (1897) of filter practice in one of the larger cities of Germany, indicates a cost there of less than $1.20 per million U. S. gallons of water filtered, for the scraping of the sand-bed, transport of the sand to the washers, washing the "fouled" sand, and finally returning the sand to the filter bed. This price would apply only to large works, in which the construction of filters and all appurtenances were modern, and when the management was the best. Allowing 100 per cent additional for other labor about the filters ; renewal of the sand lost in handling and washing ; deterioration of barrows, trucks, sand-washers, etc., and for supervision ; and increasing this cost by 50 per cent for similar works in this country, the cost, not including interest and sinking-fund charges on filters and apparatus, nor repairs of the filters proper, should not exceed $3.00 per 1,000,000 gallons of water passed through the filters.

Assuming a cost of $4.00 per million gallons of water filtered, interest charges on the cost of constructing open filters at 4 per cent, and payments to sinking-fund for 40 years invested at 3½ per cent, the total cost per million gallons of water filtered should not exceed $6.37. Allowing for a consumption of 100 gallons per capita per diem, the annual cost per capita will be 23¼ cents.

APPENDICES.

APPENDIX A.

TYPHOID FEVER STATISTICS

OF THE PRINCIPAL CITIES OF THE UNITED STATES AND EUROPE.

Compiled from the Official Reports of Health Departments, January, 1897.

DEATH RATE PER 100,000 OF POPULATION LIVING.

City.	Source of Supply.	1890.	
		POPULA-TION.	DEATH RATE.
New York, N. Y.,	Imp'd water from Croton and Bronx Rivers,	1,705,980	21
Chicago, Ill.,	Lake Michigan,	1,208,664	83
Philadelphia, Pa.,	Schuylkill and Delaware Rivers,	1,046,964	64
Brooklyn, N. Y.,	Impounded water from driven and open wells,	853,945	26
St. Louis, Mo.,	Mississippi River,	450,000	34
Boston, Mass.,	Lake Cochituate and Sudbury River,	437,245	43
Baltimore, Md.,	Lake Roland and Gunpowder River,	434,151	57
San Francisco, Cal.,	Impounded water from mountain streams,	300,000	59
Cincinnati, O.,	Ohio River,	296,000	67
Cleveland, O.,	Lake Erie,	277,488	66
Buffalo, N. Y.,	Niagara River at head,	. . .	. .
New Orleans, La.,	Drinking-water from tanks and cisterns,	254,000	20
Washington, D. C.,	Potomac River,	250,000	83
Pittsburg, Pa.,	Alleghany River,	. . .	. .
Detroit, Mich.,	Detroit River,	230,000	18
Milwaukee, Wis.,	Lake Michigan,	220,000	33
Newark, N. J., *	Impounded water, Pequannock River,	181,830	60
Jersey City, N. J ,	Passaic and Pequannock Rivers,	163,003	91
Louisville, Ky.,	Ohio River,	161,000	88
Providence, R. I.,	Pawtucket River,	132,146	29
Indianapolis, Ind.,	Driven wells and Filter Gallery,	. . .	. .
Lowell, Mass.,	Merrimac River and driven wells,	77,696	158
Lawrence, Mass.,	Filtered from Merrimac River,	44,654	123
Nashville, Tenn.,	Filter gallery, Cumberland River,	77,000	46
Dayton, O.,	Driven wells,	60,000	20
Covington, Ky ,	Ohio River,	37,400	43
Newport, Ky., †	Ohio River,	. . .	. .
Denver, Col.,	South Platte River and Marston Lake,	. . .	. .
Atlanta, Ga.,	Mechanical filter, Chattahootchie River,	65,533	151
Chattanooga, Tenn.,	Mechanical filter, Tennessee River,	29,109	145
Knoxville, Tenn., ‡	Mechanical filter, Tennessee River,	40,000	101
Quincy, Ill.,	Mechanical filter, Mississippi River,	31,500	83
Davenport, Ia.,	Mechanical filter, Mississippi River,	30,000	50
Montreal, Que.,	St. Lawrence River,	216,300	29
Toronto, Ont.,	Lake Ontario,	167,439	93

* East Jersey Water Co., Estab. April 15, 1892. † Health Department, Estab. 1893.

APPENDIX A.

TYPHOID FEVER STATISTICS

Of the Principal Cities of the United States and Europe.

Compiled from the Official Reports of Health Departments, January, 1897.

DEATH RATE PER 100,000 OF POPULATION LIVING.

1891.		1892.		1993.		1894.		1895.		1896.	
POPULATION.	DEATH RATE.	POPULATION.	DEATH RATE.	POPULATION.	DEATH RATE.	POPULATION.	DEATH RATE.	POPULATION.	DEATH RATE.	POPULATION.	DEATH RATE.
1,765,645	22	1,827,396	22	1,891,306	20	1,937,452	17	1,879,195	17	1,934,077	16
1,250,000	160	1,438,010	104	1,600,000	42	1,567,727	31	1,600,000	32	1,619,226	46
1,069,264	64	1,092,168	40	1,115,562	41	1,146,000	32	1,163,864	40	1,188,793	34
880,780	20	962,530	17	990,891	17	1,045,000	15	1,090,000	16	1,140,000	15
452,000	30	460,000	37	500,000	103	540,000	31	560,000	19	570,000	19
461,093	33	474,063	29	487,397	30	501,107	28	496,920	33	508,694	32
445,853	34	458,350	42	473,193	47	455,427	49	496,315	39	507,398	37
330,000	41	330,000	34	330,000	32	330,000	35	330,000	37	330,000	31
300,000	62	305,000	40	310,000	43	336,000	50	336,000	36	341,000	48
299,475	52	309,243	54	322,932	47	325,000	27	325,000	36	330,279	43
255,664	50	285,000	34	300,000	37	315,000	36	335,709	29	350,000	20
254,000	23	254,000	21	254,000	15	275,000	28	275,000	41	275,000	33
250,000	83	260,000	70	285,000	66	270,514	71	271,000	74	278,150	51
247,000	100	255,000	100	264,000	111	272,000	56	275,000	77	280,000	61
230,000	13	230,000	51	230,000	61	250,000	26	280,000	22	279,000	20
233,333	33	245,000	31	260,000	37	267,500	26	260,000	27	257,500	18
187,108	81	192,531	45	198,115	28	203,861	15	215,725	17	230,000	21
167,237	95	171,471	53	175,000	60	179,939	76	184,173	71	187,098	61-62
161,000	81	161,000	72	161,000	84	200,000	72	205,000	77	211,100	45
132,146	47	132,146	39	148,944	34	153,000	47	145,472	32	150,000	27
120,000	36	125,000	52	125,000	106	125,000	55	125,000	97	165,000	41
80,400	98	83,200	90	87,191	61	90,613	55	84,367	39	85,700	42
45,911	115	47,204	102	48,355	93	49,900	48	52,164	31	55,000	15
80,000	56	83,000	53	85,000	24	87,000	32	87,500	47	87,754	55
60,000	32	63,000	44	75,000	64	85,000	20	80,000	47	85,000	25
40,000	45	42,500	40	45,000	27	48,000	42	48,000	27	50,000	32
...	..	...	..	27,500	58	30,000	37	30,000	73	30,000	63
...	..	120,000	53	125,000	57	140,000	35	145,000	30	150,000	61
75,000	119	85,000	87	95,000	66	108,000	43	100,000	70	110,000	60
34,900	66	40,000	55	36,000	86	35,751	48	40,000	47-48	40,000	30
40,385	45	40,385	37	40,385	67	40,385	59	...	..	¹ 37,000 / ² 8,000	32 / 125
34,000	32	36,000	50	37,500	48	39,000	77	40,500	59	42,000	26
30,000	30	30,600	16	30,900	35	34,000	18	35,000	31	35,000	20
218,268	30	224,816	22	231,560	21	241,748	17	249,000	18	256,470	21
181,220	94	184,000	43	188,333	42	196,666	17	196,666	28	196,666	28-29

‡ (1) City proper; (2) Suburbs.

APPENDIX A.—*Continued.*

DEATH RATE PER 100,000 OF POPULATION LIVING.

City.	Source of Supply.	1890. POPULATION	DEATH RATE
London, Eng.,	From Kent wells and filtered water from the Rivers Thames and Lea,	4,180,654	16
Liverpool, Eng.,	Lake Vyrnwy (Wales),	513,493	24
Manchester, Eng.,	Lake Thirlmere (Cumberland),	379,437	31
Edinburgh, Scot.,	Impounded water, Pentland Hills,	271,135	19
Glasgow, Scot.,	Loch Katrine,	530,208	26
Dublin, Ire.,	Impounded water filtered from River Vartry,	353,082	62
Paris, Fr.,	Ourcq Canal, artesian wells, springs, Rivers Seine, Marne, and Vanne,	2,260,945	30
Brussels (with suburbs), Bel.,	.	477,288	26
Amsterdam, Hol.,	Haarlem dunes,	406,302	19
Rotterdam, Hol.,	Filtered water from River Mass,	203,486	6
The Hague, Hol.,	From sand dunes,	156,497	3
Copenhagen, Den.,	Driven wells,	312,387	9
Stockholm, Sweden,	Lake and well water,	236,350	18
Christiania, Nor.,		143,300	12
St. Petersburg, Rus.,	Filtered water from River Neva,	842,000	57
Moscow, Rus.,	Mytschia springs and ponds, Moscov and Yanza Rivers,	753,469	73
Berlin, Ger.,	Filtered water from Lake Tegel and River Spree,	1,548,279	9
Hamburg (State), Ger.,	Filtered water from River Elbe,	591,647	28
Altona, Ger.,	Filtered water from River Elbe,	143,249	19
Dresden, Ger.,	Filter gallery by River Elbe,	269,250	9
Breslau, Ger.,	Filtered water from River Oder,	324,400	15
Munich, Ger.,	Spring water from Mangfall Valley,	298,000	8
Vienna (with suburbs), Aust-Hung.	Springs in the Schneeberg and driven wells,	822,176	9
Prague, Aust.-Hung.,		314,425	33
Budapest, Aust.-Hung.,	Ground water from wells,	463,017	34
Trieste, Aust.-Hung.,		160,092	12
Rome, Italy,	Fontanadi Trevi, Aqua Felice, and Paoli,	417,392	35
Milan, Italy,	.	. . .	. .
Turin, Italy,		314,827	46
Venice, Italy,	Springs in the mountains fifteen miles distant, — cast-iron conduit.	156,800	44
Cairo, Egypt,*	River Nile by canal,	374,838	260
Alexandria, Egypt,*	River Nile by canal,	231,396	208
Sydney (with suburbs), Austr.,	Impounded water from Upper Nepean River,	. . .	. .
Brisbane (with suburbs), Austr.,		. . .	. .

* Including malarial fevers.

APPENDIX A. — *Continued.*

DEATH RATE PER 100,000 OF POPULATION LIVING.

1891.		1892.		1893.		1894.		1895.		1896.	
POPULA-TION.	DEATH RATE.	POPULA-TION.	DEATH RATE.	POPULA-TION.	DEATH RATE.	POPULA-TION.	DEATH RATE.	POPULA-TION.	DEATH RATE.	POPULA-TION.	DEATH RATE.
4,222,157	15	4,264,076	11	4,306,411	16	4,349,166	15	4,392,346	14	4,421,955	14
517,116	25	513,790	25	510,514	53	507,230	58	503,967	37	632,512	32
506,460	39	510,998	25	515,598	25	520,211	18	524,865	19	529,561	23
261,970	18	264,787	13	267,261	14	270,588	15	273,535	20	276,514	16
567,143	31	669,059	18	677,883	20	686,820	24	695,876	19	705,052	23
347,312	58	349,594	39	349,594	87	349,594	48	349,594	27	349,594	45
2,424,705	20	2,424,705	28	2,424,705	25	2,424,705	29	2,424,705	11	2,511,629	11
465,517	41	476,862	23	488,188	27	498,400	14	507,985	16	518,367	18
417,539	11	426,914	15	437,892	16	446,295	8-9	451,493	11	489,496	3
209,136	4	216,679	6	222,233	5	228,597	5	272,042	2	276,338	12
100,531	12	165,560	4	169,828	2	174,790	3	180,455	5	187,545	4
320,000	8	330,000	7	337,500	9	341,000	7	333,714	16	333,714	7
245,317	18	248,051	19	249,246	8	252,937	8	259,304	9	267,100	6
151,130	9	156,535	4	161,151	6	167,588	3	174,717	7	182,856	33
. . .	. .	. . .	. .	954,400	51	954,400	49	954,400	87	954,400	142
753,460	75	753,469	68	753,469	40	753,469	29	753,469	50	753,469	46
1,601,327	10	1,662,237	8	1,714,938	9	1,701,643	4	1,734,492	5	1,695,313	5
622,530	23	637,686	34	634,878	18	598,372	6	608,710	9	625,552	6
144,388	64	145,527	43	146,667	15	147,807	7	148,934	13	. . .	. .
276,523	8	301,400	5	308,930	4-5	316,600	8	324,341	5	342,340	4
339,000	12	346,442	15	353,551	10	360,660	6	367,769	9	377,062	8
357,000	7	373,000	3	385,000	15	393,000	2-3	396,000	3	406,000	3
1,378,530	6	1,406,933	8	1,435,931	7	1,465,537	5	1,495,764	6	1,526,623	5
310,485	37	321,167	53	327,953	36	339,172	57	351,478	46	364,632	28
513,010	23	526,263	26	539,516	15	552,769	14	566,022	20	579,275	29
156,190	11	157,343	26	158,314	17	159,739	19	160,825	5	161,886	13
427,684	36	438,123	26	449,430	34	456,777	30	465,563	62	473,296	27
. . .	. .	424,887	62	430,829	62	. . .	. .	441,948	55	. . .	. .
320,808	41	329,724	44	334,090	29	335,957	24	344,203	32	344,203	24
158,288	33	162,664	30	163,601	26	158,187	18	158,159	23	163,254	27
374,838	235	374,838	163	374,838	154	374,838	135	374,838	90	374,838	141
231,396	348	231,396	77	231,396	79	231,396	100	231,396	103	231,396	89
. . .	. .	406,480	20	411,710	19	421,030	29	423,600	20	. . .	. .
. . .	. .	. . .	. .	93,657	19	93,657	10	93,657	00	. . .	. .

APPENDIX B.*

THE BACTERIA.

THE bacteria are minute vegetable organisms, devoid of chlorophyl, and consist of a cellulose envelope containing a protoplasm described as mycoprotein.

According to Nencki † they have the following chemical composition : —

Water,	84.26 per cent.
Solids,	15.74 " "
	100.00 per cent.

Of the solids Nencki finds for the putrefactive bacteria of : —

Albumen,	87.46 per cent.
Fat,	6.41 " "
Ash,	3.04 " "
Undetermined substances,	3.09 " "
	100.00 per cent.

"The albuminous substance is not precipitated by alcohol, and differs in its chemical composition from other known substances of its class."

Nencki calls this substance mycoprotein, and gives the following as its chemical composition : —

Carbon,	52.32
Hydrogen,	7.55
Nitrogen,	14.75

* This Appendix is written with reference solely to water purification, and is intended only as a brief discussion of the bacteria. Those who may desire to pursue the inquiry further are referred to the standard text-books on this subject, of which may be mentioned, *A Manual of Bacteriology*, by Dr. George M. Sternberg, New York, 1893; *The Principles of Bacteriology*, by Dr. A. C. Abbott, Philadelphia, 1894 ; *Micro Organisms in Water*, by P. F. & G. C. Frankland, London, 1894; *Bacteriological Diagnosis*, by Dr. James Eisenberg, Philadelphia, 1892; *The Pathogenic Bacteria*, by Dr. Joseph McFarland, Philadelphia, 1896, etc.

† *A Manual of Bacteriology*, by Dr. George M. Sternberg, New York, 1893, p. 117.

Mycoprotein contains neither phosphorus nor sulphur.

The nitrogenous body appears to vary in different species, for in *b. anthracis* a substance has been obtained by Nencki which does not give the reactions of mycoprotein. This substance he calls anthrax-protein.*

The green coloring-matter of plants is known as chlorophyl, and the absence of this substance in the bacteria compels them to obtain the materials upon which they subsist from organic matter in process of digestion or decomposition ; in fact, the destruction and splitting up of organic matter into its constituent elements, is chiefly, and in some cases wholly, due to bacterial agencies.

The production of carbon dioxide, carbon monoxide, and nitrous and nitric acids from decomposing organic matter, is due to the action of the bacteria. The putrefactive bacteria are the first to attack organic matter, producing what is known as decay, with a liberation of carbonic acid and other gases, while the nitrifiers discovered by Winogradsky in the soil at Zurich, act upon the nitrogenous matters, and convert them into nitrous and nitric acids, which, uniting with lime, sodium, potash, or other bases, form the nitrites and nitrates for the support of plant life.

SAPROPHYTES AND PARASITES.

The bacteria divide into two great classes : —

1. Those which live and propagate their kind only upon dead organic matter, and known as the *saprophytes*.

2. Those which will live and develop only in the tissues or fluids of the living body, and known as the *parasites*.

The line of division between the two classes is not well marked. Some of the *saprophytes* may, under certain conditions, flourish as *parasites;* while certain of the *parasites*, known to attain their highest state of development in the animal body, will live for a limited time as *saprophytes*. Thus the bacillus of tuberculosis (consumption) is classed as a true *parasite*, but it can be cultivated (on artificial media) outside the living host ; while some of the so-called *saprophytes* may independently, or in conjunction with certain of the pathogenic bacteria, be responsible for processes in the animal body which result in disease, and should therefore be regarded as *facultative parasites*.

Bacteria which cannot subsist upon living matter are strict *saprophytes*, while those which cannot subsist upon dead matter are true *parasites;* but the dividing line is not so distinct that we can readily

* *A Manual of Bacteriology*, by E. M. Crookshank, London, 1890, p. 148.

determine with regard to certain bacteria whether they are the one or the other; and a *saprophyte* may be a *facultative parasite*, while a *parasite* may be a *facultative saprophyte*.

LIQUEFIERS AND NON-LIQUEFIERS.

The bacteria again divide into two other great classes: —

1. Those which when cultivated in gelatin will render it fluid, and known as the *liquefiers*.

2. Those which will develop on or in gelatin without liquefaction, and known as the *non-liquefiers*.

The bacillus of typhoid fever will not liquefy gelatin, while the bacillus of cholera does liquefy gelatin. Most of the pathogenic or disease-producing bacteria are *non-liquefiers*, while most of the putrefactive bacteria are rapid *liquefiers*. Certain of the bacteria will liquefy gelatin at room temperature (70° Fahr.) within a day or two, while others require a growth of two or three weeks to render the gelatin fluid, and some reduce the solid gelatin to a fluid at a rate so slow that the water of liquefaction is evaporated through the cotton plug of the test-tube as rapidly as it is formed.

The liquefaction of gelatin by bacterial agencies is not due to the production of heat in the destruction of organic matter, but to certain somewhat indistinct changes, by which the gelatin is peptonized and rendered incapable of again becoming hard at the temperature of melting ice (32° Fahr.).

AËROBIANS AND ANAËROBIANS.

Again, the bacteria divide into two other great classes as defined by Pasteur : —

1. Those which will grow only in the presence of oxygen, and termed *aërobians*.

2. Those which will not grow in the presence of oxygen, and termed *anaërobians*.

Most of the bacteria, so far as we are now aware, are *aërobians;* but it is probable that plate cultivation under strictly anaërobic conditions may demonstrate the existence of species now unsuspected which will not grow in the presence of oxygen. For example, the bacteria found upon cultivation of a sample of water in a Petri dish, or on a plate, are all *aërobians*, while the bacillus of *tetanus* (lockjaw) is a true *anaërobian*. Under the usual conditions of plate culture the anaërobic species, if any are in the water or other sample, will not grow, and of course do not enter into the subsequent count of the colonies, nor into the differentiation of species found on the plate.

The plugging of the glass test-tubes for culture media with cotton, allows the air to pass freely into the tube, while it effectually prevents the entrance of any organism in the air, however small it may be.

Naturally, because of the difficulties of cultivation, few anaërobic species of the bacteria have been found in water, but with improved and more convenient methods of (anaërobic) cultivation, more may in the future be found.

FORMS OF THE BACTERIA.

The bacteria are seen to be of three general forms when examined under the microscope.

1. The *Cocci*, or spherical forms, which for convenience of identification are divided into : —

The *Micrococci*, when the spheres are single or in irregular groups.

The *Diplococci*, consisting always or occasionally of two spheres joined, and resembling a dumb-bell with the connecting rod missing.

The *Tetrads*, which consist of triangular groups of three of the spheres, or *cocci*.

The *Streptococci*, in which the spheres are found in chains of many members.

The *Staphylococci*, in which the spheres, or *cocci*, are grouped somewhat like bunches of grapes. (To this class belong the yellow and white germs of septicæmia, or blood poisoning.)

The *Sarcina*, in which the spheres are found in cubical packets, divided in three directions, like a bale of goods tied with cords parallel to all the sides.

The *sarcina* contain 8 or more spheres. Thus, if divided once in each direction, the packet will contain the cube of two, or 8 spheres ; if divided twice in each direction, the packet will contain the cube of three, or 27 spheres. Usually the *sarcina* are seen under the microscope as broken packets, the preparation and fixing of the culture on the cover glass breaking up the characteristic arrangement of the members.

The *cocci* are regarded as non-spore-bearing bacteria.

2. The *bacilli*, or rods, straight or slightly bent.

To this class belong the organisms *b. typhosus, diphtheria, coli communis, lactis aerogenes*, the *tubercle bacillus*, and nearly all the putrefactive and pathogenic bacteria.

The bacilli grow into rods, and separate into individual cells by fission. Thus one rod becomes two rods by separation in the middle ; each of these separates again ; and as an evidence of the rate of growth and multiplication of some of the bacteria, it is stated that one rod or cell may, under favorable conditions, grow and divide within twenty minutes ; from which, by calculation, it will be seen that one rod may become the parent of nearly 17,000,000 within twenty-four hours.*

Of the bacilli, most are straight rods with round ends. *B. anthracis* is a straight rod with square ends united in chains. In young cultures of the typhoid germ long crooked strings are frequently noticed; these strings, or filaments, consist of many bacilli united together. In due time such strings, by fission, separate into the typical bacilli of varying length. The manner in which the bacilli are displayed on a cover glass preparation is an important number in the differentiation of species. Thus certain kinds, like *b. anthracis*, always are found in well-defined long chains, with some detached links or rods (probably broken from the chain by the manipulation of the specimen on the cover glass) ; others occur only as separate rods ; sometimes short chains, of two to six or eight rods, constitute the manner of grouping, but in all cases there is a method of grouping which is a property or characteristic of the species.

3. The *spirilla*, or *vibrios*, are rods always bent, sometimes in the form of the letter " S." To this class belongs the *comma bacillus* of Koch, known as the cholera germ. As a rule, the spirilla are rods which, if measured on the curve, are longer than the bacilli ; or the bacilli and spirilla may both be regarded as rod forms of the bacteria, the bacilli usually being the shorter and straight rods, while the spirilla are the longer and always bent or crooked rods. The germ of *diphtheria* is a comparatively long, slightly bent rod, but is classed as a bacillus.

The spirilla found in water are much fewer in number of kinds than the bacilli ; in fact, the majority of the bacteria found in polluted waters are of the latter form.

MOTILITY OF THE BACTERIA.

A property of the bacilli and spirilla, the cause of which is still open to investigation, is motility. Certain of the bacteria of these forms when examined, stained or unstained in drop cultures, exhibit surprising activity. Thus the germ *b. typhosus* (in a drop of bouillon) has motions of translation and rotation, and sinuous movements like a snake. Occasionally some of the rods, when taken from young cultures, will be

---

* *A Manual of Bacteriology*, by Dr. George M. Sternberg, p. 114.

observed in rotation resembling the movement of an acrobat on a horizontal turning-bar, while others have a sluggish or no motion at all. *B. fluorescens liquefaciens*, a bacterium frequently found in water, resembles in motility *b. typhosus;* it resembles also the smaller rods of this germ in dimensions; but unlike *b. typhosus*, it rapidly liquefies the gelatin in which it is grown, and in gelatin, and especially upon agar, produces a beautiful fluorescent green which permeates the whole culture material.

B. coli communis has motility, but the motions of the bacillus are sluggish and unlike those of *b. typhosus*. *B. lactis aerogenes* is not possessed of motility.

Motility of the bacteria, when viewed in drop cultures, is not to be confounded with *pedesis*, which is a swaying or oscillatory motion of the organism not due to inherent powers of locomotion. The motile bacilli and spirillā are provided with delicate flagella or hair-like appendages, which, acting as whips or oars, propel the germ through the drop of fluid on the cover glass. It was at one time supposed that the motility of the bacilli bore some relation to the number of the flagella, but recent investigations seem to negative this belief.[*]

In Germany the flagella have been regarded as an important element in the differentiation of the bacteria, but according to Dr. V. A. Moore, the flagella cannot be taken into serious consideration in the differentiation of closely allied species.[†]

With reference to the form, size, and other features of the bacteria, due allowance must be made for the environment of the culture. The culture media, its reaction, temperature of incubator, and nearness of the culture to its original source, all have an important bearing on the differentiation of species. When the bacteria are grown in a Petri dish, room temperature (about 70° Fahr.) is preferable as corresponding with the conditions under which the largest and most rapid growth will be obtained; but at room temperature most of the pathogenic bacteria develop slowly, and even if such were in a water sample, the probability of finding them in plate cultures is rather remote.

CHROMOGENIC SPECIES.

Certain of the bacteria when grown upon suitable materials elaborate beautiful colors, which rival the colors of the solar spectrum. For example, *b. prodigiosus*, a bacillus found in water, produces a deep blood red; *b. rothe*, another water bacillus, produces a raspberry red;

---

[*] *Character of the Flagella*, V. A. Moore, Washington, D.C., 1893.   [†] *Ibid.*, p. 363.

b. violaceus, also a water bacillus, produces a purple merging into blue; the *staphylococcus pyogenes aureus*, the organism of malignant pustule or septicæmia, found in water, produces a golden yellow; *b. proteus fluorescens* produces a fluorescent green; *m. candicans*, a water germ, produces a dazzling Chinese white; *m. aurantiacus*, another water germ, elaborates a beautiful orange color; and *m. carneus*, a water micrococci, produces a delicate pink or flesh color when grown on agar. The color, when a characteristic, is an important element in determining species.

Among the products of bacterial action on dead organic matter are the ptomains, some of which have toxic properties. The substance isolated by Dr. V. C. Vaughan * from ice-cream and cheese, called *tyrotoxicon*, is one of the vital products of the putrefactive bacteria. Whether the putrefactive bacteria are capable of producing ptomains from the organic matter in water is not known, but some of the investigators abroad seem to suspect the possibility of it.

The action of the pathogenic bacteria on organic matter is the production of toxins, which probably are absorbed into the circulation of the animal with the symptoms during life characteristic of specific disease, and the pathological lesions usually found upon post-mortem examination. The toxin from the growth of the bacillus of diphtheria on the mucous membrane of the fauces, when taken into the circulation, produces the symptoms and lesions characteristic of this disease. Dr. McFarland remarks upon the virulent properties of the toxin elaborated by the *diphtheria bacillus*,† "No more convincing proof of the existence of a powerful poison in diphtheria could be desired than the evidences of general toxæmia, resulting from the absorption of material from a comparatively small number of bacilli situated upon a little patch of mucous membrane."

DIMENSIONS OF THE BACTERIA.

The dimensions of the bacteria are stated in microns, designated by the Greek letter " μ," which is $\frac{1}{1000}$ of a millimeter, equal to about $\frac{1}{25400}$ of an inch. Thus the typical dimensions of *b. typhosus* are .5 to .8 " μ " wide, by 1.5 to 2.5 " μ " long; or about $\frac{1}{50800}$ to $\frac{1}{31750}$ of an inch wide or thick, and $\frac{1}{16800}$ to $\frac{1}{10800}$ of an inch long.

Taking the average length of the typhoid bacillus as 2 microns (μ), it will be seen that it would require 12,500 of these little rods placed end to end to make one inch. The human mind can scarcely grasp the

---

* *The Ptomaines and Leucomaines*, by Vaughan and Novy, Philadelphia, 1891, p. 35 *et seq.*

† *A Treatise on the Pathogenic Bacteria*, Dr. Joseph McFarland, Philadelphia, 1896, p. 227.

smallness of the bacteria; but assuming that the unaided vision is capable of distinguishing 200 lines or divisions to the inch, then each of such divisions would contain over 60 of the typhoid germs, placed end to end, or 180 if placed side by side.

The air and soil both contain bacteria which may come into water, and aside from the pathogenic species, all bacteria found in water must not be regarded as indigenous to this source. The natural water bacteria may be considered as those found in the water from deep wells after the rainfall has percolated through many feet of various kinds of soil and filtering material, and even these may be, and probably are, from extraneous sources; but for the present purpose it may be held that such belong to water because of the inability of the filtering materials in the drift and rock to restrain them.

Rain is probably free from bacteria and organic matter as it falls from the clouds; but in falling, material suspended in the atmosphere will be intercepted and carried down to the earth, and into the usual receptacles or channels of discharge of rainfall. In addition to the bacteria and organic matter from the air, bacteria and matter from the soil is washed into the streams and lakes; and the excess in numbers and gain in species of bacteria in river or lake waters, over those in deep well waters, may be attributed to the air and soil, or to sewage pollution. Any bacteria naturally in the air will be intercepted by rainfall; and if the species are capable of an independent existence in water, may upon examination be found there. Likewise storm water discharged through natural channels will contain bacteria intercepted in flowing over the ground, together with some species obtained from erosion of the earthy banks.

In the examination of a water sample for bacteria, a large number, or rapidly liquefying organisms, should suggest the probable presence of the putrefactive germs, among which are often found *b. proteus vulgaris, b. mesentericus vulgatus,* and others of like character, which usually are held to come into water from sewage sources.

SPORE–BEARING BACTERIA.

A characteristic of the bacteria not to be overlooked in differentiation for species, is the presence or absence of spores. This cannot, in all cases, be easily determined; but a germ which yields spores is known to be much more difficult to destroy than non-spore-bearing germs. The spores are small, round, ovoid or oblong bodies, of which one or more may be noticed in a single bacillus or spirillum, which will live and propagate bacteria of its kind after the destruction of the germ itself.

Of the pathogenic bacteria found in water a few develop spores. "According to Hueppe, the Koch *comma bacillus* forms arthrospores, but it possesses no form which is endowed with any considerable powers of resistance." * This view is not shared by all investigators.† *B. anthracis*, another pathogenic germ found in water, forms spores. The *tetanus* bacillus forms a spore in one end of the rod which gives it the form of a drumstick. *B. pyocyanus*, found in green pus and also in water, forms spores. Bacillus of *mouse septicæmia* forms spores. Of the twenty-three pathogenic species of bacteria found in water, the above are all that are certainly known at present to form spores.

The Franklands in their work on *Micro Organisms in Water*, give a list of 200 species of the bacteria which have been found in water, of which the following are classed as pathogenic varieties : —

PATHOGENIC BACTERIA FOUND IN VARIOUS WATERS.

GERM.	ORIGINAL DATE OF IDENTIFICATION.	AUTHORITY.
B. anthracis,	1850	Rayer and Davaine, Pollender-Pasteur, and Joubert-Koch.
B. typhosus,	1880	Eberth-Gaffky.
B. mouse septicæmia,	1881	Gaffky-Löffler.
B. rabbit septicæmia,	1881	Koch-Gaffky.
B. pyocyanus,	1882	Gessard-Charrin-Ernst.
Sp. Asiatic cholera,	1884	Robert Koch.
B. tuberculosis,	1884	"
B. saprogenes,	1884	Rosenbach.
Staph. pyogenes aureus,	1884	Rosenbach-Passet-Fick.
B. coli communis,	1885	Escherich.
B. lactis aerogenes,	1885	"
B. proteus vulgaris,	1885	Hauser.
B. proteus mirabilis,	1885	"
B. proteus Zenkeri,	1885	"
B. brevis,	1888	Rintaro Mori.
B. capsulatus,	1888	"
M. biskra,	1888	Heydenrich.
B. of tetanus,	1889	Nicolaer-Kitasato.
Coccus " B,"	1890	Foutin.
B. hydrophilus fuscus,	1891	Sanarelli.
B. proteus fluorescens,	1892	Jaeger.
Sp. Berolinensus,	1893	Neisser.
B. tholoeideum,	. .	Gessner.

* *Micro Organisms in Water*, Percy & Grace Frankland, London, 1894, p. 399.
† *Principles of Bacteriology*, by Dr. A. C. Abbott, Philadelphia, 1894, p. 314.

In addition to the pathogenic bacteria heretofore found in water, certain investigators abroad seem to think that the bacillus of diphtheria may be transmitted through the medium of water supply. In his evidence before the Royal Commission on Metropolitan Water Supply, Dr. Alfred Ashby * stated a belief that diphtheria might be so transmitted. Dr. E. Frankland † says that animal refuse finding its way into water may be accompanied by zymotic poisons dangerous to health, such as those of typhoid fever, tuberculosis, or diphtheria; while Dr. George Turner ‡ testified before the Commission that, "he had had one case where he suspected that diphtheria was conveyed by water." No proof is at hand indicating the transmission of this germ by water, although it is possible that it may find its way into water, in the same way as the tubercle bacillus, by the sputa or membraneous sloughings from a patient suffering with this disease. It, however, may be said that the remedies to be applied to polluted waters, or the precautions to be observed in selecting water from the best natural sources, will have the same influence in diminishing the chances of propagation of diphtheria (if it should be shown to have a temporary habitat in water) as upon the transmission of typhoid fever and cholera by this means.

In order to render the bacteria easily discernible under the microscope, recourse is had to dilute solutions of the aniline dyes, which as simple watery solutions, or in combination with a weak acid or alkali, are readily taken up by the protoplasm of the cell substance. The bacteria being devoid of chlorophyl, and consequently colorless in drop cultures or fixed on cover glasses unstained, are somewhat difficult to study; while by the addition of the dyes, or stains, these colorless bodies become more or less opaque, and contrast sharply with the light transmitted through the preparation, and when stained are easily viewed and examined microscopically.

The manner in which the bacteria take the stain is a material element in the differentiation of species, and in jotting down the memoranda of examination of an organism the experienced observer never fails to note the facility with which the stain is taken up. *B. anthracis* thus takes the simple watery stain readily, while *b. typhosus* can be promptly colored only by an acid or alkaline solution of the stains, and the *tubercle* bacillus stains with great difficulty. The bacillus of *tetanus*, on the other hand, is easily colored with the watery solutions, while

---

* Report of Royal Commission on Metropolitan Water Supply, London, 1893, *Minutes of Evidence*, p. 140.

† *Ibid.*, Appendices to *Minutes of Evidence*, p. 200.

‡ *Minutes of Evidence*, p. 177.

b. proteus fluorescens requires the strongest dyes to give it color. This property of taking stains is affected by the age of the culture, old cultures being more troublesome to stain than young ones.

To illustrate the importance of familiarity with the action of the aniline dyes on the bacteria, if a cover glass preparation suspected of being the typhoid bacillus was under examination, and it took the watery solutions promptly, it can be safely set down that it is not *b. typhosus*, but some other germ.

The growth of the common water bacteria is inhibited by high temperatures, while the pathogenic germs attain their highest development at the temperature of the body. Thus, while the waters in rivers, lakes and reservoirs, attain the highest temperature at the end of summer, a temperature unfavorable to the growth of many of the water bacteria, they are approaching the condition favorable to the growth and full development of the pathogenic organisms ; and it is at this season of the year when water-borne diseases should be most manifest.

In the following tables are given : —

1. A list of bacteria found in water which resemble the typhoid bacillus in some dimension, and like *b. coli communis* and *b. lactis aerogenes*, resemble it sometimes in other respects.

2. A list of the germs smaller than *b. typhosus* found in water.

3. A list of the larger bacteria found in water.

4. A list of the spore-bearing bacteria which have been found in water.

In all the tables the principal properties of the organisms are given to assist in the rough identification or differentiation of species. But for the exact differentiation, the best descriptions of the various bacteria, together with long and conscientious experience, will be found absolutely necessary.*

* In the author's forthcoming work on the "Interpretation of Water Analysis," a full description will be given of the modern methods of Bacterial Water Analysis, and the aids to identification of species of bacteria.

No. 1. SMALL BACILLI RESEMBLING IN SOME RESPECTS B. TYPHOSUS.

GERM.	DIMENSIONS. Width. Length.	MOTILITY.	LIQUE-FACTION.	SPORE FORMATION	FERMENTATION.	STAINING PROPERTIES.	REMARKS
B. Typhosus,	$.5-.8 \mu \times 1.5-2.5 \mu,$	Actively motile,	Non-liq.	No spores,	Turbidity, without gas,	Not readily,	Rounded ends, grow into long filaments.
B. Coli communis,	$.4 \mu \times 2-3 \mu,$	Slightly motile,	"	"	Turbidity, with gas,	"	Rounded ends, no filaments.
B. Aquatilis sulcatus, 1	Resembling typho,	Actively motile,	"	"	.	"	
B. Aquatilis sulcatus, 2	Resembling shorter typho,	Motile,	"	"	.	"	
B. Aquatilis sulcatus, 5	Thicker than typho,	Motile,	"	"	Turbidity, with gas,	"	Rounded, and pointed ends.
B. Lactis aërogenes,	$.5-.8 \mu \times 1-2 \mu,$	Non-motile,	"	"	.	"	Rounded ends.
B. Tholoeideum,	$.5,$	Non-motile,	"	"	.	.	
B. Fluorescens tenuis,	$.8 \mu \times .65-1 \mu,$	Slightly motile,	"	" (?)	.	Not readily,	Grows into filaments with rounded ends.
B. Fluorescens longus,	$.63 \mu \times 1.45-1.65 \mu,$	Actively motile,	"	"	.	Readily,	Grows into long filaments
B. Viridis pallescens,	Longer and thinner than typho,	Actively motile,	"	" (?)	.	.	"
B. Fluorescens liquefaciens,	$.5 \mu \times 1-1.5 \mu,$	Actively motile,	Liq.,	"	.	Readily.	
B. Termo,	$.8 \mu \times 1.4 \mu,$	Actively motile,	"	.	Turbidity,	.	Grows in pairs and clumps.
B. Rabbit septicaemia,	$.6-.7 \mu \times 1.4 \mu,$	Non-motile,	Non-liq.,	"	.	Readily,	Grows into filaments with rounded ends.
Weisser bacillus	Slender. $1.5 \mu,$	Non-motile,	"	.	.	.	"
B. Sub-flavus,	$.77 \mu \times 1.5-3 \mu,$	Slightly motile,	"	.	.	.	Forms chains
B. Aureus,	$.5 \mu \times 1.5 \mu,$	Slightly motile,	"	No spores,	.	Readily,	Grows into long filaments.
B. Fluorescens aureus,	$.74 \mu \times 1.5 \mu,$	Actively motile,	"	"	.	.	In pairs with rounded ends.
B. Hydrophilus fuscus,	$.7 \mu \times 1.5-3.5 \mu,$	Actively motile,	Liq.,	"	.	Not readily,	Rounded ends.
B. Sulfureum,	$.5 \mu \times 1.6-2.4 \mu,$	Slightly motile,	"	"	.	.	Grows into long filaments.
B. Diffusus,	$.5 \mu \times 1.7 \mu,$	Actively motile,	"	"	.	.	Long rods, often bent.
B. Janthinus,	$.65 \mu \times 1.5-3.5 \mu,$	Motile,	"	"	.	.	Becomes indigo blue.
B. Berolinensis indicus,	Resembling typho,	Actively motile,	Non-liq.,	"	Turbidity,	.	Grows in pairs and filaments with rounded ends.
B. Stedenglanzender,	$.8 \mu \times 1.7 \mu,$	Slightly motile,	"	.	Turbidity,	.	

No. 2. SMALL BACILLI FOUND IN WATER.

GERM.	DIMENSIONS. (Width, Length)	MOTILITY.	LIQUE- FACTION.	SPORE FORMATION.	FERMEN- TATION.	STAINING PROPERTIES.	REMARKS.
B. Mouse sept.,	.1–.2 μ x .8–1 μ,	Non-motile,	Liq.	Forms spores,	· · ·	Readily,	Liq. only in alkaline gelatin.
B. Pyocyanus,	.15–.25 μ x .8–1 μ,	Actively motile,	"	"	· · ·	Not readily,	Single and in groups.
B. Fluorescens non-liquefaciens,	Fine,　Short.	Non-motile,	Non-liq.,	· · ·	· · ·	Readily,	Rounded ends.
B. Tetanus,	.1–.2 μ x .9–1.1 μ,	Slightly motile,	Liq.,	Forms spores,	· · ·	· · ·	"
B. Aquatilis fluorescens,	Thin,　Short.	Non-motile,	Non-liq.,	· · ·	· · ·	· · ·	"
B. Saprogenes,	Slender,　Short.	· · ·	"	· · ·	· · ·	· · ·	
B. Rubefaciens,	.32 μ x .75–1.65 μ,	Actively motile,	Liq.,	· · ·	· · ·	· · ·	Rounded ends.
Yellow bacillus,	Thin,　Short.	Non-motile,	Non-liq.,	· · ·	· · ·	· · ·	"
B. Flavocoriaceus,	Very small,	Non-motile,	Liq.,	No spores,	· · ·	· · ·	Grows in groups.
B. Tremelloides,	.25 μ x .75–1 μ,	Motile,	"	· · ·	· · ·	· · ·	Rounded ends.
B. Nubilis,	.3 μ x 3 μ,	Motile,	Liq.,	No spores,	· · ·	· · ·	Forms long wavy filaments.
B. Cuticularis,	.3–.5 μ x 2–3 μ,	Slightly motile,	"	· · ·	· · ·	· · ·	Forms filaments.
Bacillus "C,"	Resembles mouse sept.,	· · ·	Non-liq.,	Forms spores,	· · ·	· · ·	Single and in chains.
B. Acidi lacticl,	.3–.4 μ x 1–1.7 μ,	Non-motile,	"	"	· · ·	· · ·	Usually in pairs.
B. Lactis cyanogenus,	.3–.5 μ x 1–4 μ,	Actively motile,	Liq.,	"	· · ·	Methy. blue,	Blunted corners.
B. Butyricus,	.38 μ x 2.1 μ,	Actively motile,	"	· · ·	· · ·	· · ·	Forms filaments.
B. Aquatilis graveolens,	Slender, x 1.3 μ,	Slightly motile,	· · ·	· · ·	· · ·	· · ·	Bent filaments in potato.

No. 3. LARGE BACILLI FOUND IN WATER.

GERM.	DIMENSIONS. (Width — Length.)	MOTILITY.	LIQUEFACTION.	SPORE FORMATION.	FERMENTATION.	STAINING PROPERTIES.	REMARKS.
B. Anthracis,	1–1.5 μ × 3–10 μ,	Non-motile,	Liq.,	Forms spores,		Readily,	Long filaments, with sq. ends.
B. Subtilis,	2 μ × 6 μ,	Motile,	"	"	Turbidity,	"	Long filaments, with rounded ends.
B. Vermicularis,	1 μ × 2–3 μ,	Non-motile,	"	"			Extensive vermiform filaments.
B. Megaterium,	2.5 μ × 8–9 μ,	Motile,	"	"			Slightly curved rods, with rounded ends.
B. Ramosus,	1.7 μ × 7 μ,	Motile,	"	"			Long filaments, rounded ends.
B. Mycoides,	.9 μ × 1.6–2.4 μ,	Motile,	"	"	Turbidity,	Readily,	Long filaments.
B. Ubiquitus,	1 μ × 1.1–2 μ,	Non-motile,	Non-liq.,	No spores,	"		Short filaments.
B. Superficialis,	1 μ × 2.2 μ,	Motile,	Liq.,	"			Rounded ends.
B. Reticularis,	1 μ × 5 μ,	Motile,	"	"			Filaments.
B. Circulans,	1 μ × 2–5 μ,	Actively motile,	"	Forms spores,	"		Rounded ends.
B. Hyalinus,	1.5 μ × 3.6–4 μ,	Actively motile,	"	No spores,	"		Short filaments.
B. Delicatulus,	1 μ × 2 μ,	Actively motile,	"	"	"		"
B. Rubescens,	.9 μ × 4 μ,	Motile,	Non-liq.,	"	"		"
B. Prodigiosus,	1 μ × 1.7 μ,	Non-motile,	Liq.,		"		Forms pairs.
B. Limosus,	1.25 μ × 3–4 μ,	Motile,	"	Forms spores,	"		Rounded ends.
B. Zopfii,	.75–1 μ × 2–5 μ,	Actively motile,	"	"	"		Long filaments.
B. Inunctus,	.8–9 μ × 3.5 μ,	Motile,	"	"			
B. Stoloniferus,	.8 μ × 1.2 μ,	Actively motile,	"				
B. Guttatus,	.93 μ × 1–1.13 μ,	Actively motile,	"	Forms spores (?)		Stains with Safranin,	Singly, pairs, or chains.
B. Gen. Nov.,	3–5 μ,	Motile,	"	(?)			Forms oval bacilli .9 μ × 1.5 μ sometimes grows 8–9 μ long.
B. Filiformis,	1 μ × 4 μ,	Motile,	"	Forms spores,			Forms long filaments.
Bacillus "D"	1 μ × 5–20 μ,	Slightly motile,	Non-liq.,	"		Readily,	Thinner at the poles, with rounded ends.
B. Lactis viscosus,	.8–1.25 μ × 1–1.5 μ,	Slightly motile,	Liq.,	Forms spores,	Turbidity,		Sometimes chains of 3–6 cells.
B. Crassus Aromaticus,	1.5 μ × 3.5–5 μ,		"	"	"	Poles stain deeper than center.	Fat double bacilli, with rounded ends.
B. Ureae,	1 μ × 2 μ,		Non-liq.,				Rounded ends; converts urea into ammonium carbonate.
B. Fusarium-Aquae-ductuum,	1–1.5 μ × 7–13 μ,	Non-motile,	Liq.,	Forms spores,	Turbidity,	Readily,	Spores are meniscus, sausage, or club-shaped.

No. 4. LIST OF SPORE-BEARING GERMS FOUND IN WATER.

GERM.	ACTION ON GELATIN.	ENDS.	COLOR.	MORPHOLOGY.
B. Anthracis,	Liq.,	Square,	Gray white,	Forms filaments, 3–6–$10\ \mu \times 1$–$1.5\ \mu.$
B. Subtilis,	"	Round,	Opaque white,	Long filaments, $6\ \mu \times 2\ \mu.$
B. Vermicularis,	"	"	Gray,	Forms extensive filaments, 2–$3\ \mu \times 1\ \mu.$
B. Megaterium,	"	"	Whitish,	8–$9\ \mu$ long, $2.5\ \mu$ broad.
B. Ramosus,	"	"	Gray,	Long filaments, $7\ \mu \times 1.7\ \mu.$
B. Mycoides,	"	. .	White,	Long filaments, 1.6–$2.4\ \mu \times .9\ \mu.$
B. Tetanus,	"	Round,	. . .	$.9$–$1.1\ \mu \times .1$–$.2\ \mu.$
B. Pyocyanus,	"	. .	Greenish white,	$.8$–$1\ \mu \times .15$–$.25\ \mu.$
B. Mouse septicaemia,	"	. .	Yellowish white,	Frequently in pairs, $.8$–$1\ \mu\ .1$–$.2\ \mu.$
B. Brunneus,	Non-liq.,	. .	Milk-white brown,	Fine and slender.
B. Circulans,	Liq.,	Round,	Translucent,	In twos and fours, 2–$5\ \mu \times 1\ \mu.$
B. Erythrosporus,	Non-liq.,	"	Fluor-green,	Slender and short filaments.
B. Der Rothe,	Liq.,	"	Raspberry red,	Small, forms filaments.
B. Cuticularis albus,	Non-liq.,	"	White,	Bent filaments, $3.2\ \mu$ long.
B. Granulosus,	Liq.,	. .	Yellowish white,	Long slender filaments.
B. Limosus,	"	Round,	White,	Two or three joined, 3–$4\ \mu \times 1.25\ \mu.$
B. Zopfii,	"	. .	Whitish yellow,	2–$5\ \mu \times .75$–$1\ \mu.$
B. Mesentericus ruber,	"	Round,	Yellow brown,	Slender.
B. Mesentericus fuscus,	"	. .	Brownish yellow,	Short, in twos and fours.
B. Mesentericus vulgatus,	"	Round,	Yellow,	Small, fat, pairs and fours.
B. Iridescens,	"	. .	Greenish yellow,	Bent filaments, 3.5–$5.2\ \mu$ long.
B. Guttatus,	"	. .	Bluish white,	1–$1.13\ \mu \times .93\ \mu.$
B. Thalassophilus,	"	. .	Light gray,	An anaerobian, with slender, variable filaments.
B. Amylozyme,	Non-liq.,	Round,	White,	Pairs and chains, 2–$3\ \mu \times .5\ \mu.$
B. Filiformis,	Liq.,	. .	White,	Forms filaments, $4\ \mu \times 1\ \mu.$
Bacillus "C,"	Liq.,	. .	Pale brown,	5–$20\ \mu \times 1\ \mu.$
Bacillus "D,"	Non-liq.,	Round,	Pearl,	1–$2\ \mu \times .1$–$.2\ \mu.$
B. Acidi lactici,	Non-liq.,	. .	Gray white,	Pairs and fours, 1–$1.7\ \mu \times .3$–$.4\ \mu.$
B. Lactis cyanogenus,	"	Blunted corners,	Gray,	1–$4\ \mu \times .3$–$.5\ \mu.$
B. Butyricus,	Liq.,	. .	Dirty yellow,	$2.1\ \mu \times .38\ \mu.$
B. Crassus aromaticus,	"	Round,	White	3.5–$5\ \mu \times 1.5\ \mu.$
B. Aerophilus,	"	"	Greenish yellow,	Slender, in twos and filaments.
B. Muscoides,	Non-liq.,	. .	Opalescent,	$1\ \mu$ broad.
B. Putrificus coli,	Liq.,	. .	White,	Slender filaments, $3\ \mu$ long.
B. Thermophilus,	Non-liq.,	. .	White,	Forms filaments.

APPENDIX C.

THE LEGAL LIABILITY OF CITIES AND WATER COMPANIES FOR DAMAGES BY SEWAGE POLLUTED WATER.

EXCEPTING cities are compelled by law to procure water from satisfactory natural sources, or adopt the most perfect methods of water purification, progress in the hygiene of public water supplies will be comparatively slow. When, however, judicial decrees are obtained against vendors (whether municipal corporations or private companies) for the distribution of polluted and unwholesome waters, then the interest of water purveyors in the quality of their commodities will be great indeed.

If cities and private companies are held legally responsible for all losses of life, time, and money by reason of polluted public water supplies, the problem then will not be, — is improvement in water quality desirable, but rather how can satisfactory improvement be obtained. The cost will not be seriously debated then ; because the possible loss of money by damage suits, for a brief period of time, will more than balance the cost of water from proper sources, or of the most perfect works for the artificial purification of polluted waters.

Let it be understood that every gallon of water sent through the public mains must carry with it the seal of approval of conscientious as well as competent water analysts, and our public supplies will then come from sources beyond the reach of sewage pollution, or will be brought to the highest state of artificial purification which is attainable.

A successful suit has recently been fought upon these lines in the lower courts of the State of Wisconsin. There, in the city of Ashland, an epidemic of typhoid fever occurred during the winter of 1893–94 ; and notwithstanding repeated complaints by the local and state health officials, the Water Company continued to supply a sewage polluted water to its consumers. Among the victims of this epidemic was one Lars G. Green, a laboring man, whose widow, Mrs. Julia L. Green, upon advice of counsel, began a suit against the Ashland Water Company for the legal value of her husband's life.

The source of water supply for Ashland was Chequamegon Bay, an arm of Lake Superior. The same bay also serves as the receptacle of the city's sewage (Chap. II.) ; and the water supplied to the patrons of the public mains was a mixture of water as received from natural sources into the bay, and the city's sewage.

The suit was based on the theory that the water from Chequamegon Bay contained the specific germs of typhoid fever, which came into it through the city sewers in the dejections of typhoid fever patients then in Ashland ; that this water was drunk by Mr. Green, and laid the foundation for the disease by which he perished ; and that the Water Company, knowing the condition of the water in the bay, was negligent in supplying to their customers water for dietetic uses which was sewage polluted and therefore unwholesome.

The suit was tried in the Circuit Court of Portage County, Wisconsin, during the last week of November (1897), before Hon. Chas. M. Webb. Upon trial of the case, it was proven that Mr. Green was a railway employee living and working continuously in Ashland ; that he was taken ill with and died of typhoid fever ; that his premises were supplied with water from the mains of the Ashland Water Company ; that the only water available in Ashland was that supplied by the water company from Chequamegon Bay ; that this water was polluted with the sewage from the city of Ashland ; that previous to Mr. Green's illness typhoid fever had prevailed in Ashland, and the dejections from the patients had gone into the city sewers and been discharged into Chequamegon Bay ; and that with the exception of four days just prior to his illness, Mr. Green was exposed to the influence of no other water than that supplied to his premises and the city of Ashland.

From the testimony offered, the jury found that the typhoid

germ was transmitted to Mr. Green through the medium of the public water supply, and held the water company liable in $5,000 damages. (The legal value of a human life under the laws of Wisconsin.)

Similar suits doubtless will be brought elsewhere, to settle the question of liability of municipal corporations and water companies for delivering to their citizens or customers a fluid which is carrying the germs of dangerous disease.

AUTHORITIES QUOTED OR REFERRED TO.

ABBOTT, DR. A. C.,	Philadelphia,	"Principles of Bacteriology."
ALESSI, DR. G.,	London,	" Putrid Gases as Predisposing Causes of Typhoid Infection."
ANDERSON PURIFIER CO.,	London, 1896,	" Water Purification."
ANKLAM, F.,	Berlin,	" Filters at Lake Müggel."
Annales de L' Institute Pasteur,	Paris, 1892-04.	
Annual Summary of Vital Statistics,	London, 1890-96.	
BAKER, M. N.,	New York,	"Mechanical Filters," etc.
BAUMEISTER, PROF. R.,	Carlsruhe,	"Cleaning and Sewerage of Cities."
BERTSCHINGER, DR. A.,	Zurich,	"Analyses of Zurich Water."
BINNIE, SIR A. R.,	London, 1894,	"Available Sources of Water Supply for London."
BLESSING, JAMES H.,	Albany, N.Y., 1897,	"An Address to the Common Council."
BRYAN, W. B.,	London,	" Cleaning Filters." East London Water Company.
CARMICHAEL, PROF. H.,	Boston, 1896,	"Reduction of Iron in Ground Waters."
Centralblatt für Bacteriologie,	1892,	" Freudenrich's Tests of Pasteur Filters."
Consular Reports, U.S.,	Washington, D.C., 1897,	"Fischer Filter, Worms."
CROOKSHANK, E. M.,	London,	"Manual of Bacteriology."
DE VARONA, I. M.,	Brooklyn, 1896,	" Report on the Future Extension of the Water Supply of Brooklyn."
DEVONSHIRE, E.,	London,	"Anderson Revolving Iron Purifier."
DIBDIN, W. J.	London,	"Analytical Investigation of London Waters."
DROWN, DR. T. M.,	Lehigh University, South Bethlehem, Pa.,	"Reduction of Iron in Ground Waters," etc.
DUNBAR, PROFESSOR DR.,	Hamburg,	"Reduction of Iron in Ground Waters," etc.

DUPRÉ, DR. A.,	London,	" Anderson Iron Purifier, Worcester, England."
ENGINEER Commission on Extension and Betterment of Cincinnati Water Works, 1890,		" Report on Filtration of Water."
Engineering News,	New York, 1896,	" Removal of Iron from Ground Waters," etc.
Engineering Record,	New York, 1894,	" Typhoid Fever Statistics."
ERNST, DR. H. C.,	Harvard University, Boston,	" Examination of Sample of Well Water."
Fire and Water,	New York, 1894–95,	" Typhoid Fever Statistics."
FLAD, EDWARD,	St. Louis,	"Subsidence of Ohio River Water."
FRANKLAND, DR. E.,	London,	" Operation of London Filters," etc.
FRANKLAND, PROF. PERCY and G. C.,	Birmingham, Eng.,	" Micro Organisms in Water."
GILL, HENRY,*	London,	" Filtration of the Müggel Lake Water Supply."
HAWKSLEY, THOS.,	London,	" Area of London Filters."
HAZEN, ALLEN,	New York,	" Filtration of Public Water Supplies," etc.
HOLLIS, F. S.,	Boston,	" Bacterial Efficiency of Lorain Filters."
JORDAN, DR. EDWIN O.,	Chicago,	" Identification of Typhoid Fever Bacillus."
Journal für Gasbeleuchtung und Wasserversorgung,	Karlsruhe, 1897,	" Cleaning Sand Filters under Ice."
Journal of the Sanitary Institute,	London, 1894–95.	" Filtration," etc.
Journal of the N. E. W. W. Association,	1896.	"Influence of Light on Micro Organisms."
KIRKWOOD, J. P.,*	New York,	" Filtration of River Waters."
KLEIN, DR. E.,	London,	" Quality of London Waters."
KÜMMEL, W.,*	Altona, Ger.,	" Rates of Filtration."
LANDOIS–STERLING,	London,	" Human Physiology."
LANDRETH, PROF. O. H.,	Schenectady, N.Y.,	" Epidemic of Typhoid Fever at Elmira, N.Y."
LANKESTER, PROF. E. RAY,	Oxford University,	" Origin of *b. typhosus*," etc.
LEFFMANN, DR. HENRY,	Philadelphia, 1897,	" Unfiltered Surface Waters always Unsafe for Town Supply."
MAGER, ED.,	Hamburg, 1897,	" Process of Cleaning the open Filters of the Hamburg Water Works."

Manual of American Water Works, New York, 1897.

MASON, PROF. WILLIAM P.,   New York, 1896,   " Water Supply."

MASS. State Board of Health,   Boston, 1890-95,   Annual Reports.

MCFARLAND, DR. JOS.,   Philadelphia,   " The Pathogenic Bacteria."

MEYER, F. ANDREAS,   Hamburg, 1894,   " Das Wasserwerk der Frien- und
Hansestadt, Hamburg."

MIGULA, Dr. W.,   London, 1893,   " Practical Bacteriology."

MILLS, H. F.,   Lawrence, Mass.,   " Sterilization of Filter Sand."

MIQUEL, DR. PIERRE,   Paris,   " Sedimentation of Waters," etc.

MOORE, DR. V. A.   Washington, D.C.,   " Character of the Flagella."

MORISON-JEWELL FILTRATION COMPANY,   " Experimental Filters for Philadelphia," 1897, etc.

MUNN, DR. WILLIAM P.,   Denver, Col., 1896,   " Preliminary Report of Health
Commissioner."

NICHOLS, WM. RIPLEY,   New York, 1883,   " Water Supply."

ODLING, DR. WILLIAM,   London, 1893,   " Filtration of Surface Waters."

Ohio Sanitary Bulletin,   Ohio, 1897,   " Lorain Filters."

OSLER, DR. WILLIAM,   Baltimore,   " Typhoid Fever in Baltimore."

PETTENKOFER, DR. MAX VON, Munich,   " Cause of Typhoid Fever."

PIEFKE, HERR,   Berlin,   " Die Principien der Reinwassergewinnung vermittelst Filtration."

PRELLER, CHARLES, S. D.,   London,   " Water Works of Zurich, Switzerland."

Proceedings American Water-   " Use of Sterilized Water at
Works Association,   1894,   World's Fair." (1893.)

Proceedings Institution of Civil
Engineers,   London, 1892-1895, " Filtration of Water in Europe."

PRUDDEN, DR. T. M.,   New York,   " Typhoid Bacillus in Water."

RAFTER AND MALLORY,   Rochester, N.Y.,   " Report on Spring Water Epidemic."

RAVENEL, DR. M. P.,   Philadelphia, 1897,   " Bacterial Tests of Chemung
Water, Elmira, N.Y.

REINCKE, DR. J. J.,   Hamburg,   " Epidemiology of Typhoid Fever
in Hamburg and Altona."

ROGERS, DR. EDMUND,   Denver, Col.,   " Cause of Mountain Fever. "

ROSENAU, DR. M. J,   San Francisco,   " San Francisco Water Supply."

ROYAL COMMISSION,   London, 1893,   " Metropolitan Water Supply."

SANARELLI, DR. G.,   Montevideo, S.A.,   " The Typhoid Bacillus and Etiology of Typhoid Fever."

SCHRÖDER, RUD,   Hamburg,   " Operation of Hamburg Filters."

SEDGWICK, PROF. W. T.,   Boston,   " Bacteria in Spring and Well
Waters," etc.

SHEDD, J. HERBERT,   Providence, R.I.,   " Sand Filtration."

SMITH, DR. THEOBALD, Boston, "The Fermentation Tube."
Statistische Zusammenstellung
der Betriebs Ergebnisse von
Wasserwerken, Munich, 1895. "Sources of German Water Supplies."
STERNBERG, DR. GEO. M., Washington, D.C., "Manual of Bacteriology."

THOMAS, R. J., Lowell, Mass., "Water Supply of Lowell."
THOMAS AND MARSHALL, DRS., Philadelphia, Report on Philadelphia Water Supply.
THORNE, DR. THORNE, London, "The Caterham and Redhill Epidemic."
Times, Daily, New York, 1894, "Typhoid Fever."
Transactions American Society
of Civil Engineers, New York, Vols. xxxi., xxxii., xxxiii., and xxxv.
Tribune, Daily, New York, 1894, "Typhoid Fever and Water Supply."

VAUGHAN, DR. V. C., Ann Arbor, Mich., "A Bacteriological Study of Drinking Water."
VAUGHAN AND NOVY, Philadelphia, "The Ptomaines and Leucomaines."

WESTON, EDMUND B., Providence, R.I., "Providence Experimental Filter Tests."
WHIPPLE, G. C., Boston, "Some Observations on the Relation of Light to the Growth of Diatoms."
WOODHEAD, DR. G. SIMS, Edinburgh, "Seasonal Distribution of Typhoid Fever," etc.

ZEIMSSEN, PROFESSOR VON, Munich, "On Typhoid Fever in Munich."
itschrift des Vereines Deutsch- "Apparatus for Washing Filter
r Ingenieurie, Hamburg, 1895, Sand."
schrift für Hygiene, 1896, "Reduction of Iron in Ground Waters."

INDEX.

295